REFUGEE SANDWICH

REFUGEE

Stories of Exile and Asylum

SANDWICH

PETER SHOWLER

McGILL-QUEEN'S UNIVERSITY PRESS

Montreal & Kingston • London • Ithaca

ISBN-13: 978-0-7735-3094-2 ISBN-10: 0-7735-3094-0 (cloth)
ISBN-13: 978-0-7735-3096-6 ISBN-10: 0-7735-3096-7 (paper)

Legal deposit second quarter 2006
Bibliothèque nationale du Québec

Printed in Canada on acid-free paper that is 100% ancient forest
free (100% post-consumer recycled), processed chlorine free.
Reprinted 2006

McGill-Queen's University Press acknowledges the support of
the Canada Council for the Arts for our publishing program.
We also acknowledge the financial support of the Government
of Canada through the Book Publishing Industry Development
Program (BPIDP) for our publishing activities.

Library and Archives Canada Cataloguing in Publication

Showler, Peter
Refugee sandwich : stories of exile and asylum / Peter Showler.

ISBN-13: 978-0-7735-3094-2 ISBN-10: 0-7735-3094-0 (bnd)
ISBN-13: 978-0-7735-3096-6 ISBN-10: 0-7735-3096-7 (pbk)

1. Refugees—Government policy—Canada.
2. Refugees—Legal status, laws, etc.—Canada. I. Title.

HV640.4.C3S48 2006   325'.21'0971   C2005-907431-0

This book was designed and typeset by studio oneonone
in Sabon 10.6/14

Author's note:
Readers who are inspired by these stories to seek ways to
support protection and fair hearings for refugees may send
donations to the Canadian Council for Refugees, 6839 Drolet,
no. 302, Montreal, QC H2S 2T1. Further information about
CCR is available at www.web.ca/ccr.

This book is dedicated to the genuine
refugees who have come to Canada's
shores seeking asylum and to all of those
in Canada, volunteers and professionals,
who have assisted in the telling and
hearing of their stories.

CONTENTS

ACKNOWLEDGMENTS

Books with long gestation periods incur significant debts of gratitude. For advice, inspiration, and encouragement, each in their own way, thank you to Alice Elman, Alan Fleischman, Audrey Macklin, Barbara Blouin, Basha Rahn, Denault Blouin, Eunice Harker, Gillian Whyte, Gladys MacPherson, Ian Kagedan, Janet Dench, Janet MacEachen, Janet van der Vink, Jim Hathaway, John Leon, Judith Kumin, Lisa Gilad, Lorne Butchart, Marie-Andrée Lalonde, Michael Bossin, Michael Finner, Michael Ross, Michel Shore, Maxine Miska, Ninette Kelley, Paula Thompson, Ray Dare, Richard Elman, Richard Stainsby, Robert Edwards, Sheldon Posen, Stephanie Brancaforte, Susan Lightstone, Virginia Shaw, William Fizet, and, most of all, to Ellen, Adri, and Zani for their love and patience.

In addition, I deeply appreciate the impeccable editorial ear of Suzannah Showler during early drafts of this book as well as the astute and gentle editing of Claire Gigantes, who made invaluable contributions to the final manuscript.

CAVEATS

All of the thirteen stories in this book are solely fiction. They are based on the experience of the author as both a lawyer and Immigration and Refugee Board member but they do not refer to or portray any individual, whether refugee claimant or any other person involved with the refugee claim process. This must be stated most emphatically since refugee hearings are, by law, confidential. Additionally, where massive and chronic persecution occurs in a particular country, resulting in hundreds and even thousands of claims, it is inevitable that many claims will appear similar and even refer to common events. Any similarity between any actual claim and these stories is purely coincidental and not intended.

One story in the book, *Looking for the Little Things*, is dedicated to Lisa Gilad, a former member of the Board, now deceased. The principal character in that story, Hester, does reflect some of the exceptional qualities of Lisa's decision making. But she remains a fictional character and does not come close to capturing Lisa's personal warmth, brilliance, and lively sense of humour.

Most of the stories are based on claims made between 1989 and 1999. History has moved on. There are inevitable anachronisms. Some of the worst human rights situations have evolved or been resolved. Civil wars have ended, totalitarian regimes have fallen. Each story should be read in its historical context. Comparably, the Immigration and Refugee Board has evolved and improved. Some of the worst member and RCO conduct described in some stories is less likely to occur today. On the other hand, claims are now decided by a single member, not by two, as in most of the stories. To that extent, the possibilities for miscommunication, misunderstanding, and uncorrected error have increased.

INTRODUCTION

I WILL NEVER FORGET MY FIRST refugee claim. I was a law student in Halifax. The claimant, also a student, came from a small African country where a junior military officer had declared himself president of the country and then backed that declaration with ruthless military force. In those days, the refugee claim process was different. Claimants told their stories to a tape recorder, prompted by questions from an immigration officer. The claimants never met the officials of the Refugee Status Advisory Commission, located in Hull, Quebec, who read a transcript of the tape and made a decision. Yes, you are a refugee. No, you are not.

My client and I were ushered into a small room at the offices of the Department of Immigration in Halifax, not far from Pier 21 where thousands of new immigrants had first entered Canada. At times, the immigration officer's interview seemed surreal, like the touching of two dream worlds. He was a kindly man with a gentle voice and no discernible knowledge of the claimant's country or culture. Fortunately my client, I will call him Samuel, spoke English well although he scarcely understood the law or the refugee claim process and I fear that I, his legal counsel, was of limited assistance. There was one particular moment when Samuel was telling of his escape through the window of his bedroom as the soldiers were breaking through the front door; of the sound of his mother screaming; of running into the bush and later learning what they did to his sister. During the telling, his face shone with sweat and fear although his voice was calm as his words spooled into the tape recorder that captured none of the incongruous contrast between the excruciating horror of his story and the quiet, almost indifferent setting in which it was being told. Intent upon his duty, the immigration officer appeared oblivious to the meaning of the words he was hearing. "And then what happened?" he prompted.

Since that time, the law has changed dramatically. Refugee claimants now tell their stories directly to the person who decides their claim, a member of the Immigration and Refugee Board (IRB). Rather than an interview, there is a full quasi-judicial hearing with a panel of one or two Board members,[1] a Refugee Claim Officer[2] (RCO) to assist the panel, an interpreter, and the claimant's lawyer, who takes an active role in the hearing. I have participated in hundreds of refugee hearings, both as a lawyer representing claimants and as a member of the IRB deciding them. And still, despite the many improvements to the process and the training of Board members, there are invariably moments in every hearing where the profound gap between the realities of the claimant and the Board member suddenly becomes apparent. Illusions of meaningful communication are momentarily shattered. The best of the Board members and lawyers find ways to bridge those gaps. Others, because of indifference or hardened world views, founder in them, usually to the detriment of the claimant.

Although more than thirty thousand refugee claims are decided in Canada every year, most refugee stories are never heard by the Canadian public. The claims are necessarily confidential to prevent additional persecution of claimants and others and so their stories rarely escape the hearing rooms of the IRB. Yet for immigration lawyers and IRB members, the hearing room is a fascinating place, a crucible of truth and falsehood, where the most remarkable stories of abuse and violence, overwhelming fear, extraordinary courage, and improbable events are told every day.

1 In all but one of these stories, claims are decided by two-member panels. Since amendments to the legislation in June 2001, most refugee claims are decided by a single member.
2 Throughout various legislative changes, the IRB official assisting the Board members has been called a Refugee Hearing Officer, a Refugee Claim Officer, and currently, a Refugee Protection Officer. For consistency, I have employed the one term, Refugee Claim Officer (RCO).

This is a book about hearing and deciding refugee claims in Canada. The stories are fictional, although they may more accurately be described as mosaics composed of pieces broken from hundreds of refugee claims heard by myself and other members of the IRB. No single individual or case is contained within these covers.[3] The stories seek to illustrate the profoundly difficult process of communicating the experience of refugees within a judicial context, a difficulty that is shared by all participants. Board members must decide whether or not the refugee claimants have a well-founded fear of persecution in their home countries. If the board decides that they do, they will be granted refugee status and permitted to remain in Canada. If it is decided that they do not, they will be removed from Canada.

The refugee definition is complex, legally technical, and meaningless to most claimants. The full definition of a refugee under the 1951 UN Convention Relating to the Status of Refugees and the even more complex definition of a "protected person" are contained in the afterword. Here is a quick summary of the definition:

1 The claimant must have fear of persecution, which may be any form of serious persistent harm, not just death or torture.
2 There must be an agent of persecution. The persecutor may be a state agent or a non-state agent. In the latter case, claimants must prove that the state will not or cannot protect them.
3 There must be a reason for the persecution. Reasons include the claimant's race, religion, nationality, political opinions, or membership in a particular social group, which in Canada is defined broadly to include gender, sexual orientation, and family as well as unions or professional groups that may be targeted by persecutors. Fears of random violence or personal vendettas, no matter how well founded and no matter how harsh the potential injury, are not included. Fears of natural disasters, drought, starvation, plague, no matter how certain it is that such calamities will occur in the future and no matter how damaging they have been in the past, are not included.

3 Most of the hearings in these stories take place in the early to late 1990s. The country information is historically accurate for the relevant time periods.

4 The claimant must harbour a future fear. Refugees are not protected because of past persecution. The question is whether there is a reasonable possibility that they will be persecuted if they return to their home countries.

5 There can be no alternative protection. If a claimant has the right to enter and be protected by another country, Canada will not grant that person protection.

6 The claimant deserves protection. Some people who have committed crimes against humanity or serious non-political crimes are excluded from refugee protection on the grounds that they are not worthy of protection.

During the refugee claim process, the obstacles to communication are numerous and formidable. A vast chasm of potential miscommunication lies between the claimant and the decisionmaker. Most genuine claimants experience a profound sense of vulnerability due to their inability to understand the refugee claim process and their fear of being returned to persecution. The process is frightening because it does not make sense to them and because the stakes are so high. Their fear is magnified in the hearing room when questions are incomprehensible because of language, different cultural perspectives, or false assumptions on the part of the questioner. Claimants may be uneducated, inarticulate, traumatized, or simply unable to remember culturally irrelevant facts. They may be telling the truth as they perceive it, they may be exaggerating, or they may be telling a big fat whopper.

Board members may have a partial or thorough understanding of refugee law, some objective knowledge about the claimant's country, and often, some experience with prior claims from that country. They will have a detailed document, the Personal Information Form, reducing the claimants' life histories to dry, objective facts that may or may not capture their reasons for fearing persecution. They will have the lawful authority to decide claims on the facts and the law without interference from any other person or authority. They will have strong administrative pressures to complete the hearing within a half day. They will unavoidably bring their own cultural baggage to the hearings and, with luck, have some knowledge of its contents.

Members will also have a powerful ethical imperative to get their decisions right and some humility, one hopes, about the impossibility of getting it all right all the time.

The challenge, for both sides, is to find a means of bridging the chasm, of conveying and understanding the information necessary for the Board member to decide the refugee claim accurately. It is a daunting task requiring great skill, genuine empathy, and moral courage on the part of the Board members. For most claimants, at least the sincere ones, the process demands even greater courage. For them, the stakes are obviously higher and the confusion, fear, and lack of comprehension greater.

This book is also about storytelling: true stories, false stories, true and false stories. It is about the possibility and impossibility of relating and assessing the refugee experience within a judicial and bureaucratic context. It is about the genius and absurdity of human communication. It is a tribute to those who try to do it well and a condemnation of those who do not. It is a recognition that all parties to the process are sandwiched between the demands of fairness and efficiency, between the differences in cultures, between wealth and poverty, between the fearful chaos of the refugee experience and the logical and unrealistic expectations of law and government.

Refugees are most obviously and desperately sandwiched between the expectations of the law and their own limited abilities to meet those expectations. In subtler and less painful ways, refugee support workers, lawyers, interpreters, Board members, judges, and judicial institutions are also sandwiched between the demands of high-volume justice and the obligation to get every decision right. The refugee arriving on our shores, asking for our protection, unavoidably connects us all to the brutalities that humans inflict on humans and to our sense of being powerless to stop them. Ultimately, the refugee claimant places us all in the refugee sandwich.

REFUGEE SANDWICH

1

TWO EXERCISES

BEFORE YOU BEGIN THIS BOOK, you may wish to undertake two brief exercises.

EXERCISE ONE: THE CLAIMANT

Imagine you are a man or woman from a small town in a country located in Southeast Asia. Your country is hot, your house is made of wood, bamboo, and tile. You have a grade eight education, which is two years more than most people in the country. You are a respected member of the community: you make a decent living. You have a family with four children. You speak a little English – you studied it for five years at school. You own a bicycle; only wealthy people own cars. Only the main street of the town and the highway leading to the capital city are paved. Add whatever details you wish. Think about who you are.

The government is controlled by one political party whose leader is the president. You believe in democracy and have participated in secret meetings of an opposition party. Over the years members of the party have been imprisoned and even killed. You are careful and only share your political ideas with trusted friends.

Soldiers come to your house in the middle of the night, breaking down the door. They accuse you of being a member of the illegal opposition, which you deny. There is a lot of yelling, the children are crying, soldiers search the house, they hit you with their rifle butts, then your spouse. Pamphlets are found and you are thrown into the back of a jeep, shoved down on the floor, and taken to a military prison outside of town. For two weeks you are detained in a cell without light. It is filthy. You sleep on the floor with one torn blanket. There are lice on the blanket, things crawl over you at night, you defecate in a bucket in the corner. After a while you ignore the stench. You have always been a very clean person. Once a day the guard brings watery rice and beans. Three times you are taken to a room where a military officer accuses you of planning to overthrow the government. You are beaten every time you deny your involvement. Your nose is broken but you are not tortured in the way some others are. You hear the moaning from nearby cells.

After two weeks, a guard opens your cell door at night and leads you through a fence to the back of the camp where men are waiting for you. They take you to a house in the capital city. Your father-in-law and members of your party have bribed prison officials to release you. You will be arrested if you go back to your home. Your spouse and children are in hiding with a maternal aunt in another town. One week later you are given false documents and airline tickets to leave the country. Your father-in-law, with the help of other family members, has arranged everything through professional smugglers. A man who only gives his first name walks you through the airport security controls. It is your photograph in the passport. He accompanies you to Singapore where he transfers you to a plane going to a place called Caracas. A man who is not from your country but speaks your language badly meets you at the airport. You stay two days in a house where no one speaks your language. You stay in your room and think about your family. The man returns to take you to the airport where he gives you a different passport. He says you are going to Canada, a country that is kind to refugees and has human rights, but you must tear up the passport in the toilet of the airplane or the Canada Immigration officials will refuse you at the airport and send you back to your country. He gives you pieces of coloured paper which he says is Canadian money.

Please close your eyes for five minutes and think very carefully about your story and all that has happened to you before continuing.

Now, imagine walking off the airplane at Pearson International Airport in Toronto. It is nighttime. You follow the stream of passengers off the plane until they separate to form lines leading to people in uniform. You stay behind the white man walking in front of you. There are many people from other airplanes. You have never seen so many white people. A door opens and very cold air comes in. You did not know air could be that cold. There is talking on the loudspeaker but you cannot understand it. There are two policemen walking around with guns on their belts. Another policeman has a large dog on a chain who is sniffing at people. You are at the front of the line. Your leg is shaking, you feel frozen. The man behind the window motions you forward. He wears glasses and says something to you in English. You shake your head. He indicates he wants your document. You have practised saying "No passport, please" and you say it now. The man looks angry.

You say the second phrase that you have practised. "Refugee, I am refugee." You repeat this in your own language from the notes in your hand. The man looks around and waves at a woman who wears the same uniform as the official. The woman walks towards you and speaks to the official. She does not look like a police officer. They speak briefly and then she signals for you to follow her to a small room where a third official, a large man with no hair, gestures for you to sit down in a chair before his desk. Here you say your third phrase: "I speak no English."

The man says several words in English and points to a map. Finally you understand that he wants the name of your country. You say the name several times until the man seems to understand. He takes you to the hallway and indicates that you should sit in a chair. There are many officials leading passengers into different offices. One woman with two children looks very frightened.

Suddenly a man speaks to you in your language. He says that he is an interpreter and you are supposed to come back into the office to talk to the immigration official. He does not offer the traditional greeting. His accent is strange. He is from another region of your country but you understand him. You wonder what his political affiliations are. He is neither friendly nor unfriendly. You wonder if he can be trusted. He leads you back into the room where the immigration officer is sitting. Through the interpreter, the officer asks many questions. He says that you must always tell the truth. You do not understand all of the questions and the officer does not seem to understand all of your answers.

Finally he says that a UN convention refugee is a person who is outside of his or her country of nationality or, if there is no country of nationality, outside his country of former habitual residence and is unable or unwilling to avail himself of the protection of those countries by reason of a well-founded fear of persecution for reasons of race, religion, nationality, membership in a particular social group, or political opinion.

Now, here is your exercise. With the help of the interpreter, please explain why you are a refugee.

Good luck.

EXERCISE TWO: THE DECISION MAKER

You enter a room, a small room with four people sitting at tables organized into a hollow rectangle. They stand when you enter and wait for you to be seated on a dais at one end of the rectangle. The person sitting opposite you on the far side of the square is a refugee claimant, seeking the protection of Canada. An interpreter is seated next to him. You have read his file, which includes the details of his life and a badly written statement about his reasons for fearing persecution. The file also contains a thick document of information about the claimant's country: its history, politics, government structures, human rights record. Much of the information is general and irrelevant. You skimmed through it last night, reading the more obviously relevant portions. You know something of the political history of the country, its record of human rights abuses, its geography. You know the names of the president and the leader of the opposition but not the minister of defence nor any poet, singer, or sports star. You know the acronyms for the two largest political parties. You know it is a quasi-democratic state but do not know if there are one or two houses of Parliament. You know the names of the three largest cities, the two principal ethnic groups, and the security police. You do not know whether remote towns and villages have electricity, telephones, or paved roads. You have heard a few previous claims from the same country. You have never visited the country. You do not share the language, religion, skin colour, or calendar of its citizens. You have never had an intimate private conversation with any citizen of the country.

You have three hours, allowing for coffee and bathroom breaks, to listen to the testimony of the claimant, consider the evidence, and decide whether he or she is a convention refugee. The interpreter's English is poor. The claimant seems to be very nervous. He does not look directly at you and does not seem to understand all of the questions posed by you or his lawyer. Some of his responses make sense, some do not. You have sixty days to write clear, cogent reasons for your decision. If your decision is negative, your reasons may be reviewed by a Federal Court judge and quashed if they are found to be inadequate in law.

If your decision is positive, the claimant will likely be granted permanent residence in Canada. If the claimant has successfully lied to you, it is unlikely that you will ever know it. If the claimant has himself committed human rights abuses, it is unlikely that you will ever know it. If your decision is negative, there is a possibility that he will be deported. He may also remain in Canada for years under a quasi-legal status, separated from family abroad, with limited rights to work or study. You will not know which occurs. If the claimant is returned to his country and persecuted, tortured, or killed, you will likely never know it. You do not enjoy the benefit of the scientific method. You do not get to test your conclusions.

Now, think about hearing six refugee claims a week from several different countries, week in, week out. Good luck.

2

EXCLUDING MANUEL

IT SEEMS A SIMPLE PRINCIPLE: do not give refuge to the persecutor. It is the corollary to the UN convention's central commitment and axiom: we shall give refuge to those who fear persecution in their home country. In the refugee business, it is known as exclusion. If you commit crimes against humanity, you are excluded from the refugee definition. There is no safe haven for the torturer even though he now fears torture.

There is an obvious good purpose to the rule. People who persecute refugees should not themselves be granted asylum. There are too many stories of Haitians out for a stroll on St Catherine's Street suddenly encountering the member of the Tonton Macoute who terrorized their neighbourhood in Port-au-Prince, killing innocents, or of a Tutsi who has lost all of her family meeting the Hutu administrator who fanned the flames of madness in her village, a man known to be without remorse. And of course there are the nations that give refuge to the Baby Doc Duvaliers, Mobutus, Idi Amins, Pinochets. These are not moral ambiguities and yet, and yet ... even with torture, we are dealing with affairs of the human heart and mind. There are subtleties, exceptions; time passes, a kindness follows a killing. The torturer seeks to atone for past misdeeds. And redemption, what about redemption?

So it was with Manuel who had been in Canada more than seven years with his family after he had escaped from his country. Now a janitor in a school, he had allegedly been a torturer for the security police before fleeing to Canada. There were no details about specific acts of torture in his file and he had vehemently denied the allegations at his first hearing several years before. He had sworn that he was a simple policeman who only did his duty, but it was a thinner, more urgent man who appeared before the second panel.

The case was a procedural nightmare. His claim was first heard in 1989, one of the early cases to be heard by the new Immigration and Refugee Board. The panel members, suspicious of his police work but new to their job, could not find their way through the thicket of his denials. In frustration, they refused him on the ground that his fear of persecution was not well founded, although his country was still consumed by civil war and he had deserted from the Technical Police, an offence punishable by death. In those days the Federal Court, buried in its own backlog, was slow to review Board decisions, and so it took nearly three years for the court to quash the Board's decision and send Manuel's case back for a new hearing.

In the meantime, Manuel had moved to a small town in Ontario, the file was transferred, the file was lost, there had been letters to the Board's chairperson from two bishops, one Catholic, one Anglican, speaking of the hard-working immigrant, the family well liked, the daughter first in her class, the concern, even indignation, of the community. Finally, seven years after his arrival in Canada, he would again sit before a different panel of the Board sent to hold a new hearing in the local courthouse. A representative of the Minister of Citizenship and Immigration also attended, determined to prove that Manuel had twisted screws in human flesh and had to be deported as a danger to Canadians and an embarrassment to the community that had spoken for him.

The panel convened on a Monday morning in the badly lit basement of the courthouse, a dry stale room smelling of old documents. Thankfully, one small window was open to the light, sounds, and smells of a soft spring day, apple blossoms, birdsong, a shaft of sunlight reaching halfway to the hollow rectangle of tables that occupied the centre of the room. Bingo hall furniture, plywood tables, metal chairs. The courthouse staff had clearly indicated the measure of their respect for the Immigration and Refugee Board.

On a bench along the wall, Manuel sat with his family. A small man in a short-sleeved white shirt, with black heavily oiled hair and dark hollows in a haunted face. His wife was shorter, heavier; the children, five in a row, all daughters, were aligned in descending order according to size, their dark hair neatly tied back with bright ribbons; they wore pastel dresses, probably their confirmation dresses, shiny black shoes, and white socks: a picture-book family. The three youngest girls were Canadian by birth. Probably none could remember their home country. And Manuel? Did he remember?

"Por favor, señor Judge, I am Manuel."

"Good morning, Mr Benitez. I am Mr McDougall and this is Mrs Chiarelli. We are the Board members who will decide your claim. And this is Ms Pacek, she is the Refugee Claim Officer who will assist us. Is your lawyer here yet?"

"No, I do not have. The lawyer is too much money. But I do not need the lawyer. I will tell the truth. I take what you and God decide."

McDougall was a tall spare man with faded red hair and too many lines in a long, thin face. He appeared uncomfortable talking to the much shorter man. His colleague, Mrs Chiarelli, was a large woman wearing a dark business suit and lipstick that was either too thick or too bright – McDougall couldn't decide which. With a look around the room, she clearly indicated her displeasure with her surroundings.

"Well, it's certainly not the Supreme Court. You'd think they could do a little better than this, even in a one-horse town."

Ms Pacek, a thin, nervous woman, went directly to the tables where she began to unpack two large briefcases. Mrs Chiarelli walked over to what would clearly be the panel members' table at one end of the rectangle, plunked down her briefcase, and opened her purse to remove a gold cigarette case.

"I don't suppose they'd mind my smoking in here since no one has apparently used the place in years." She removed a cigarette from the case and lit it with a flourish, returning the lighter to her purse, which she snapped shut.

McDougall, still standing near Manuel, appeared lost in thought. He didn't know his colleague well. She was relatively new to the Board. Member rumours said she had been the volunteer president of a major arts charity before her appointment and was well connected to two cabinet ministers from Toronto. He was troubled by Manuel's lack of a lawyer. Clearly the man had no idea what exclusion meant, or complicity, or duress, or any of the legal principles that contributed to the complicated body of case law surrounding exclusion. McDougall had been a successful lawyer before coming to the Board, real estate and estate planning, nothing to do with refugees. Successful in a minor way; he was well off, not rich, and had wanted something different for the latter part of his career, to put his legal skills to work for some good, something with flesh and blood. Through good fortune, his best friend, who was also his local Member of Parliament, had been pleased to express his gratitude for a lifetime of personal and financial support. After three years on the Board, McDougall was still overwhelmed by the vividness of the suffering that so frequently filled his hearing room.

"Well, let's get this show on the road."

Mrs Chiarelli had finished her cigarette and was unpacking her briefcase. She was the presiding member, responsible for all procedural decisions in the case. McDougall found her to be crass, insensitive to claimants and to the effects of her remarks on others. He had learned that claimants secretly scrutinized the judges, looking for any signs of positive or negative inclination, reading too much into too little. During their few cases together, Mrs Chiarelli had seemed totally oblivious to the claimants. She had barely acknowledged Manuel or his family. He also knew she was smart and decisive, brooking no nonsense from claimants or colleagues.

Ms Pacek was still untangling the wires of the various tiny microphones that would be placed before each participant. She was a competent, dutiful RCO who did her job while disclosing as little as possible about herself. This was a nightmare case; she had avoided it and wouldn't be here except for a screw-up at scheduling, which of course should surprise no one. Chiarelli was a blunderbuss and should never have been put on a case like this, certainly not as the presiding member. McDougall was okay, a trifle insipid, but he didn't put his foot in cow plops, as her uncle used to say.

Chiarelli was not pleased that McDougall had been assigned as her partner. The man was a twit. She normally travelled with Helen Carstairs, who was a delight. They saw things the same way, never disagreed on the outcome of a case. She was someone who knew the pleasure of a cigarette and didn't mind the odd off-colour joke. She imagined McDougall's long white body in a bathing suit at the hotel pool, probably a sunken chest, wrinkles on his knees. This would definitely be a business trip. No hanky-panky with the punky-wunky. Hopefully they wouldn't have to stay over. With luck this fellow would admit to having tortured people and they could all go home.

"We're still missing the Minister's rep and the interpreter."

McDougall was standing beside her. God he was lanky. What did he expect her to do about it? Couldn't anyone show up on time in this organization? Compared to the Foundation, this was a joke. God, when she thought of her former office – the carpeting, great view, prestigious address, everything but a salary. Still, compared to this. A basement for God's sake. Board members of the largest federal tribunal, practically judges, hearing cases in a basement. She looked over at the claimant, cute little family all in a row. Her son had had a bunny dish like that when he was a boy. Momma rabbit and all the dressed-up little baby rabbits. He hadn't phoned in a month. Stanford education, doing well in Silicone Valley. He could bounce e-mails off satellites but he couldn't pick up a telephone. She was irritated to see McDougall standing there, obviously waiting for something.

"Can't we start without them? Just get the start-up nonsense out of the way?"

He looked uncomfortable, twisting his long body into unusual positions.

"I don't think so. The claimant doesn't have a lawyer so we're going to have to explain the law and procedure fairly clearly. He's not going to understand. What do you think Ms Pacek?"

Ms Pacek had finally untangled the wires of the tape recorder and was on her knees trying to insert the extension cord into a wall socket, which for some reason was cut into the baseboard.

"I don't believe we can start without benefit of an interpreter, un-less you are satisfied that he is sufficiently competent in English to proceed without interpretation."

"The man's been in Canada for seven years. What's his problem? He doesn't need a college degree. He just has to understand ordi-nary English. He probably watches more TV than any of us. Maybe the daughter can translate. She's old enough. She must be in grade ten or eleven, top of her class according to the bishop."

McDougall turned a bland eye on her, thinking it was going to be a very bad day. Great idea. Let's ask the fourteen-year-old daughter to interpret while the father tells us about all the crimes against humanity that he's committed. Oh yes. A fourteen-year-old claimant becomes the interpreter while the family has no legal counsel. The Federal Court will love this one.

"She's a claimant herself. She can't act as interpreter. Besides she hasn't been certified. We could never challenge his credibility. The court would strike it down in a minute. Do you agree, Ms Pacek?"

"I agree. I'll call the office and see if they have a number for the interpreter. We also have to wait for Gilles. The Minister could appeal if we proceeded without him."

"I take it Gilles is the Minister's rep. Why would he appeal if it's going to be a negative?"

Ms Pacek, looking for the cellphone in her briefcase, pretended not to hear her. Nothing like starting the hearing with an open mind. McDougall looked away, watching Manuel's wife bending over the youngest daughter, straightening a sock. She was squatting, not bending, her thick legs surprisingly pliable. Probably women had been squatting like that in fields in her country for hundreds of years. He found it refreshing, an honest body posture. He remembered the psychiatric report in the file, speaking of her extreme stress; she was under medication due to the endless delays and anxiety about being sent back to her country.

There had been a lawyer on the file at the time, pleading for an early date for the hearing. That was more than a year ago. McDougall had not been too surprised to find Manuel without counsel. The legal aid cutbacks would have greatly reduced his chances of getting a lawyer. His home country was no longer considered to be refugee-producing. Wonderful expression that, refugee-producing. It made refugees sound like a product, a natural resource. Mind you, they still killed deserters from the army. Not all was forgiven after ten years of civil war. Why couldn't the bishops pay for a lawyer? Or the community, if they were genuinely concerned.

"Bonjour. Comment allez-vous, Monsieur le Commissaire? Salut, Sandra. Ça va?"

"Bonjour Gilles! Oui, ça va. Et toi?"

McDougall mumbled a responding bonjour. Ms Pacek had clearly brightened with the arrival of the Minister's rep, a cheerful, breezy man in a black leather sports jacket and thin leather tie. His receding hairline was partially disguised by the half-inch buzz cut. McDougall felt he would never get used to the French Canadian thing. He had been designated as functionally bilingual, which meant that he could say hello and thank you and catch half the gist of what was said at bilingual meetings. He was willing to speak his heavily anglicized French but he felt hesitant and uncomfortable. It wasn't the language, it was the personality change that went with it. At the same time, he despised the hypocrisy of the bureaucrats who began their comments in French, usually written by their francophone secretaries, and then switched as soon as politically possible to English, for "the remainder of my remarks." They were suckholes. Buzz cuts and suckholes. Two expressions he'd learned from his daughter, a commercial artist who moved with a very fast crowd in Toronto. Fast by his standards anyway, a lot of sexual ambiguity and very little commitment. But his daughter claimed to be happy and looked the part. Gilles had shaken hands all around although he studiously ignored Manuel who still sat with his family on the far side of the room.

McDougall strolled self-consciously over to the family. "I am sorry we cannot begin until the interpreter arrives. We are trying to locate her, to find her. Good morning, Señora." He nodded to Manuel's wife, who remained seated with her children.

"I do not wish to wait. I can speak some English and my daughter is very good in English. She is *primera* in the classe. My wife is very sick. She does not want to wait."

"We do not want to wait either. We know it has been a long time but we also want to be fair to you, to make sure you understand everything." McDougall had learned the knack of speaking English to claimants, clearly enunciating his words, no contractions, no colloquialisms, slowing his speech yet maintaining a rhythm so he didn't appear to be talking down to them. He did not confuse limited language ability with lack of intelligence.

"It is more fair to decide today, Mr Judge. I am sure. It is in the hands of God."

McDougall nodded and sighed inwardly. In the hands of God. God willing. Inshallah. The number of times he had heard that naive fatalism from claimants of every major religion. All so confident of some exterior beneficence. The Lebanese Shiites, so many of them refused a few years back because of one Board member, a staunch Orangeman from rural Ontario who was suspicious of all Arabs. God had some peculiar ways of looking out for his own. In God's hands indeed.

"We're all here. Let's get underway!" Mrs Chiarelli called from the other side of the room. A quiet well-dressed woman stood beside her. She signalled urgently to McDougall to join them. "This is Diane Cord, our translator. Let's go before I need another smoke break. Mrs Cord, please tell the claimant and his wife to join us. His name is Manuel Benitez. I don't know the wife's name."

McDougall wondered how well she had prepared the case. He had spent the previous evening making meticulous notes of all the relevant details of Manuel's military career, the family's flight, and a summary outline of the civil war and subsequent political violence. He knew from experience that it would be very difficult to follow the twists and turns of the testimony without an outline of names, dates, and major events.

"Now Mr Benitez, you sit over there. And talk loudly so the microphone can pick up your testimony. Mrs Cord, could you tell him all that in Spanish? And Mrs Benitez, you can sit back there. The children don't need to be here. Some of the testimony may be messy. I don't think they should be here." Mrs Chiarelli was arranging the parties around the table, apparently oblivious of the children who huddled around their mother although their eyes followed Mrs Chiarelli. Manuel's dark face was already shining with sweat. McDougall watched as the mother spoke quietly to the eldest daughter who then led the children out of the room, the second oldest casually brushing her father's shoulder as she walked behind him.

"Is everyone ready?" Mrs Chiarelli looked at Ms Pacek, who nodded and pressed the start button on the tape recorder.

"Now, this is a hearing into the Convention refugee claim of Manuel Benitez, file number 89-00759, as well as that of his wife and his two eldest children, whose names and file numbers are on file. This is a rehearing of the claim upon order of the Federal Court, which quashed the Board's original decision upon judicial review in April 1995 and ... Oh, excuse me, Mrs Cord, I forgot to allow you time to translate; perhaps you'd better do that now. Just summarize what I said."

McDougall wondered who looked more confused, the interpreter or Manuel. She turned to Manuel and began to speak in hesitant Spanish. Even McDougall's inexperienced ear could hear the anglicized accent. Manuel nodded encouragement to her several times.

With that rocky beginning it took more than half an hour to complete the formalities of the hearing introduction, to enter the exhibits and have Manuel swear an oath to tell the truth. The file clerk had inadvertently packed a Koran instead of a Bible. Mrs Chiarelli said it had the same effect but Manuel could make a solemn affirmation instead. Mrs Cord did not know how to interpret "solemn affirmation." Manuel crossed himself and said in English that he would tell the truth before God, crossing himself again. Mrs Chiarelli said that was probably good enough.

McDougall's best friend on the Board, John Barstow, had a theory about problem files. He said they were like positive ions that attracted all the negative factors in the claim process, thus keeping the file flow relatively clean for the other cases. Barstow was a very clever cynical man who constantly complained about the ineptitude of the Board and the civil service in general. He had been loudly proclaiming his imminent retirement for two years. McDougall didn't buy the theory but he suspected the current file might make him a believer. It was definitely a Murphy's Law case. Whatever could go wrong, would go wrong.

Two of the tiny microphones weren't recording. Mrs Chiarelli said everyone should speak louder. The Minister's representative had not received the Board's letter outlining the principal issues that were to be decided. McDougall listened to Gilles's protests with half a mind. Weren't the issues obvious? Had Manuel committed human rights abuses? And would the military still prosecute him for desertion after all these years? And what did the Minister want, another adjournment? Manuel had received the disclosure package, a large thick document that he had not read, explaining that he did not read English so good and it was not something for his daughter to read. Mrs Chiarelli said that that was his decision but the hearing should proceed.

The interpreter, Mrs Cord, was a disaster, stumbling over the legalisms in English. McDougall could not imagine what she was saying in Spanish. He was bemused to observe her confusion as Mrs Chiarelli droned through her opening spiel. "The Convention Refugee Determination Division hears and determines claims in accordance with the law and in a manner which reflects Canada's humanitarian tradition ... if you are outside your country of nationality or formal habitual residence ... those who have a well-founded fear of persecution due to their race, religion, nationality, membership in a particular social group, or political opinion." McDougall had long since discarded the spiel, finding it to be virtually incomprehensible in English or any other known language.

Barely pausing for breath, Mrs Chiarelli plowed on into the elements of the definition that spelled out the grounds for exclusion – if the claimant had committed crimes against peace, a war crime, or a crime against humanity, as defined in the international instruments drawn up to make provision in respect of such crimes.

Obviously defeated, Mrs Cord was making no pretence of interpreting everything, mumbling a few words in Spanish out of the side of her mouth whenever Mrs Chiarelli paused for breath. McDougall finally leaned toward his colleague to whisper, "I don't think she's able to follow you."

Mrs Chiarelli gave him an irritated look. She wasn't blind. God the man could be inconvenient. It was all just mumbo-jumbo to satisfy the court that all of the procedures were followed. Of course the interpreter didn't understand it. It had taken her months of reciting the damn thing before she understood it. The world wasn't all lawyers after all, just the bloody judges. What did he expect? And what was that little Hispanic man going to understand in any language? He didn't read English and had a grade four education in Spanish.

"Mrs Cord, are you understanding the substance of my recitation?" She gave the interpreter a stern look that admitted of only one answer. Mrs Cord said she did.

"And you, Mr Benitez, do you understand the interpreter?" Manuel nodded his head vigorously, not waiting for the interpretation.

"I am satisfied that all parties understand the gist of the procedure and law and that we can continue."

McDougall wondered how Mrs Cord would interpret "gist."

By three o'clock Mrs Chiarelli had a piercing headache. Lunch at the little diner across the street had been most unsatisfactory – lovely gingham tablecloths but godawful club sandwiches; too much mayonnaise, no low-fat. She should have known when the waitress asked, "Brown or white?" The town had not yet discovered the concept of whole wheat bread. God in Heaven! Dyed Wonder Bread and Club Soda masquerading as mineral water. And the hearing was going badly. She couldn't decide who was the principal culprit, that little Frenchman who spoke inexcusable English, the interpreter who truly was as clueless as the waitress, the little Hispanic who seemed too ignorant to lie or the bloodless doorpost next to her, scribbling endless notes as though the claimant had anything meaningful to say.

McDougall found the questions from the Minister's rep to be truly surreal as he attempted to dissect the minute details of Manuel's duties with the Technical Police. "So dese tings dat you did for dis oder man who is de commandant, is dis de same ting dat you did for the oder officer, de one wit de power to make de arrest to de suspected person?"

"Loopy." That was another word McDougall had learned from his daughter. The questions, the entire testimony, were definitely loopy. He could not imagine what metamorphoses the mangled questions underwent as they passed through Mrs Cord's Spanish meat grinder and Manuel's comprehension to elicit unconnected responses.

"I went many times to the home of the officers."

Manuel appeared to be working hard, his brow deeply furrowed with vertical creases, desperate to give a meaningful answer and knowing it wasn't going well.

It was three o'clock and McDougall had no clearer idea of what Manual actually did for the police. The Technical Police appeared to have a wide range of duties, everything from traffic control to security work. Manuel, frequently breaking into English, was trying to describe the different divisions and sections of the police. Mrs Cord's translation of "section" as "field" had not assisted

McDougall. For a while he thought they were talking about field duties. Meanwhile Chiarelli harrumphed and snorted but was generally ineffective in forcing her way through the thickets of miscommunication.

McDougall leaned over to whisper. "Perhaps we should have the RCO ask the questions directly in English. Manuel's English seems to be as good as Mrs Cord's Spanish."

"Yes! An excellent idea. Mr Archambault, perhaps we will make more progress if Ms Pacek asks the questions in English." Gilles looked relieved. "Is that all right with you, Mr Benitez? Ms Pacek will ask you the questions in very simple English so you can understand and make your answers in English?"

"Yes please, Señora. Is much better. I understand."

And they made progress. Pacek asked the questions well, simplifying the English and following clear lines of logic that Manuel began to anticipate. They soon understood that he had been originally conscripted into the army, then transferred to the Technical Police, which was a separate military branch under the direct control of the minister of the Interior. He had first worked as a traffic policeman responsible for "civil control" of particular neighbourhoods. McDougall made a note, he would go back later to ask what civil control actually meant, entailing what kinds of police action. He had heard previous refugee claims from Manuel's country where the military had kicked in the doors of suspected guerrilla sympathizers and arrested male suspects, later leaving them on the outskirts of town frozen in the kneeling position, blindfolded, hands tied behind their backs, a single bullet in the base of the skull, sometimes marks of torture on hands and bare feet, often smashed teeth. Had Manuel done these things to other humans? Is that why his face was heavy with sweat? Chiarelli interrupted his thoughts.

"Let's take a break. Miss Pacek, fifteen minutes?" He knew that meant enough time for a cigarette on the back steps of the courthouse, the kind of hideaway smokers soon ferreted out in smoke-hostile environments. Surprisingly Chiarelli signalled for McDougall to join her. The back stoop was pleasant and sheltered, if a little cramped. It looked onto a small park filled with the greenery of large leafy trees. Chiarelli lit her cigarette in silence. McDougall stood on a lower step to allow her more smoking room and to equalize their heights. He waited, knowing she had brought him there for a reason.

"We're going to have to adjourn. We'll never get done today and I'm not available for two months."

He was taken offguard. "Can't we finish tomorrow? This case needs to get done."

"Well you can do it. I have plans at home and there's no way I'm staying in some second-rate Holiday Inn."

McDougall looked off into the shadows cast by the tall stately trees in the park. Elms. Didn't see them so often, nearly wiped out by Dutch Elm disease. "What about the psych report on Mrs Benitez? She's in bad shape. Another adjournment could put her back in the hospital."

"Well whose fault is that? She's the one who married the human rights abuser." McDougall didn't say anything, waiting, standing his ground. Silence was a powerful persuader.

Chiarelli broke first. "God, I hate it when these people lay their problems on others. Besides, the interpretation was terrible. He's not understanding half of it. We should really start again with another panel and a real interpreter."

McDougall bit his tongue. He should be amused by Chiarelli's sudden concern for natural justice. Instead he had an irrational urge to physically strike her – better still, aim a kick at her well-padded posterior. He hadn't struck anyone in his life. Not even the boy who had deliberately stomped on his model airplane in grade three. How ridiculous. He probably couldn't even raise his leg that high.

"Leonora, I don't like you and I am perfectly aware that you do not particularly like me. This hearing has already been buggered up in more ways than I can count, mainly due to the inability of the Board and Minister to even approximate compliance with their own procedures. But there's a man and woman and five children in there who are going through a living hell and we have a job to do. If this fellow has committed human rights abuses, and I say 'if' because we have not yet heard one scintilla of evidence to establish that he has, despite all your presumptions, then we send him back. If he hasn't, we decide if he still has a fear of persecution. But we decide. We do not adjourn, we do not dump the dirty job on some other panel to come down two months from now. We use our intelligence and common sense to bypass the interpreter and Minister's rep and we decide. And I don't care if we sit until midnight or we adjourn for supper and resume in the morning. We will decide this case."

He was shaking as he walked back in, not looking behind to see her reaction. "Buggered." Another one of his daughter's words. He could never recall uttering the word. And Ralph Dempsey. The name kept repeating. He hadn't thought about the man in five years, a real estate lawyer, not particularly successful but known for sharp practice, a bully who had twice attempted to force him to close a deal after last-minute irregularities had occurred and he had given ground, comprising, suggesting alternatives that had worked out but left him feeling weak, somehow sullied.

Manuel was again seated on the bench across the room, huddled with his wife and two eldest daughters, who had returned. Who was caring for the younger children? They all turned to watch him, sensing that something of import had occurred. He nodded to them, nodded at Pacek, then took his seat. Manuel and his wife returned to their chairs as did Gilles, Mrs Cord, and Ms Pacek. He busied himself with his notes as did the others except for Manuel, all studiously ignoring Chiarelli's empty seat.

The lingering silence was painful. He could hear the scratching of Gilles's pen. Pacek occupied herself with the tape machine. Manuel and his wife sat with stony faces. The quiet was choking, claustrophobic. The old courthouse creaked in the full heat of the day, making long strange sounds, quite distinct when you listened, like some old plow horse labouring up a slope. Gilles cleared his throat and finally, McDougall heard the bang of the door as Chiarelli entered behind him. Manuel didn't move and stared straight ahead, his black eyes, shiny as buttons, fixed on some object. It suddenly hit McDougall that Manuel thought this was it, the final decision. My God, they weren't halfway through the evidence. The poor fellow didn't have the faintest notion of what the hearing process was about. Beside him Chiarelli was struggling with her chair. He scraped his chair sideways without looking at her.

"Mr Benitez. This panel would like to acknowledge the difficulties in interpretation that have occurred during your testimony today. Through no fault of Mrs Cord's, I might add, who has been

asked to perform duties outside the range of her normal professional experience as a Spanish language instructor."

McDougall felt his shoulders tighten. Damn. She was going to
adjourn anyway. She was presiding, there was nothing he could do
except make a complaint to the Deputy Chair, a fruitless gesture.
Chiarelli's power lay elsewhere with the unknown cabinet ministers. She had little to fear from a Deputy Chair whose word would
carry little weight with the Minister of Immigration.

"And I must say that, in the view of the panel, we have made little progress in assessing the material issues in your case. Given the
lateness of the day and the lack of progress, an adjournment is inevitable."

Damn. Manuel moved for the first time, squirming in his chair.
Clearly he understood that word, adjournment. How could he not,
having heard it so often? McDougall looked away, seeing nothing.

"However, I am also cognizant of the considerable stress the
refugee determination process has placed on you and your family,
in particular Mrs Benitez." McDougall heard his own intake of
breath, felt his throat constrict. "We realize that an extended adjournment would be cause for considerable distress to all concerned. As well, we are encouraged by your ability to testify in
English. Consequently we will resume the hearing tomorrow morning. We stand adjourned."

Manuel was struggling to understand. "Tomorrow, Señora?
Here? *Nueve hora?*"

"No. Eight o'clock. Mrs Cord, tell him he must be here at seven
forty-five. We will start promptly at eight and we will finish this
damn thing. Mr McDougall, I trust you will not object excessively
to the profanity. Ms Pacek, speak to whatever clerk upstairs is responsible for this dungeon to ensure it will be open before eight. Mr
Archambault, I trust you will be able to attend? I should have asked
prior to my decision."

"Oui, Madame. No problem, an' I will be ver' happy if de RCO
ask de question."

"Good. Mr McDougall, since this was your idea, I trust you will
take responsibility for finding us a decent place to stay. No motels
and I prefer a double bed. Also a restaurant that can spell hors
d'oeuvre."

McDougall found himself hopping to, part of the entourage receiving his assignment from the queen. And pleased to be of service, Ma'am. Manuel looked glum and worried, talking to his wife in Spanish. McDougall had an urge to clap him on the shoulder, to reassure him. This was good news. What did he expect? A same-day decision? If the decision was going to be negative, it would be two or three months before he received it with written reasons. A one-day delay was nothing. He still had a chance. McDougall had to remind himself that this man might still turn out to be a torturer. He was the decisionmaker. He wasn't supposed to be rooting for the little guy.

While Mrs Chiarelli was reorganizing her files, he quietly spoke to the RCO. "Ms Pacek, could you please reassure Mr Benitez that we will make every effort to complete the testimony tomorrow?"

Ms Pacek nodded, thinking of her concert ticket for Yo-Yo Ma, now worthless. As usual, no one had asked the RCO about her schedule. At least the Minister's rep got an apology. The man earned about ten thousand more than she did and couldn't ask four competent questions in English. His logic was so convoluted, she suspected he wasn't that much more effective in French. So she would be spending the evening in her room preparing the questions that Gilles wasn't capable of asking and not even a thank you for a job well done. McDougall was a nice man but he might think about someone besides the claimants. Without further comment, she went over to Manuel to explain that the bad news was really good news. It was difficult to believe this scrawny little man had been a policeman, let alone a torturer. She supposed they all looked big with a weapon in their hands.

McDougall had a surprisingly pleasant dinner with Mrs Chiarelli. The hotel dining room proved to be charming, with beautiful linens from another time and fresh-cut flowers on every table. They had a small table overlooking well-kept gardens and a grassy slope running down to the small river for which the town was named. His wife would enjoy the view as the lowering sun softened the outline of trees and flowers, filling the gardens with a rich golden light. He thought of Thomas Hardy who wrote so well of that time between day and night, a daily equinox with its own particular stillness. There were cows in the pasture across the river. Bucolic. A good word. These were his sunset years, he should be softened by the lowering of his energies and expectations. He should be thinking of retirement, of leaving the fray.

Mrs Chiarelli pronounced the Chianti excellent. It appeared she was something of an expert; her father had made wine for years. She told him of her father's immigrant struggles, arriving in Canada after the war with little but the skill in his hands and the will to succeed. She remembered a succession of houses in downtown Toronto, big houses with the noise of student tenants and endless renovation. Her father was a tireless man. A stonemason by day, he renovated at night, and they moved once the house was completed, a family of hermit crabs. By the time his back gave out, he owned six properties, enough to support his children while he passed his time with the older men in the Cafe Calabria and became a presence in the back rooms of the Liberal party. Angelo could deliver the vote.

She said she knew something of poverty. The only stain on the evening occurred when she claimed to be able to understand "these people," meaning, McDougall assumed, refugees, and she was endlessly sympathetic to the ones who were willing to work hard and told the truth. He played with the notion of a new refugee definition based on sincerity and effort – and what then of the persecuted with broken lives or the frightened dissemblers, the inarticulate? – and found it an unkind thought as the golden light descended further into the grasses of the lawn and distant pasture; he did not want to fight with Chiarelli or anyone else on such an evening.

———

The morning started well. Everyone was in the room early, Manuel and his family looking fresh and apprehensive, the children again in their Sunday dresses. He wore the same shirt he'd had on the day before but freshly laundered and pressed. Again the daughters departed and Pacek was already asking questions as the town clock sounded the hour. Even in the basement, McDougall could feel the heavy waves of bronze sound rolling out over the town, a real bell, reassuring the residents of time and continuity. Most of these people had marked the days of their lives by that sound. This was a place out of time, perhaps a place to retire. Far enough from Toronto for lower property values and his wife would be pleased with the large gardens. How had Manuel found such a haven?

"And did you carry weapons when you went on patrol?"

"Si, Señora, it was very dangerous."

Pacek was trying to isolate Manuel's more serious military activities. Over the first hour she had roughed out the outlines of his military career. As a sixteen-year-old peasant boy working in his father's rented fields, he had been drafted early into military service and had served as a dutiful soldier fighting guerillas in the north. The army arbitrarily extended his service by one year, then transferred him to the Technical Police where, upon re-enlistment, he was offered more money than any of his brothers could earn labouring as tenant farmers. He could marry and have a family and send money to his father and so he accepted, remaining with the police for five years before suddenly leaving the country one year before the civil war ended. Questions about torture had disclosed nothing. Manuel was unwavering in his denial that he had ever smashed teeth, twisted limbs, attached electrodes. Idly, McDougall wondered why Manuel had left. His rapid departure from service and country had never been explained.

"Were these patrols in the city, into people's homes?"

"No, Señora, they were in the field."

"And this was still with the Technical Police, not with the military?"

"Yes, with the Technicals but they are the militaries, Señora."

They had been over this ground twice before, once with the Minister's rep in a very haphazard manner, then with Pacek, moving very carefully, thoroughly, the way, McDougall imagined, a good platoon commander would move over terrain, missing nothing. They had at least partially uncovered the metamorphic relationships between various units of the police and the army. The Technical Police, the National Police, the Military Police, the Security Service, the Army, the Traffic Police, who were ironically some of the most serious people, accused of numerous atrocities against the families of suspected political dissidents. It was difficult to establish a pattern. The army did what appeared to be police work and the police carried out military missions. McDougall was certain that it was all a shell game perpetrated by political leaders and commanders who did their best to hide the worst of the abuses from international eyes. The civil war had been going on for years before human rights reporters were able to link the atrocities with particular units. And then there were the death squads, the nighttime murderers with balaclavas whom everyone knew to be security police of some form. But never proven, just as the American military presence had never been proven beyond a few "military advisors" captured after the downing of a government helicopter.

So Pacek was careful, reversing her field, always ascertaining which police unit Manuel was referring to, for McDougall knew she was cautiously moving toward one damning piece of evidence buried in the two-hundred-odd pages of documents. It was a report by the local human rights commission on one of the most "active" police units, known as Unit B or the White Division, which maintained a secret detention centre on a military base near the capital city. The commission had documented the testimony of several torture survivors before the commission's offices were ransacked and burned by persons unknown. The government alleged that guerrillas were responsible, purportedly trying to destroy evidence of their own human rights abuses. No one believed the government but it didn't matter. Nothing could be known for certain. Fortunately some of the commission's documents had been smuggled out of the country by a Protestant church group, including the document that stated quite definitively that Unit B was attached to the Technical Police.

By the coffee break, Pacek had established that Manuel had fired his gun on several occasions, but it was always during military skirmishes while on patrol. He had not shot at civilians. So far he had held up fairly well, answering the questions promptly in bad English.

After the break, Pacek asked Manuel directly about Unit B. McDougall had seen this technique before. Meander around laying groundwork, then suddenly hit the claimant right between the eyes with the crunch question. With manifest liars, McDougall thought it a good technique.

Manuel seemed surprised. His brow had instantly furrowed. "Unit B? Que es Unit B? Is that a Section B?"

A peculiar time to lapse into Spanish. Pacek smelled a rat and went after it like any good terrier. "Yes. Unit B. Do you know of a police group known as Unit B?"

"There are many militaries with that name, Señora."

"I am interested in one particular police section. It is known as Unit B. They wear regular army uniforms with a white patch on the shoulder." Pacek paused, then added, "The right shoulder," looking directly into Manuel's eyes.

Again this was excellent technique. Scare the hell out of him by dropping a very precise detail but don't disclose how much you really know. Keep him guessing and see if he starts to shift and evade. Manuel couldn't win. If he denied all knowledge of the unit, they would find him not to be credible since he would surely know of its existence. Early in the morning's testimony, he had said he was assigned to the military base where the detention centre was located. If he admitted knowing about the unit, there would be many more questions.

"Si, Señora. Los Blancos. Yes, I know these people. They are militaries."

McDougall noted the sweat beads that had popped out amidst the furrows in his forehead. He was getting that strained greasy look again.

"Why didn't you tell me this the first time I asked you about Unit B?"

Manuel looked puzzled and worried. "The first time, Señora?"

"Yes, the first time, Mr Benitez. Ms Pacek just asked you about Unit B and you appeared not to know what in the devil she was talking about. Now suddenly you do. So why didn't you just say so the first time?"

This was Chiarelli, barging in before Pacek could respond. McDougall found it irritating when she did this. Moving in for a clumsy kill after other members of the pack had brought the quarry to bay. Often she moved prematurely before all the pieces were in place. It must drive Pacek crazy after all her careful work, like a clever junior detective watching the police chief stumble around the crime scene contaminating evidence.

Manuel's reply was urgent. "But Señora, there are very many Unit B. Is a Unit B for the Brigado in the norte when I fight the guerrilleros, is a Unit B in la Policia Trafico, is a Unit B in everything."

Chiarelli turned to Pacek. "Well Ms Pacek, which Unit B are we talking about and what is its relevance?"

McDougall winced. A bull in a china shop was the better analogy. Whose side was she on? Then he realized that she hadn't read the document. She didn't have the faintest idea where Pacek was going with this.

Pacek paused, uncertain of her response. She glanced at Mc-Dougall who leaned over to whisper into Chiarelli's ear, "Let's let her run with this. There's a document."

Chiarelli gave him an irritated side glance. He knew she didn't like whispering in her ear and she didn't like being left in the dark. He also knew she would not want to admit that she hadn't read the document by asking which one.

"Please continue, Ms Pacek. Let's get to the bottom of this Unit B business."

Pacek nodded, resisting the temptation to glance a thank you to McDougall. "Mr Benitez, could you please tell us again why you did not tell me about Unit B when I first asked you."

"Is many Unit B. No one say, Unit B. Is paper name. People say, "Los Blancos." When you tell me white patch, I know you talk about Los Blancos."

"Do other units have different patches on their uniforms?"

"Yes. Different colours. Some no colour. Or same colour but far away in the norte."

"So why did you know that the white patch was Los Blancos?"

"Is very important. Is very big. Everybody know Los Blancos. It mean the white ones."

"Yes. I understand. And what section or area of the military are the Blancos related to?"

McDougall was amused to hear how quickly they all assimilated Manuel's vocabulary. They had all been saying "guerrilleros," even Chiarelli. Now it was "Blancos." He was never sure if it was the vitality of particular words or the utility of using the claimant's words to avoid unnecessary ambiguity. He shifted back to Manuel's answer; this was important. Which way would he go?

"Area, Señora? What is area?"

Pacek was patient. "I will rephrase the question. This Unit B, the Blancos, they are connected to which part of the military or the police?"

"Yes, I understand. Los Blancos are part of the Technical Police."

He said it almost with a sigh. McDougall watched Manuel's head slowly descend, as though it were too heavy, made of iron, his neck suddenly too weak to support it, until his chin was almost touching his newly washed shirt. His black hair, heavily oiled, fell partially forward, like a rooster's comb. A bantam rooster, the little fighters who never give up. His head rose slowly; there was more sweat on the brow.

"But Señor, I am not a Los Blancos." He was looking directly at McDougall, his black button eyes, flat and opaque, somehow communicated the depth of his pain. Why him? McDougall had not asked the question. Did Manuel see him as the soft touch, the easy one on the panel? He looked away as Pacek asked her next question.

"So I want to be sure I understand. The Blancos, this Unit B, were a part of the same Technical Police that you were a part of?"

"Yes, Señora. But not the same. The Blancos are very difficult, very different."

"What do you mean by different?"

"They no go with us. Always secret. Alone. Very dangerous men."

"Were you ever a member of the Blancos?"

"No, Señora, never. I am never with the Blancos. I was a Technical Police."

Again Chiarelli interjected, "Yes, but the Blancos are Technicals as well. That's what you told us already. It seems there's some sort of contradiction here."

The sparring went on for more than an hour with Pacek probing for some connection between Manuel and the White Unit with occasional interjections from Chiarelli and even Gilles. On two occasions, Manuel gave his answer in Spanish then corrected Mrs Cord's interpretation. Sweat stains darkened his neatly pressed shirt. Just before the noon hour, Chiarelli announced a lunchtime adjournment, saying that they were all drawing blanks. McDougall thought it an amusing if inadvertent pun as he walked out into the brightness of the day through the heavy ringing of the noon hour. Perhaps that town clock would become irritating in time.

He spent the lunch hour carefully reviewing his notes, ignoring Chiarelli's attempts at conversation. He knew there was something missing. Pacek had attempted several lines of inquiry to establish some relation between Manuel and Los Blancos. There was none. Privately he had given up the notion that Manuel had himself committed serious human rights abuses, either torture, rape, or murder. But there was still complicity, the doctrine that said that if you were implicated in the commission of human rights abuses, you were also excludable. You didn't have to pull the trigger or the switch as long as you were either directly involved or a member of a group whose primary purpose included the commission of human rights abuses. If Manuel had been a member of Los Blancos, the claim would be over. But he wasn't. The real question was whether or not Manuel had assisted in some way. Manuel was telling the truth, McDougall was fairly certain of that. He had truly sworn before God. But something was missing, there was something he wasn't talking about.

McDougall found a promising line of questioning immediately after lunch, a lucky guess. "Manuel, you have told us about the patrols you made with the Technical Police, I don't mean the early patrols in the north with the army, but later, after 1985, with the Technical Police. Did you ever arrest people?"

"Yes, Señor. Sometime but not too many times."

"And these arrests, did they happen in the city and in the country?"

"No, Señor, not the city. I told the Señora that we do not make the patrols in the city."

"Yes, I remember, but you did make them in the country near the capital, during these one- and two-day patrols you told us about?"

"Yes, Señor, sometime."

"And who were these people that you arrested? What were they accused of?"

"Sometimes they were bad people, Señor. Criminales."

"All the time? Or were there other kinds of people you arrested?"

"I did not do the arrest, Señor. I go with the patrol."

"Yes, I remember, you said you were never the commander, but sometimes you were second-in-command. Is that right?"

"Yes, Señor."

"And was it always the decision of the commander to make the arrest?"

"Yes, Señor."

"Never the second-in-command?"

"No, Señor. The commander decide to take the people. Is long walk or he have to make the order for the vehiculo. Is commander who decide."

"And these people who were arrested, you said that sometimes they were criminals. Who were the other ones, the ones who were not criminals?"

"Is jus' people, Señor." Manuel was showing considerable distress, sometimes attempting to glance at his wife who sat perfectly still except for her hands, which lay in her lap quietly squeezing one another.

"Guerilleros?"

"No, Señor. The guerilleros fight, Señor."

"Did they arrest civilians? Women and children?" McDougall had switched to the third person, making it less personal, it would come more easily if "they" were making the arrests.

"No children, Señor." The sweat was now flowing freely from his brow. He had taken a red neckerchief from his pocket, which he used to wipe his forehead, holding it in his lap, working it with the same nervous gestures as his wife. McDougall had an open view of his legs under the table.

"But civilians, men and women. They were arrested?"

"Yes, Señor."

"And what were the charges, what were they accused of?"

"Sometimes crimes, Señor."

Manuel was still resisting, telling the truth but evading at every possible turn. McDougall was relentless. "I am not interested in the criminales, the bad people you told us about. I am talking now only about the other people, not the criminales. The civilians, sometimes women. What were they accused of?"

"They say they help the guerrilleros."

"Who is 'they'?"

"The commandante. Or sometime we have report. They say, you go to this place and you find the people who help the guerrilleros."

"And how often did they make arrests?"

"Not too many time. Many time nobody home."

"I need you to be more precise if you can. You were a Technical Police working on the military base for about three years. During that time, about how many patrols did you make where they arrested civilians, the men and women accused of helping the guerrilleros?"

"Is difficult. It was long time ago. I try to forget that time."

"I understand. And I know this is painful for you but it is important so I want you to try as best you can. It doesn't have to be an exact number but we do need to have a general idea. About how many arrests would you say over the three years?"

"Maybe three, Señor." He paused, wiping his brow, then looking down at his hands. "Maybe little bit more, Señor. Maybe six."

McDougall had to decide if Manuel had started to lie, if the pressure was too much. "Six arrests. That would be about two times a year?"

"Not every year, Señor. Sometime no arrest or only criminale. Sometime I only go in the city. Is always different. But not too many times, Señor. Before God, not too many times."

Whether or not it was true, Manuel probably believed it and so McDougall decided to move on, he had to close the other half of the net.

"And what happened to these people, I will call them the civilians, what happened to these civilians when you brought them back to the military base? You did take them back to the base?"

"Yes, Señor."

"In the vehicles or sometimes walking?"

"Yes, Señor."

"And what happened to them?"

"Is go in a jail, Señor."

"A jail? What jail is that?"

"Is a jail. Is a place, you know, with big wall and a ..." He paused, obviously seeking a word, making vertical hand motions, "metales."

"Bars? Iron bars?"

"Si, Señor. Iron bars."

"And what happened to these people once they were put in the jail?"

"No se. I don't know, Señor. Is different police."

"Not the Technical Police?"

"Yes, Technical Police, but different."

"Unit B? Los Blancos?"

"No, Señor, different. Is a guardia for the jail."

"Did Los Blancos work in the jail?"

"No, Señor. Los Blancos have different place. Is ... is ... is in a campo, very high wall."

"A separate prison? In a separate camp but still on the military base?" McDougall was going to help him out. The report said that the Unit B detention centre was in a separate walled area within the base.

"Yes, Señor. Separate."

"And have you ever been inside this other jail? Or been inside the Los Blancos area?"

"No, Señor. Never. Is very secret. Very dangerous."

It was all so neatly done, so neatly compartmentalized. McDougall had seen it in other countries, Iran under the Shah, Lebanon, Argentina, the Soviet Union. The regular army or police deliver the prisoners to a neutral detention centre containing ordinary criminals. Who knows what happens to them then? Later the security police remove them to a separate clandestine torture centre. Nothing to do with the police. Clean hands, just doing their duty. The Nazis were probably the architects of the system. It lets the leaders and the Manuels off the hook.

"Did you ever do guard duty in the regular jail?"

"Yes, Señor. Sometime. Not too many times."

"About how often over the three-year period?"

"Maybe four-five time. Sometime they not have enough guardia for the night. Is very quiet."

"And did you ever see any torture victims in the jail? People with injuries?"

"No, Señor. Is not like that. The people okay. Is very unhappy but nobody is torture."

Questions about the jail were going nowhere. Being a part-time jailer of arbitrarily detained people who weren't going to get a fair trial was not going to be seen as complicity in human rights abuses. He had to try a frontal assault.

"When you were working on the base, did you know what the Blancos did to people?"

"Maybe a little bit, Señor. Is very secret."

"Did you know that they tortured people?"

This time Manuel turned his head to look directly at his wife. "Is stories, Señor. Los Blancos do many bad things. But is secret, muy confidencial. No one know for sure. Is very dangerous to ask question."

"But you must have had a pretty good idea that they were torturing these people inside that hellhole, isn't that the way it really was? Everyone knew and no one was talking."

Manuel looked confused. Chiarelli's question was too blunt, she had spoken too quickly. McDougall quietly laid a hand on Chiarelli's elbow. He didn't want her screwing this up.

"Manuel, what are some of the bad things that people talked about?"

"Is very bad, Señor. Is hurt people very bad. People say they hear the people crying in the night, is make big noise. But no one know."

"Sounds in the night. Like screams and people crying out?" Manuel nodded, looking at McDougall now, as though he were afraid to look away. "And so the other Technicals knew the Blancos were hurting people, the prisoners, inside the prison?"

Again a nod. McDougall spoke very gently, he didn't want to spook him. "Manuel, I need you to say something for the record, to speak. The tape cassette is recording the testimony so there have to be some words, not just moving your head."

"Si, Señor. We hear the noises, the scream, and we know Los Blancos doing bad things to the people. But nobody talk. Is very dangerous to talk."

"I understand. And were there any other signs, any other ways that you suspected the Blancos were doing bad things to people?"

"Yes, Señor. Is one other thing." He seemed almost eager to talk, as though a small dam had overflowed. "My friend, Enrique, is a driver. He say at night sometime he drive truck for Los Blancos, special job. He no work for Los Blancos full time. They go in country and put people, los muertos, in ground."

"Enrique drove the truck? He transported dead bodies from the Los Blancos prison into the country where they buried them. Is that what you are saying?"

"Yes, Señor. But Enrique no touch dead people. He is driver solamente. But he know."

"I understand." If there were more time McDougall would ask questions about the number of bodies but he could see that Manuel was tiring and he did not want to lose the rhythm of the questions. "And you think the bodies, the dead people were the same people making the noises in the nights, the screams in the prison?" He was careful not to say the word torture.

"Yes, Señor. We know is same people."

It was time to close the net. "Did the Blancos sometimes come and take people from the Technical Police jail? Take them from there to their own prison?"

Although his face still glistened with sweat, Manuel seemed calmer. His eyes did not leave McDougall's face. "Yes, Señor. Sometime they take the people."

"And did the Blancos return the people to the Technical jail, later. Did they bring them back?"

"No, Señor. No one come back from Los Blancos."

"And could some of these prisoners be the ones making the noises in the night or the ones being killed?"

"No se, Señor. I not know. Some people maybe go home. Make the interrogation and go home. Is possible."

Fair answer. Dumb question, smart answer. Manuel had no way of knowing who was tortured and killed in that place. Some probably were released. In court his counsel would have objected to the question – "Calls for speculation, your Honour."

So far, he really didn't have a lot. "Bupkes," as his best friend, Morty Silverstein, would say. And he would be right. He had established that Manuel had been a member of patrols that had occasionally arrested people who were delivered to a central prison. And the security police who did commit torture occasionally removed prisoners from that same prison. In terms of complicity in the commission of human rights abuses, he had bubkes. There had to be a more direct link between Manuel and the abuses. But where was it? He thought of asking for a break, maybe retrace his line of questions, what had he missed? And then, it fell into place. It was suddenly there, like finding his missing car keys which had been lying there in plain view the whole time.

"Manuel, these six arrests of the civilians that you told me about, did you ever know that the people would be taken to the Blancos?"

Manuel visibly started, his bony shoulders jerking sideways. He had been staring off into space before the question, possibly lost in some nightmare. At first he didn't answer, simply staring at Mc-Dougall – no, not staring, the black button eyes were almost sightless, opaque, nothing but surface reflection. For some bizarre reason, the word Rumpelstiltskin popped into McDougall's head. Manuel's lips were moving but there was no sound. Finally, "Si, Señor, una vez, one time. Si, Señor."

The quality of his voice had altered, become softer and, ironically, more relaxed. He had ceased to look at McDougall or anyone else. Manuel was no longer sitting in the basement of the courthouse with the bright sound of red-winged blackbirds coming through the window. He was standing on the edge of a clearing in heavily forested hills watching the seven people tied to the tree and the patrol resting in the shade after a heavy two-day march and brief firefight. The men squatted down eating US army field rations watching flies gather on the bodies of three guerrilleros lying in the sun. One of their own men was wounded, sitting against a tree, needing more than his share of water. They would have to carry him out to the main highway. He knew that headquarters would not risk the loss of a helicopter for an ordinary soldier.

The story came very quickly. McDougall was careful not to interrupt, occasionally prompting with brief questions when Manual appeared to lose the flow of his thoughts. The patrol had not been expecting to find guerrillas, only supporters. If they found signs of a guerilla presence, they would burn some houses, destroy the gardens scratched out of thin acidic upland soil, ask some questions, scare the peasants and their families. But there were three guerrillas playing soccer in the clearing, chasing a ball made of rags. Coming up the trail, the patrol had heard their laughter and been warned. Two had fallen in the first hail of bullets. The third one had somehow scrambled to a weapon and released a burst of shots, wounding Carlos, before his body jerked backwards from the impact of their second volley. Manuel knew his own burst had struck the man in the chest, knocking him backwards. And now they must do something with the seven people tied to the tree. The men were excited, they had never shot a guerrilla before but they were also very angry because of the wound to Carlos since they knew they must carry him. They were also angry because all the prisoners were very old, except one. Where were the young women? They had all heard of the rapes, of the commandantes allowing them, even ordering them to violate the women of the guerrilleros. Here there were six old people, two men and four women, farmers, very old. There was the one woman, very thin but not too old, and maybe they would violate her.

The commandante wanted to kill her. He said she was different from the others. She was not from the region and so must be with the guerrilleros. The old people, he would burn their houses and small field of corn, take their chickens. But the younger one they should kill or she would go to the guerrilleros, possibly identify them. Perhaps the men would violate her first but she was as skinny as the chickens. He did not think it was worth the trouble. Manuel said they should not kill her, they should take her with them back to the base. If she was with the guerrilleros, she would have information that might interest Los Blancos. And if the men violated her, she would not be able to walk. They did not want to carry both her and Carlos. Besides, if they radioed to say they had a prisoner with information, the colonel might send a truck to take them all back to the base. Manuel did not tell him that the name of the woman was Milagro and that she had been the friend of his older sister in his village. Milagro had not always been thin. He remembered her with a round face and beautiful hair. She had a big laugh and sometimes gave him candy. She had been the daughter of the schoolteacher and the first girl from the village to go to the university.

The commandante had said Manuel was right and perhaps they would send a truck if Los Blancos were eager to talk to the prisoner. He would give the men three of the chickens instead of the woman and only keep two for himself. Manuel could also have a chicken for his good advice as the second-in-command.

It was difficult to carry Carlos down the trail and he cried out many times. Manuel loosely held the rope tied to Milagro, having already loosened the knot around her wrists where it was bleeding. She gave no sign that she recognized him. A truck was waiting for them at the highway, which made everyone happy except Manuel. If they had walked back to the base, Milagro might have escaped in the night while they slept. Three Los Blancos drove up in a cloud of dust while the men were unloading at the barracks. They spoke briefly to the commandante who pointed at Milagro. One had a knife to cut the rope which the commandante had tightened in the truck. Without speaking they placed her in the jeep and drove away. All three men were big with faces of stone. Milagro stared straight ahead, apparently sightless, but Manuel could see her body shaking through the thin dress. Manuel said he did not want his chicken and gave it back to the commandante. He knew the bad taste in his mouth would not leave for a long time.

McDougall had forgotten the other people in the room, had become lost in Manuel's story. Likely, it was the same for the others since no one had spoken. It required a few more questions to learn that Manuel had waited two more months before deserting from the police and his country, before selling his few possessions for bus fare to the north, his wife following without asking questions. She knew about his nightmares and inability to eat. Chiarelli asked if he had news of Milagro and he nodded slowly, as though considering a difficult problem. His father had told him on the telephone that she lived with her father in the capital city. He knew only that she had been hurt very badly by the police and did not leave the house. There were many bad stories from the war, it was one of many and Manuel asked his father only a few questions.

McDougall and Chiarelli later sat at their same table overlooking the gardens. He had been surprised by the lateness of the hour by the time all the questions were finished. Without consultation, Chiarelli had told Manuel that they would return with a decision after dinner, they would not keep him waiting. Over dinner, they had briefly reviewed the law on complicity. The issues were knowledge of the human rights abuses and proximity to their commission

and Manuel fell within that definition, certainly in regard to Milagro but also probably the other five arrests. He knew that anyone
suspected of supporting the guerrillas was likely to fall into the
hands of Los Blancos. Perhaps they should have asked questions
about the other arrests but there had been no time and another adjournment was unthinkable. There was never enough time. There
were always unanswered questions.

They also discussed the law on duress, which did not help Manuel.
He had had a choice. He had actually re-enlisted, although it was
unclear how much he knew at that point. However, he definitely
had not taken the first opportunity to leave once he did know.

McDougall had never been fully comfortable with the law on
complicity. It was one thing to reject the butchers, but what about
the teenagers dragooned into military service, complicit yet frightened, peasants like Manuel who had never had a sense of choice or
alternative in their lives, having been raised within hierarchical cultures to do what they were told? Manuel should have left at the first
opportunity, he should have refused. "Should" seemed like a pretty harsh word. Still, it was the law and he was, presumably, a man
of the law. He looked over at Chiarelli, who hadn't said a word.

"Ironically, he's honest and hard-working. He fits very niceley
within your definition," he offered tentatively.

Chiarelli nodded, absent-mindedly fiddling with the overlarge
piece of lemon in her soda water. Her face had softened, become
more pensive. With the briefest of peripheral glances, she scanned
his face, assessing his mood.

Those large eyes contained such a quick intelligence. She was
more complex than he had at first thought and he wondered if she
were waiting for him to suggest a way out of the box, an alternative logic. They would have to decide, one way or the other. Poised
on the brink of some precipice, they both looked off into the garden and to the cows lowing in the pasture across the river.

3

AND NOTHING BUT
THE TRUTH

"I AM AFRAID OF THESE PEOPLE. They will kill me."

"That may well be but that is not the question which was asked. You did not answer the question which was asked."

The claimant hunches his shoulders, appearing to sink into himself. He does not look directly at the two men sitting across from him, he knows they are the judges and he must not lie, he has promised, and now he has not given the correct answer. The small judge with the pink face is not happy. Confused, the claimant looks to his right to a young woman dressed in a high-collared dark suit, a small ruffle at the throat, his lawyer. She is looking at the two judges, not at him. Perhaps she will say something, tell his story to the judges. He watches his index finger rub the surface of the table where he sits, back and forth. It looks like a worm trying to burrow into the table, a fat blind worm. In the garden, his mother would crush such a worm between her fingers.

It is a small windowless room used for the hearing of refugee claims. The voices are muted within the sound-resistant walls, the faces drained of colour by the fluorescent light and neutral grey colours of the room. The participants are seated at four tables grouped in a rectangle whose dull surfaces absorb the fluorescence from above. Empty chairs have been placed at the back of the room for observers.

The judges sit across from the claimant at the opposite end of the rectangle. A microphone rests on the table in front of him like the head of a big silver snake, too close. It obscures his view of the small pink judge but it is not difficult to see the big judge who has a big voice. This judge has told him to speak up because the microphone records his words on the machine. He would like to move the microphone but is afraid to touch it. The lawyer sits on the right side of the rectangle opposite a tall man with a large nose. The judge has said that this man is there to help the judges ask questions, but he has not yet spoken.

"Please listen carefully to my question before answering." The lawyer is talking. "I asked you if you knew who it is who wishes to persecute you. Who are these people?"

"I do not know their names. They are from the government."

"Do they wear uniforms?"

"I do not know."

"You don't know?" The young woman's voice is sharper than she intends, suggesting surprise, perhaps irritation. Again the claimant hunches down in his chair.

"Who were the men who came to your house? Who killed your brother? Did they wear uniforms?"

"They were from the government."

"But did they wear uniforms?"

"Yes."

"So do you think the men you are afraid of, these other men, do you think they wear uniforms?"

"I do not know those men."

"But you just said that ..."

"Excuse me, Mr Board Member. Counsel is leading the claimant." It is the silent man who speaks. He looks only at the judges.

"Yes, it is a leading question. Counsel, please try to avoid leading the claimant."

The young woman appears uncertain, looking down at her notes, recrossing her legs under the table. She does not see the silent man watching her legs. The claimant looks away, down at his finger still rubbing the table; there is now a discernible mark where heat and moisture have begun to darken the oblivious surface.

"I apologize. I was simply trying to elicit a more focused response to my question. I will rephrase the question."

"It's not necessary. We have heard his answer. He does not know the people he fears and does not know if they wear uniforms. You can move on, Counsel."

Again she hesitates, as though to speak, then looks down at her notes, turning the pages. The claimant can see she is without confidence. His cousin told him to get a man lawyer but this is the lawyer who took his Legal Aid paper and talked to him at the lawyer's office. She helped him write his story and asked him questions with a soft voice. She knows the bad things that happened to his family except she cannot say the names of his father and brothers in the right way.

"I am going to ask you about something else now, about your family. Can you tell us how many people are in your family?"

"Yes."

They are all looking at him, waiting. He has not said anything incorrect this time. The big judge smiles as though he knows a secret joke.

"Mr M_____, please tell us about your family."

And he tries to tell them about his father and mother, his wife and two children, his four brothers and his sister. The lawyer asks if they all live in the same house and he tells her yes. He wonders why she asks him the question. She is supposed to know about his family, she has written his story in the paper he gave to Immigration. The words were better than his own and he did not completely understand them until his cousin read the story to him in their own language. The Immigration man had said his English was good and he did not need a translator, but he often cannot find the words to tell these people and wishes his cousin were there to help him.

"And what happened when the policemen came to the house?"

He swallows and looks at his finger, which is not moving. He knows he must answer. She has told him he will have to tell the judges even though she has written it in the paper. He can feel the choking in his chest, he has no air and the lawyer tells him to take a drink of water. He has the taste in his mouth again, the horrible taste and he knows his leg is shaking. The silent man will be able to see it under the table.

"They broke the door and came into the house. My father was talking to them."

"And then what happened?"

"They hit my brother and he fell down."

"Hold on a minute. Let's get this straight." It is the big judge talking. He sounds angry. "Who is 'they' and which brother are we talking about here?"

He looks to the lawyer. Should he answer? She nods her head. "My brother, Y_____, the militaries were beating on him and he fell down."

"And where did all this happen?"

"In my father's house."

"Yes, but where *is* the house?"

"In my village."

"And what is the name of your village?" He has written all this many times in the paper that the lawyer gave to Immigration and he wonders why the judge is asking him again. The judge said that everyone had read his paper. They had asked him if it was true after he held the Bible and he had said yes, it was true. He repeats the name for the judge.

"In your Personal Information Form you refer to it as a town, now you say it is a village. Can you tell us which it is."

He is confused. They do not understand. Perhaps he has used the wrong word. He looks at the lawyer who asks him how many people are there in his village.

"There are many people."

"Yes, but how many?"

"Very many."

The big judge makes a sound in his throat and puts down his pencil. Before he had been writing many notes.

The lawyer changes her voice like the language teacher in the school. "Mr M_____, I want you to tell the board members how many people are in your village. Are there one hundred, five hundred, or more than a thousand? It can be an approximation, of course."

He does not know what that word means and the numbers are very big.

He has promised to tell the truth. There are more than one hundred people, that is only ten families and there are many families.

"Five hundred."

"There are five hundred people in your village?

"Yes."

"Well we've got that straight. It's a village, not a town. Now let's go back to the beating. Counsel?" The big judge picks up his pen and starts to write. He does not seem to be so angry now. Perhaps the answer was correct.

"Mr M_____, tell us what happened after the men came into your house."

"It is the house of my father."

"Yes, I'm sorry, your father's house. Please describe what occurred to the board members."

"The policemen hit my brother with the thing on the end of their guns and he fell down and they hit him again."

"Once again, which brother?" The voice of the big judge is still not happy.

"Y_____."

"And what was it they hit him with, something on the gun?"

The claimant raises his arms to mime a shooting motion, holding the rifle, then touching the big part near his shoulder.

"The butt of the gun?" the lawyer asks. He nods.

"Have you ever fired a gun?" This question comes from the silent man. The claimant shakes his head. He is confused. Perhaps the silent man does not understand that it was the soldiers who had the guns.

"I ask the question because you seemed pretty comfortable making that shooting motion. Do you know what kind of guns the men were carrying?" Again the claimant shakes his head.

"You have to speak up. You cannot just move your head. All of the proceedings are being recorded." It is the big judge speaking. "You should move the microphone closer."

The claimant touches the base of the microphone pulling it forward an inch. The head of the snake comes closer and he now must move his head to see the small judge. He would like to move his chair back but is afraid to.

"So I repeat the question: do you know what kind of weapons the soldiers were carrying?"

The claimant says he does not know. He guesses that the weapon word means a gun.

"Excuse me, Mr Board Member. I would like to continue the direct examination of my client. The Refugee Claim Officer will have his opportunity to pose questions later. I also object to the RCO raising exclusion issues without giving written notice prior to the hearing."

He knows the lawyer's words are important because the big judge sits back in his chair. He pulls at his tie which is long and red, like the tongue of a lizard, and then he leans toward the small pink judge who whispers in his ear.

"Well, I'm not sure exclusion has been raised at this point. There is no allegation that the claimant has participated in crimes against humanity. The RCO's question really just goes to credibility, which, as you know, Counsel, is always an issue. But we don't want to unnecessarily impede the claimant's testimony so we'll get the direct out of the way, then we'll give Mr Barnard his chance."

The corners of the lawyer's mouth make a little smile. Maybe it is a good thing what the judge has said.

The big judge now removes his glasses and looks directly at the claimant. There are bright red marks on the nose where the glasses fit and the judge looks tired. His skin is shiny with sweat. "So let's keep going, Mr M_____. Tell us what happened to your father."

"It was my brother."

"Yes, sorry, your brother ..." He looks at his notes and says a sound that must be the name of his brother but is a funny sound that would make his brother laugh. Y_____ was very clever with words and could imitate the sounds of the tourists in the capital city where he worked as a waiter and the blood was bright red coming out of his hair and again the horrible sound of the rifle butt on his skull. As small boys, they used to break melons in the neighbour's garden with sticks at night with the same sound except not so heavy and his father falling as he tried to pull at the military's arm and his mother screaming, begging the policeman who was from their village while the militaries were kicking his father and he could not move.

"Tell us what happened to your brother."

The claimant reaches for the water, which tastes like metal.

His leg will not stop shaking. "The military hit him with the thing on his gun."

"With the rifle butt?" He nods his head and then remembers to say yes.

"How many times did they hit him?"

"I do not know."

"Can you give us an approximate idea?"

"Many times." The big judge makes a sound and looks at the lawyer.

"Maybe three times." He knows the judge would like to hear a number.

"*Maybe* three times? Are you sure? Was it three or not?" It is the big judge talking and again he is not happy.

The lawyer speaks to him quietly. "I know this is difficult, but please try to recall. Did the soldiers hit your brother three times with their rifle butts or was it some other number?"

His mother is screaming and he is pulling his wife away, pushing her, and they are kicking his father who is on top of his brother, covering him, and he can see the face of the policeman who is afraid and who had been a friend of his older brother.

"I do not know."

"You don't *know?*"

He is afraid of the big judge who gets angry so quickly and is unhappy with his answers. It is not possible to say how many blows if he was not counting and he was too frightened to count and he does not know how to tell this man the truth.

"In your personal information form you said 'several blows to the face and head.' Three does not sound like several to me." It is the tall quiet man talking.

"Perhaps it was more."

"How many more?"

"I do not know."

"Would it be incorrect to say seven or eight?"

"I do not know."

He does not hear his mother or see his brother anymore. He watches his finger, which has been rubbing the shiny part at the bottom of the microphone. There are little drops of water clinging to the surface of the table, which tremble when the judge talks. He must have spilled his water and something collapses inside. The room is dark in the corners and the big judge is a long way away although his tie is bright red and shiny like blood and he does not want to hear his wife who has been screaming with his mother after the militaries had taken them to the bedroom.

The lawyer is standing now. "Mr Board Member, could we have a five-minute break please?"

"Okay, Counsel. It's almost 10:30. We could all use a break. We'll take fifteen minutes for coffee but I would like the testimony to move along a little faster after the break. Please speak to your client about answering the questions a little more precisely. His responses are unnecessarily vague. It's a straightforward case. My colleague and I certainly expect this to be wound up before lunch."

4

A REAL NOWHERE MAN

"I AM A NOWHERE MAN. This is my problem."

He was smiling when he said it. A large black face, dusty black, smiling, solicitous. Clearly concerned for our predicament; for despite his concern, it was somehow *our* predicament, not his.

You might ask why that should be since he was the claimant, not we. It was *his* obligation to establish that he had a fear of persecution, his burden of proof. Yet somehow, and I am not sure how, perhaps through inflection, the reluctant shrugging of shoulders, the softened timbre of his voice, or possibly the occasional falsetto crack when he told a real stunner, whatever the reason, the burden had somehow shifted to us to make sense of something that made no sense at all.

I am not a fool. I am not a gullible person. Neither is my colleague. Between the two of us, we have more than twelve years' experience hearing refugee claims from all of the continents of the world except for Antarctica and Australia. We both have ears trained to distinguish deception from desperation and lack of comprehension. We are both women who have achieved some measure of success in masculine professions by listening well. I believe we also both have the humility to know that we can be fooled, but not often and not easily.

Both of us agree that this claim was an extraordinary exercise that tested our wits and stretched our sense of reality far beyond anything called for by the facts of the case. Now we can laugh about it over lunch. It is the laughter of people who have just emerged from a hall of mirrors at some carnival where the tiny moments of disorientation and panic quivering in the half-light of multiple distorted reflections are once again ridiculous in the warm evening air that is thick with the sweet smell of fried meat and cotton candy.

Of necessity his story was long and complicated. I cannot take you through all the shifts and turns of his narrative. I am not sure I remember. However, I have found the transcript of the hearing and will make reference to specific passages that were particularly relevant. Certainly I could never imitate his peculiar manner of speech, which was both perplexing and persuasive as he testified in English.

He was a Christian living in the north of his country where the majority of residents were Muslim. Perhaps I will leave it at that for the moment. He also had other fears of persecution in the Christian south and the capital city where both religions coexisted peacefully. That will come later. In the north he had lived in a large city, working as a street vendor with little interest in politics or religion.

He was selling in the street the day his life was lifted and altered as suddenly as Dorothy was pulled up and out of Kansas by a wayward tornado. A tumbling dust storm of angry Muslims, protesting the construction of a Christian church in a mixed neighbourhood, suddenly spilled into the street where he sold carpets, clothes, and watches. His broken but intelligible English made his recounting of the event all the more vivid, as though the story could not be told in any other way.

"The peoples were coming very quickly, very quickly, and I was not understanding the purpose of their appearance. They were not looking at me. I was beside the street in the shade of the market where it is cooler. There was much anger and shoutings. I have seen goats go by in this manner in the villages. I know them to be Muslim peoples and I had no fear for their purpose was not to do with myself. And then a man with a long beard rose up from the crowds of peoples and pointed in my way and shouted that I was a Christian man and had befouled the temple of the Muslim peoples. I did not know why he was saying this thing but many peoples turned to me. There was a very big man with a big stick and much anger in his face. He was shouting that I am an unbeliever. He was looking crazy and he was coming very quickly to me. I was not moving because I was not understanding why this thing was happening when first he hit me and I was falling. I was smelling his very bad breath he was so near to me. He was a very ugly man.

"They were hitting many peoples with sticks, not only myself, but other merchants. The big man hit me many times. Here, I can show you. See, he hit me here and here and also on my back many times where I can show you. I will be a dead person if I am not running away."

I recall this portion of his testimony, the claimant bending forward, almost deferentially, pointing quite precisely to small scars on the top of his head. I told him that it was unnecessary to remove his shirt, which he was about to do. He looked puzzled but did not persist. I did not want to interrupt the course of his testimony and would later try to explain that my colleague and I are Board members, not doctors, and do not have the expertise to determine whether his scars were the result of the beating or some other incident. To add to his difficulty, he did not have legal counsel, who, if she or he were competent, would have filed a medical report as evidence. The report would describe the scars and confirm that their age and appearance were consistent with the claimant's account of how they were incurred.

He pointed again to one particular scar on his forehead. "This was a very bad one and the blood began to come into my eye. I was not seeing and was very afraid. The big man was shouting and was hitting other peoples. I was seeing the blood on the end of his stick which was very shiny and red. My neighbour John was lying on the ground crying very loudly. He sold rugs like me. There was some blood on his rugs. I was able to crawl into a little street. I was hearing the sound of the breaking of many things in the market. They were breaking all of the trade goods of the merchants. There was very much breaking. I put a cloth on my head because I must hide my blood or other Muslim peoples will beat me. I ran away leaving all of my worldly goods."

There is a break in the transcript at this point. I recall that the claimant was shaking, his hands jammed between his legs, and he would not look at us. Under such circumstances, the members will ordinarily adjourn for a fifteen-minute break in order for the claimant to compose himself, even where there are suspicions about the claimant's credibility. The members' job becomes more difficult if an apparently traumatized claimant has no lawyer to act as an interlocutor. It is the lawyers who can speak to their clients privately, outside the hearing room, and who can then advise us of a claimant's state of mind and ability to testify. Of course, unethical counsel can exacerbate the problem, exaggerating and even encouraging their client's purported psychological stress.

I will not repeat the transcript verbatim. The testimony went on in a similar manner for most of the morning and you might ask, what is my difficulty? Why is this claimant so very different from the many other uneducated, unrepresented claimants who come before the Board? I would respond that the claimant was remarkable for the very great contrast between the utter improbability of his story and the wonderfully colourful and believable manner in which he recounted it.

The claimant said that he crawled into an alleyway where he was then able to slip away from what appears to have been a religious riot. Despite his awkward English, he was able to paint a very real and immediate picture of a mob that had overturned and pillaged the stalls of Christian merchants, a story supported by the country information documents, which described periodic pogroms in the north, street riots, and the burning of churches; where the authorities permitted the occasional spasm of religious violence to play itself out, a medieval bloodletting to relieve the vitriol of the body politic.

To that point, his story was quite plausible. He hid in the home of a fellow Christian, an acquaintance, and then slipped out of the town at night, without returning to his own home where he feared that Muslim rioters who recognized him would be waiting.

It's only when you look more carefully at his story that pieces of it start to flake off. His life was strangely unencumbered by the trappings of a normal life. He had neither wife nor children, although he was well past the average age for marriage in his country. Throughout his testimony, there were no references to parents, siblings, or relatives, although for most people of his country, Muslim or Christian, the bonds of the extended family are essential to personal identity and, without overstating the case, to existence itself.

His story, both his written narrative and oral testimony, consisted solely of foreground action with little context or background.

There was a curious disconnection between the events of his life and his surroundings. It reminds me of watching one of those films where the actor is a singular image on a blue screen before the backdrop is filled in by a computer.

When we asked questions later about his background, we had the sense that he was making it up as he went along, although his answers were fluent and detailed, ordinarily a sign of truth telling. Most liars have prepared simple plot lines but can only offer barren backgrounds, without texture or detail. For example, I asked him where he lived in the town. A false answer might come out as "I stayed in a room," or "I lived in the house of a family." I hasten to add that a truth teller might also provide little detail simply because of fear or an inability to describe or even, I suppose, notice the circumstances of his life. But fresh detailed descriptions are often a mark of truth.

From the transcript of the hearing, I have noted his response to that particular question. "I was living in a very small room in the house of my friend, Simon. He was a man who was selling in the marketplace such as myself. His selling place was in the next street to myself and his trade goods were of the very highest quality. He was giving me the room for a very good price and it was near to the church. I was sharing the room with his two sons who were of the same age. They came out of their mother at the same time."

"Did this man Simon also flee the city after the attack on you and the other Christian merchants?"

"I do not know. I was not returning to my room. I was running away to the country where it was safe for me. I had nothing and I was very afraid. It was the time of year when the grains in the fields were very high and it was possible to hide in this place. Simon was not fleeing without his family and his wife is a very big woman but he owns a motor car, a very good one, very new, and maybe he was fleeing with his family in his car."

Well, I can see that I have not yet proved my case. I must admit that so far his story seems believable. Related in bad English, somewhat stilted with interesting biblical overtones, which I suppose confirms that he is a Christian. Certainly it was never evident where he learned his English. He only had three or four years of schooling, but it is reasonable to assume he was taught by priests or missionaries.

But please, do not judge me or him too quickly. I assure you there were gross anomalies that could only lead to one conclusion. Let me start with his flight to the capital. On his Personal Information Form he wrote that he "went directly to the capital city." In testimony, he said that the journey took less than a week. Soon after his arrival in the capital, he was arrested on suspicion of political activity. But there was a serious discrepancy in dates. His arrest occurred three months after the riot in the north. Where was he during that time? This may seem mundane and very picky, but it is the nuts and bolts of assessing credibility. When questioned on this point, the claimant said that he had remained hidden near his town for about six weeks before coming to the capital and his journey may have taken longer than a week.

I admit that time is elastic and even irrelevant in certain cultures. But why had he not mentioned the six weeks' delay? I note his answer in the transcript; I have highlighted all the passages where he used this most interesting expression: "I do not know. It was very confusing for me at this time. Everything was very busy and very confusing. I was a nowhere man."

And where did he hide for this six-week period? He first said in the "fields with the tall grains," which later became "a place with plants," and finally, in response to the question how he could hide in the field during the day when it was being worked, he said he had hidden in a small shed during the day and the shed was in a large "patch of garden."

My youngest son uses the word "morph" a great deal. He has been raised in an era of computer-generated images where cartoon and even live images can easily "morph" into something quite different. In response to any implausibility or inconsistency that we raised, the claimant's story would morph seamlessly into something else, always with the small graphic details suggesting truth.

Trying to comprehend how he could live in a tiny agricultural shed in a working field for six weeks without being discovered, we asked questions, many questions. He was able to describe the interior of the little shed so persuasively that I can see it to this day. It was dark and hot and he said that it smelled of a certain plant whose name he knew only in his own language, but his description suggested something like a skunk cabbage, large leafed with a strong odour. He had to remain quiet when the workers were nearby and would have to rub the mosquitoes off his skin rather than slap them for fear of making noise. Sometimes the workers would eat their lunch in the shade of the shed and he would smell the rice and bannock and feel "very, very hungry." He remembers the jokes that they used to tell and one woman who made beautiful beautiful laughter. There was a man with a big voice named Ahmed who bragged of beating and killing Christians in the city.

No, the workers did not come into the shed. Only the farm manager entered the shed and then only rarely. The shed was used in the spring mainly for storing fertilizers and seeds and then for harvesting in the fall. He was able to hide under burlap grain sacks at the back of the shed when the manager entered. It was very warm under the burlap and one time he almost sneezed because of the dust in the sacks. The sacks would not be used until the fall harvest so there was little danger that the manager might find him.

How was he able to sustain himself? He would sneak into the nearby town at night to get food and water.

If these local workers were hostile, how was he able to get food? There were a few Christian families in the town. One man he knew from his church and this man gave him food and water.

Was it not dangerous to go into the town every night? Yes, it was dangerous and so, after a while, a small boy, the son of the Christian man, brought packages of food to his shed at night. The boy made a scratching noise so the claimant would know it was him. For two nights, during the full moon, the boy did not come for fear of being seen, and so for two days he had neither food nor water, although he sneaked into the nearby forest to chew on some plants. One of the plants made him very sick, gave him a very bad stomach ache, and so he was afraid to eat other plants and decided to wait for the boy.

Gratuitously, he offered that he would "do his business" at night on the edge of the field, in a hole, covering it up since unidentified human faeces would cause suspicion.

Why did he stay so long in such an uncomfortable and dangerous situation? He was very afraid. He did not know where else to
go. He had never been in the south. He was hoping that the situation would improve in the city so that he could return to his home.
Also the wound on his head had become infected; he had some fever
and was very weak. In the shed he could rest and stay quiet.

Where were the tools kept? Presumably in the shed?

The workers took them home at night. Yes, there were a few
tools in the shed but only a few speciality tools, something called a
"bandu," which as best we could understand was a tool for remov-
ing small stumps or very deep roots of the "kasudu" plant. You can
imagine that neither of these precious jewels of information were
obtained without numerous questions and elaborate descriptions
and I recall taking a break after this particular session, watching the
snow swirling outside my office window, wondering how we had
just spent three-quarters of an hour on African agricultural imple-
ments. Progress was slow.

I fear that my colleague and I had become fixated on his experi-
ences in the field and the shed. He was so graphic in his descriptions, yet we could not shake our profound scepticism. We even
questioned ourselves in private. Were we too sceptical? Was there a
failure of imagination simply because these events lay so far outside
our own narrow middle-class experience? Desperate times breed
desperate measures. Why could this not have happened?

Certainly, as a Jew, I had grown up on extraordinary stories of
survival during the Holocaust. There were so many stories from my
grandparents' generation. My husband's aunt had been hidden by
a Polish family for nearly three years, passing days and weeks in
tiny enclosures in the house and barn. The Nazis searched the farm
three times. Once a bullet had been fired into a crawlspace less than
two inches from her head. It was unbelievable. Crazy. And I have
heard her tell the story myself. So why could our claimant not hide
in a shed for a scant six weeks? Why did we not believe him? I can
only tell you that we questioned ourselves and took nothing for
granted.

I recall that we adjourned for the day never having completely
escaped from the shed or the field. It was nearly two months before
we were able to resume the hearing. Although neither of us were

fully satisfied with the claimant's explanations, we decided to move on to his adventures in the capital city. Again, it was difficult to locate his story in time or space. He had been arrested and badly beaten by the police soon after his arrival in the city on suspicion of illegal political activity, which he swore was completely unfounded. Possibly he did not understand that arrest *because of* his political activity would only strengthen his case.

He seemed to know that his fears of religious persecution would not follow him to the capital. Although the country's religious tensions swirled through the capital, large areas of the city were inhabited by Christians who dominated the economic life of the country and were not subject to persecution for that reason alone. He also understood those affiliated with any one of a half dozen nascent political parties were liable to arrest and detention. Some of these parties advocated violence, some were dedicated to achieving democratic change through the rule of law. Most were ineffectual and closely tied to particular tribal groups. All were subject to arbitrary arrest and, for the more serious parties, torture.

The claimant had been walking in the street one night when he was stopped and questioned by a police patrol. The police were apparently looking for men recently dispersed from a clandestine political meeting. His lack of identity papers was sufficient reason to throw him into the back of a truck with several other men who were not of his tribe and who also viewed him with suspicion. One of the men lay moaning on the floor of the truck with one arm bent at an impossible angle.

Again his testimony was vivid and compelling. "The place where they were bringing us had a very bad smell and very high walls. The soldiers were very bad, hitting the peoples with the guns when they were falling on the ground from the truck and kicking the peoples on the ground. I was not knowing the language of these peoples, what they were speaking to each other, but I was knowing they were very afraid, a very big fear.

"In the place where they were putting us, there were many peoples, many many peoples, very close and a very bad smell. There was no place to do our business and people were doing their business in a vessel in the corner. I was not knowing the language these peoples were speaking. They were not peoples from the city and I was alone in the corner. One man was speaking to me in the language of the city and he said that the other peoples were not trusting me and that maybe I was a friend of the soldiers. I was telling him that I was a good Christian man and a merchant and I was coming to the city because of my big fear and I was hiding. This man was saying these things to the other peoples in their language. He was speaking very fast. This man was very kind and gave me a small biscuit to eat. It was very dry but I was hungry. He did not have any water to give me.

"I was staying five days in the jail. The soldiers were taking many peoples from the jail and they were not walking when they were bringing them back. There was very much blood on their faces and one man had a very big pain in his back. He was making sad noises all the times until the soldiers took him away again and he did not come back. We were hearing the crying noises in the nighttime, very loud, and many of the peoples were very afraid. I was very hungry. The soldiers were giving us goma two times or maybe sometimes one time in the day, but it was very unsatisfactory for me to eat. The other peoples were taking the bucket first and were only giving me a very little part.

"They were taking me to the officer soldier one time but they were not hitting me and they sent me from the jail when they were understanding that I am not the same peoples. They were telling me that I must come back to the jail with my papers or they will come to get me again and it will be very bad for me if I do not bring the papers. This man was an officer with only one eye and he was looking very hard at me. He was speaking the language of the north and he was telling me that I am better to go to the north. He was a Muslim person and he said there was no Christian killings in the north and it was Christian lies.

"But I do not want to go to the north and in two days I bring him my papers. If I do not bring the papers I know there will be a big trouble for my friend where I am living. I am very afraid and so I was telling them the house of my friend.

"I know it was very bad for me. I know the police peoples will come again to find me or they take me in the street. I am not having money and I am a Christian man from a very small tribe and I am not with job. I am not going to the south. The peoples are maybe

Christian but they are a different tribe and will not be buying my trade goods. I am nowhere man. It is very bad for me."

I must admit that at this point my colleague and I were stymied. If the claimant's story was true, he probably was, in law, a Convention refugee. He could not return to his home city because of the continuing religious violence. He may or may not have been individually targeted by the Muslim extremists but that is the sort of thing where the claimant should receive the benefit of the doubt. The appropriate test is whether or not there is a *reasonable possibility* that the claimant would be attacked again. And in the north, the state was clearly not protecting the minority Christian population. In the capital he was now known to the police and under suspicion. Given his Christian and tribal identities as well as his lack of livelihood, he was vulnerable to arbitrary arrest from a police force with a well-documented record of human rights abuses.

The situation in the south was more ambiguous. It was Christian and he had never lived there. However, he was correct in believing that a stranger without tribal support had little possibility of earning a living as a merchant. Family and tribal connection was the essential bond of the community. Without it, his chances were slim. Some would say that his problem was poverty, not persecution, and poverty was not a reason to grant protection under the Convention. Some would say that, but it is a harsh analysis and not one that persuaded me or my colleague. In our view his problems stemmed from his religious and tribal identities. *Our* problem was that we did not believe him but were unable to frame our doubts in the clear, lucid logic of the court. Or, more honestly, we could not resolve our own uncertainties. Both my colleague and I were always conscious of the potentially terrible results of making a mistake. We did not want to send any claimant back to death, torture, imprisonment, or even a life of endless fear and profound discrimination. We also did not want to grant Canada's protection gratuitously to scoundrels, or worse, to criminals or killers, and we did not yet know where our claimant fit on this spectrum of fear and falsehood.

But I have not told you his entire story. You have yet to hear about his flight to Canada, although I do not think it will be of much assistance to your assessment of his case. He said that in desperation he had gone down to the harbour with "a bag of hard bread, some dates and a can of water." The capital was a busy port with a large international freighter traffic. He had slipped aboard a ship at night and had hidden under a tarpaulin in a lifeboat.

He had been discovered three days out of port when he ran out of water. He said that he had been caught doing his business over the side of the ship. At first the captain had been very angry but decided to put him to work rather than throw him over the side. He had worked very hard and had stayed with the ship for five months. He was happy on the boat but knew he could not stay forever. The captain gave him money and he left the ship in New York City, using a shipmate's identity papers to pass the security controls within the harbour's restricted area. A trucker heading north to Canada offered him a ride. He did not know the name of the man. It was a blue truck, very big, filled with cardboard boxes. He did not know what was in the boxes. He fell asleep in the back of the truck and awoke in Montreal. He came to Ottawa to make his refugee claim because it was the capital city and many people did not speak English in Montreal.

And that was all of his story. To our eyes, he arrived in Canada without documents, speaking a language that is common to several African countries. He had produced no documents at the hearing and had told a story that was complicated, colourful, persuasive, and as thin as tissue paper. We were not certain of his identity, his nationality, his means of entering Canada, or his real motives for coming. Our only certainty was that he could genuinely claim to be a nowhere man.

It was late in the afternoon of the second day of testimony. We were all tired after backtracking too many times through the minute details of his story, details that had begun to blur and fade through overexamination, like a photograph that has been handled too many times. Discouraged and worn out, I suggested that we adjourn for yet another fifteen-minute break. Perhaps a cup of tea would clear our heads or suggest a way out of the confusion.

But my colleague intervened, touching my arm. Perhaps just a few questions before the break. She spoke softly, which was always a sign to me that she had picked up the scent of something. I could hear the hounds baying in the distance.

She brought the claimant back to the garden shed, saying she wanted to clarify a few points. She asked why the manager was the only person to enter the shed. In retrospect, a very clever question. And the claimant had a very good answer: he said that although the workers were responsible for their own tools, they could not be trusted to enter the shed where there were seeds, sacks, fertilizer, and something called "donde," which turned out to be a kind of netting, protection against birds. It was interesting, although we did not pursue it, that this city dweller had such a thorough knowledge of gardening techniques. We did not ask about it, because we feared the elaborate answer that would inevitably follow. As my grandmother, herself a farmer's wife, would say, "He was never stumped for words."

So presumably these farm items were all valuable? Yes, of course, quite valuable. He thought it was the manager's job to take care of them. One day he heard the manager speaking harshly to a worker, telling him not to think about entering the shed.

Then quite elegantly, she closed the trap, saying that since these items were so valuable, she expected that the shed would have been locked at night to keep all the valuable items safe from thieves, leaving the claimant trapped inside his little shed that smelled of skunk cabbage.

He tried to escape, of course, acknowledging that the shed had been locked but continuing with an excellent story about a loose board at the back of the shed that left just enough space for him to slither through, although sometimes he received splinters in his stomach since the hole was so narrow, which was another reason for the boy to bring food to him since it was easier to pass food through the hole than for him to go out, which was very difficult but still possible.

But had he not said at the last hearing that the shed was made of tin? Both tin and boards, some places tin and some places boards. It was tin on the roof and it made a very big noise when it rained, which was not very often because it was not the time for rain but it was a very big noise.

Although we had stopped seriously listening, my colleague could not resist a small *coup de grâce*, inquiring about the faeces that could then no longer be buried in a hole on the edge of the forest each night and would the skunk cabbage mask the odour in the shed during the manager's visits?

Probably the non-credibility of the claimant's account of his six weeks in hiding was sufficient to undermine the core of his fear of persecution in the north. If he was lying about that, why should we believe that he had fled Muslim rioting in the first place? However, good Board members are cautious members. In judicial review, some judges of the Federal Court are more demanding than others. Some want each stone of material evidence turned over and are not generous to members who are too brief in their reasons for doubting claimants.

For insurance, my colleague had found a second large hole in the claimant's story, a gaping one that I should have seen myself. The claimant said he had returned to the police station with identity papers. My colleague asked where he obtained the identity papers. He said he had brought them south with him.

But he did not have identity papers at the time of the riot and he had not returned to his home. He said he had fled with nothing. How could he have gotten the papers?

Yes, it was true that he fled without papers but he had arranged for the small boy to be sent to his home. The father of the boy had spoken to members of his church in the city. They had made the arrangements.

What arrangements?

For the boy to go to his house during the day, for the Muslim people would not bother a child and he was able to get his identity papers.

So, if the boy had gone to his house, why did the claimant say he did not know what happened to Simon and his family?

Because he did not know what happened.

Why not? Did he not ask the boy?

No, he did not ask. The boy put the papers through the hole with the bag of food. Normally the boy did not talk to him. It was too dangerous. Besides, the boy did not know anything.

How did he know that if he had not asked?

The boy was very quiet and respectful and would not have asked such a question. He was a very good boy.

Our incredulous reaction to this string of nonsense must have been obvious. After a lengthy pause, the claimant offered that the story about the boy was not true. He apologized for not telling the truth. He was feeling very badly because he did not want "to bear false witness." At this point, the claimant covered his face with his hands and appeared to be crying. No tears were visible but his entire body shook with dry sobs. I turned off the tape recorder and we waited, saying nothing. Undoubtedly, if there had been a lawyer, she would have asked for a break and perhaps it was unfair, there being no lawyer, that we allowed the silence to linger.

After several minutes, the claimant removed his hands from his face. His cheeks were wet. Shaking his head without looking at us, he repeated that he had not told the truth and this was like "a knife in his heart." He had gotten the documents in the capital from the government office. He was ashamed that he had paid a bribe for the document and had not wanted to tell us of his sinful conduct. But he knew he must and did not want to commit an additional sin by telling more lies. This was God's truth. The information on the paper was true but it was forged by a government clerk.

There was no national registry of births in his country and he was born in the north, so why would the police be fooled by a document issued in the capital city?

All the information was true except for his place of birth. That part was changed. The clerk had written what he told him to write. He had to pay five American dollars. The clerk was a Christian man or he would have charged twice as much.

Why did he not bring the papers with him when he escaped the country?

He left the papers with his friend so that he would have something to show the police if they visited. Besides, they were false papers and he did not want to cause more trouble for himself in foreign countries, and besides, they were not international papers, they were no good to others who did not speak his language.

Before adjourning the hearing, I asked the claimant if he had anything else he wished to say. He appeared dejected, sensing our disbelief. The play was over, the lights in the theatre had come on, the magic had left the room. His head slowly descended toward his chest, like a flower wilting. After an interminable moment, he rose suddenly and stood, his arms outspread, his voice breaking.

"I am loving your Canada so much! It is the promised land. It is very very beautiful and the Canada peoples are very kind to me. I have been travelling very far. I am a stranger in a stranger land. Please. I am asking that the Canada judges know my suffering. I am a nowhere man."

His head was bent to one side, beseeching, arms spread even wider, his face now shiny with sweat. My colleague shifted quietly by my side. There was no denying the raw plaintive quality of his voice and demeanour and I would like to say that we responded to the stark urgency of another human being begging for protection, and perhaps there was a time when I might have, rather than seeing him as an old vaudevillian who was attempting one final soft-shoe shuffle before the lights, hoping to create once more a magic of laughter and tears that had irretrievably disappeared.

I nodded and thanked him for his testimony, saying that we would consider his remarks in making our decision, which would be sent to him by mail within the near future.

And where is he now? The short answer is that I do not know, although, perhaps more informatively and equally true, he is almost certainly somewhere in Canada. For the Government of Canada, he is unremovable. To deport someone from Canada, the government must have somewhere to deport him to. Without knowing his identity or country of nationality, there is nowhere to send him and no country would accept him without clear evidence that he was a citizen of that country. So he is ours, floating about the country as a person subject to a removal order and unremovable.

After five years, he will be able to apply for permanent residence and will receive it as long as he has not committed any crimes during his time in Canada. In that sense, Canada's law is humane and reasonable. It does not leave the world's unwanted in purgatory forever. If he has committed crimes in Canada, he will remain on temporary status, but still he will remain. If, through the miracle of fingerprinting, he is identified as a national of a particular country, he will be removed post-haste. The possibilities are slim. He is ours and let us hope that he will thrive in this northern garden and not simply languish in poverty, still trapped by colour, language, lack of education, and lack of legal status.

I would be pleased if one day I opened the newspaper to page three of the arts sections, weekend edition, to find that the Citadel Theatre in Halifax was staging a new and original work by Jan Grosmenteur, a graduate of the Berkeley School of the Arts, who had adapted the work of three storytellers from three different African traditions for the stage. The narrative traditions of many countries contained all the elements of great dramaturgy, according to Mr Grosmenteur, including large epic themes, intense particularity of emotion and event, and a mesmerizing use of language and movement. He wanted to transpose the genius of those traditions for Canadian audiences. There would be a photograph of Mr Grosmenteur with the three storytellers, who were to assist with both the writing and performance of the piece. The face on the far left, the face with the largest smile, would be the claimant, there identified as Louis Gikende.

I would be very happy if this came to be. I fear it will not and that the only subsequent reference to the claimant will be a four-line, one-column squib on page three of the city section of the paper, the page that lists the detritus of the local criminal court, the minor convictions with which the editor sees no hope of tweaking the prurient or voyeuristic interest of the reading public unless they know the accused personally. And of course the name will pass unnoticed before my eyes, just another name, a man of no fixed address, unknown to me or anyone else. Just another name of just another nowhere man.

Now, however, years later, with my beloved colleague long since gone from the Board and our friendship reduced to an annual exchange of Christmas and Chanukah cards, I must confess that I can still feel the dark heat of the shed, hear the laughter of the workers outside, smell the dry comforting odour of the burlap as though I had been there myself, or had dreamed my time in the shed.

5

GHOST

THERE IS NO STARTING POINT for this story and even as I
say those words two possibilities, two beginnings, emerge and both
are troublesome. This is something that cannot be approached directly and I have avoided speaking about it for some time. The
words stick to the roof of my mouth and I know what causes the
adhesion, the dryness of throat. So I shall begin stupidly: her name
was Celestine.

She was a thin woman with a dark skin of the most amazing
sheen stretched tautly over the delicate bones of her face and shoulders. There were dark hollows in the shallow valleys around her
throat and collarbones, shadowed valleys instead of flesh as though
nothing lay beneath the taut silken skin, nothing, not flesh, not air,
just an unspeakable emptiness given a semblance of shape by a desperate covering of bone and skin.

I am attempting to describe a ghost, a real ghost, not the hobgob-
lin or Halloween variety. A living ghost who sat before me in the material world of Planet Earth, in Montreal, Canada, sitting in a room
of the Immigration and Refugee Board, sitting amongst humans like
me who were attempting to decide whether she was a Convention
refugee. The room must have seemed both bare and opulent to her,
if she noticed at all. Soft grey walls, indirect fluorescent lighting,
large silver microphones set on heavy sculpted tables, padded er-
gonomic chairs covered in a rich fabric, all intended to make her feel
comfortable, a word she would no longer recognize in any language.
I think of aliens beamed aboard the starship *Enterprise*, simple

aliens, not the exotic variety, with human shapes, abruptly introduced to the technologies of the twenty-fourth century. Could this setting be any more foreign to this woman who had lived on a small farm in the northern regions of Rwanda without electricity or an interest in much more than her bit of land and her family?

Possibly she had an interest in her neighbours, both Tutsi and Hutu, who lived together, gently tolerant of each other if not overtly friendly, largely indifferent to the palace coups, civil disputes, and occasional pogroms that had swept over the countryside like tropical storms for more than thirty years. She may also once have had an interest or belief in God, decked out in the trappings of the small wooden church and priest, a young man of her own country who wore a beautiful robe and shiny shoes when he greeted her family at the door of the church on Sunday mornings. He spoke French in the manner of the voices on the radio in her uncle's home and it was rumoured that he had lived in the land of "les Blancs," the Whites, and had been blessed by the pope. He spoke like the government officials from Kigali but his voice was strong and he was not afraid to speak loudly in his church despite his lack of years, and he told them how God loved them all and that they should love God and one another. It seemed unimportant that he was Hutu.

It is strange that I have not yet spoken of her eyes for they were the beginning and end of her story, which was no different from many that come before the Board, stories of the most stunning and unbelievable human brutality. They were acts by human beings upon other human beings and we Canadians were not so distant as most would think. Although not a player in the first rank, Canada had its connections to this particular holocaust. A member of the international claque, we watched the fomenting violence from a distance, did deals with the companies and nations that pillaged, abused, and civilized throughout the Grand Lac region. We held our tongue at the fork-tongued utterances of those nations with an "interest" in the region; we watched the white man bear his burden to the bank. But "we" is an unkind, too-demanding word; for we think and act as individuals, without a sense of knowledge or power, overwhelmed by the subtlety and complexity of our nation's connections to the world's not-so-random violence, and in that sense, we are far less guilty than Celestine herself who lived so much closer to the causes of her children's deaths. Yet we need not praise ourselves for being around to pick up a few of the salvaged remnants of the violence. And Celestine, if she does share a greater portion of the guilt, has certainly paid the price.

On 6 April 1994 the airplane carrying President Habyarimana of Rwanda was shot down by a missile as it circled the capital city of Kigali. Habyarimana was the Hutu strongman who had controlled the country since the military coup of 1973, when a brushfire genocide sent a generation of Tutsis scrambling to nearby countries for safety. The killing started almost instantly, leading many to think that the assassination of Habyarimana had been planned by dissident elements within his own party, those disgruntled by his negotiations with Tutsi leaders, by his apparent willingness to grant some civil equality to the detested Tutsi, who made up only fourteen percent of the population and who had not fully paid for their historical dominance over the Hutu before Independence in 1962, when Tutsis had been so unjustly favoured by the white colonizers. They had not yet fully paid and surely it was easier to remove the problem. Eighty-five percent could obliterate fourteen percent. Kill the cockroaches.

The assassination of President Habyarimana set off the conflagration of killing. Rwandan soldiers and, worse, men of the Interhamwe militia entered the homes of Tutsis to kill the men, women, and children inside. The killing quickly spread throughout the country. Government radio broadcasts ordered Hutus to do their civic duty and kill all Tutsis in their village. Without hate or malice, too many Hutus obeyed those orders, slaughtering neighbours as they would their pig when its time had come. With considerable malice and forethought, the Interahamwe also entered the homes of politically moderate Hutus. Within one hundred days, eight hundred thousand people, give or take a hundred thousand, had been killed, usually in the most personal manner possible, with hammers, scythes, and machetes, workman's tools.

Three days after the destruction of President Habyarimana's plane, Celestine was in her home, which formed part of a cluster of farmer's houses, less than a village, only four kilometres from a large town, not too far to walk to market on Saturdays. Her seven children were with her and her husband returned home shortly before the neighbours arrived. Her husband had talked of the family leaving the previous night but they did not know where to go. Their eldest son had said they should hide in the banana field.

Her husband opened the door to Nahimana, the neighbour who had wanted to buy their second field last year but could not pay the price. He was a tall man with bloodshot eyes who held a machete as did the other men who came into the house without invitation. Two of the men she did not know. They would be men from the town.

Celestine awoke under the bodies of her family. No doubt there was a great weight upon her, possibly a slim child's arm resting across her forehead or the bridge of her nose. We did not ask for details. There was a twenty-two-centimetre scar running in a semi-circle from the rear cranial region along the side of her head to the left cheekbone. According to the medical report, the scarring was consistent with her description of how the wound had been incurred, as were the scars on her left arm and shoulder, right buttock, thigh and shin.

Left for dead, how had this woman arisen? How had she removed the arm of her child and pushed herself upward from the weight of the bodies of her seven children and husband? How had she found the will to continue, to open and close the door of her home, leave her unburied family, and walk like a somnambulist the twenty kilometres to the home of her uncle at night, somehow avoiding the rampaging gangs of killers?

There was a psychological report as well, badly written, which described the symptoms of Celestine's post-traumatic stress disorder: depression, lassitude, lack of motivation (motivation to do what, exactly?), nightmares, inability to concentrate, sudden involuntary jerking of various body parts.

Despite the documentary evidence, it is necessary to ask a few questions, to mime the appearance of a hearing. It *is* conceivable that her story is concocted, that she is really a Ugandan or Zambian attempting to escape poverty by slipping into the stream of human suffering flowing from a neighbouring country. Worse yet, she might be a Rwandan Hutu who had herself participated in the butchering of her neighbours. The Rwandan genocide is historically unique in this respect, that the killings were committed by the many, not just the military or mercenaries. Women and children, even young children, had swung the machete. A few questions to confirm that she spoke Kinyarwanda, the native tongue of Rwanda, would not suffice; some portion of her story would have to be tested, and so I ask, looking into the eyes of a woman who is not there, who finds herself somehow not dead, her body sitting in a strange chair in a strange land answering strange questions from a white man, questions that are repeated in her language by the large kind Hutu man sitting next to her.

I ask about her life in Rwanda after the defeat and flight of the Interahamwe and Rwandan army. I ask about the stones on the roof thrown by the unknown men at night and the notes. She remembers seeing her neighbour in the marketplace and screaming his name, Nahimana! The police came and took him away, her uncle says he is in the prison with the other Hutu.

The country documents tell me there are 120,000 accused genocidaires languishing in filthy makeshift prisons awaiting trials that will require more than a century to complete at the current pace. The government should hire more judges, more prosecutors, more defence lawyers, more courtrooms, say the international agencies concerned with human rights and justice. These agencies do not speak about the other desperate needs of an impoverished country devastated by civil war and genocide; widows, orphans, hunger, hospitals, transportation, electricity, employment, commerce, insanity – these are not their areas of expertise or concern. They do know something about the continuing violence, which is on the increase.

In December 1996 the government permitted more than one and a half million Hutu exiles to return from festering refugee camps in Zaire. Most of them were probably innocent of genocidal acts, victims of the Interahamwe and former Rwandan soldiers who controlled the refugee camps, brutally repressing any dissidents who wanted to return, controlling these pawns in their game with the complicity and funding of international aid agencies and the United Nations. Tens of thousands of refugees escaped the camps to wander starving through the dense and hilly jungles of eastern Zaire, only to be hunted and killed by various militias and soldiers as Zaire heaved and struggled in its own civil war.

The Banyamulenge, who were tenth-generation Tutsi residents of eastern Zaire, oppressed by the local Bantu tribes, arose finally to defend their farms and families. They were joined by Tutsi soldiers from Rwanda who were well armed, well fed, well trained. They set out to kill the hated Interahamwe militia and the soldiers of the former Rwandan army; too often they found Hutu civilians, women, children, and the elderly who had fled through the forests until they could no longer flee, falling by the wayside with wasted limbs to accept death in whatever form it took; starvation, a bullet, the butt of a rifle. Thousands of people, unknown, unnamed, disappeared, vanished with the mystery of old leopard bones.

The Tutsi army eventually would join with the rag tag army of Laurent Kabila, a local warlord, former communist, former smuggler, who had hidden in Zaire's hilly jungles for more than thirty years, dreaming of dethroning President Mobutu – a hopeless dream until the arrival of the Rwandans. Within months, Kabila would be crowned the new president in the distant capital of Kinshasa and would be applauded by Nelson Mandela of South Africa and therefore by the world. The Americans and the West, lavish in their praise of the possibilities for democracy, would fail to mention that Kabila had already made several generous deals with American, Canadian, British, and South African corporations to take over the country's mineral, oil, and diamond deposits. The French would stand embittered on the sidelines, outmanoeuvred. Days after he assumed the presidency Kabila would ban all political activity, and the West would wring its hands when he refused to allow the United Nations to investigate his army's own atrocities in eastern Zaire. But all this bloodletting came later and only serves as an ironic background to the claim of Celestine, who now sits before me with eyes of burnt smoke masking black empty space.

Her problems lie in Rwanda where many of the Interahamwe and unidentified genocidaires slipped back into Rwanda with the flood of returning refugees. They bided their time, unrepentant, looking to complete the job, eighty-five percent to fourteen. They whispered in the night, "We will kill all Tutsi, we will kill the dogs." They whispered in the street in passing, behind the curtains of market stalls, snatches of phrases floating on the wind, kill, Tutsi, dogs; malevolence was in the air, subtle, untouchable. The Interahamwe conducted border raids from Zaire, coming in the night, destroying families; boarding schools and convents were favourite targets.

Hutu students betrayed their Tutsi classmates to the invaders. They killed moderate Hutus, mayors, anyone who cooperated with the government, and the Rwandan army responded ferociously, killing Hutus, anyone suspicious, and sometimes just anyone.

Celestine heard the whispers, the pebbles tossed upon her roof at night over the courtyard wall; she saw the shadowed figures disappear before the tardy arrival of overworked police. Notes were found under her door – All Tutsi insects will die, Tutsi die, Tutsi gone – endlessly banal, endlessly evil. And: You will not speak, your mouth will be filled with offal.

Celestine was a genocide witness; Nahimana is one of the one hundred and twenty thousand awaiting trial. You will not speak, you will not speak. The voices floated behind her shoulders as she walked in the street, a cloud of gnats, persistent without biting. She did not turn quickly to catch them like real gnats as she did when she was a young girl. She walked ahead, hearing, not feeling, until her uncle said, enough. Money was found among the relatives to send her to Canada. Here she is safe, here she is frozen in the kind Canadian north. The voices have gone and she remains in purgatory alone, surrounded by the professional kindness of aid workers, nuns, immigration judges.

After summarizing the evidence, I say, looking into her eyes, I conclude that you are a Convention refugee. Congratulations. I hope that you will be happy here in Canada. My voice trials off as she rises to leave the room she never entered.

6

A BALANCE
OF PROBABILITIES

YOU DON'T UNDERSTAND. These people aren't what they seem. Half of it's sham. It's not just them, it's the lawyers, the immigration consultants, the smugglers. They're the worst. They're called "coyotes" but that's just the US-Mexican border. They operate all over the world, the Middle East, the Far East, Eastern Europe. It's the same thing everywhere. For the right price they can get you anything, false documents, visas, a prepared story, the works. The Iranians, those guys are a piece of work. Organized? You wouldn't believe. Immigration once intercepted a whole planeload of Iranians coming over, all with phoney stories already written out and hidden in their luggage. And the Chinese gangs are probably worse. There's a story about one smuggler in Fujian Province who has a picture of himself sitting pretty with the entire Surrey Board of Education. The guy's a Canadian citizen. I'm telling you, we've sold the farm.

You want another beer? Okay, this'll be the last round for sure. I gotta get home too.

So like I was saying, the smugglers get hold of PIFs from successful claims – eh? PIF's? Sorry, personal information forms Big long form, thirteen pages, it's got everything about the claimant, where they went to school, addresses, stuff you and I forgot years ago, as well as their story, why they fear persecution. Some of the stories are actually true. It's not like the Ayatollah and the Revolutionary Guards haven't been kicking the crap out of the political opposition in Iran. If you're in trouble over there, you're really in trouble. They don't mess around. If the Revolutionary Guards, they're called the

Pasdaran, if they think you're really involved with the mujahedeen – they're the opposition, the ones who want to take down the Ayatollah – if they think you're mujahedeen, you're gone. Right off to Evin, which is this fortress of a prison in Tehran. You disappear. They won't acknowledge that they've got you, doesn't matter if the Guards arrested the guy at home in front of his wife and kids, they just say, "No, we don't have him, he was released five hours after the arrest. Go look somewhere else."

Like who are you going to complain to? And what they do in there, you don't want to know. Those Amnesty reports would curl your hair. Not that I'm any great fan of Amnesty International. They've got their own axe to grind and you can't trust half the stuff they write. But it's serious business in Evin.

Which is why I get so damn mad when all these phoney refugees come over here and say they're afraid they'll end up in Evin when it's all bullshit. They're usually some businessman, a car dealer or something, who just doesn't like the regime. Who does? They maybe got knocked around once by the Pasdaran because they had a garden party where the women wore Western dresses, showed their knees, or they drank a little wine, played a little Western music and bang, in come the Guards. But that's small stuff, they get a fine or probation. It happens to everyone over there and it sure as hell doesn't add up to persecution. But if they want a better life, they buy some phoney story from a smuggler and come over here and say they're going to be arrested and tortured, which is just a load.

Take the case I heard yesterday. It's a doozy and really why I'm telling you all this, because I shouldn't be talking about it but sometimes the stuff drives you crazy. Here's this claimant, a young guy, twenty, twenty-one, with a wife and kid already. They marry young over there. Here he is, a mechanic, saying his ass is grass because he was involved with this revolutionary group and somebody blew his cover and now the Guards are going to turn over every stone in Tehran looking for him, except he's not from Tehran, it's some city in the north with this long name that nobody can pronounce, but it's basically the same thing as Tehran.

Now how is a mechanic going to be a political revolutionary? Like he's got a grade ten education, doesn't know the difference between communism and Catholicism, doesn't know the names of half the opposition parties, or the government ministers for that matter. He just knows he hates the Ayatollah and the mullahs. Shit, almost everyone hates the mullahs except for the fundamentalists, your hard-core true believers. Let's face it. Iran was pretty Westernized under the Shah. A lot of Iranians went to Europe, got a taste of freedom, the good life, and they sure don't like having to hide their light under a basket now. Everybody has a story about getting dumped on in school by some zealot teacher or getting hassled by the Pasdaran in the street with their girlfriend, who's wearing lipstick or unacceptable head covering. Everybody has a story about that shit but it sure doesn't make them a refugee.

People don't understand you gotta have a fear of persecution, real persecution, the serious stuff, hanging by your thumbs in Evin. Well I guess they do understand, or the smugglers do anyway. That's why they come up with the bullshit stories.

So this claimant comes into the hearing room and starts talking about his little revolutionary group, which consists of about five people sneaking around the city at night sticking pamphlets under doors and putting posters up saying the mullahs are a bunch of jerks and they're the reason the economy's going down the toilet. Which is probably true. But he can't tell you anything about the party because he doesn't know anything except about his own little group. They call them cells. He doesn't know who wrote the pamphlets. He says the "party leaders" but doesn't know who they are except the head guy, who's living in exile in France. It's true he did know about him but he's this revolutionary hero who everybody knows about. He doesn't even know what the pamphlets say, except in the most general way.

"It says the freedom is important and the human rights and the people should have democracy." What are you going to do with something like that? Mind you, it's all coming through the Farsi interpreter whose English isn't so hot either, so sometimes you're not sure who's screwing it up, the interpreter or the claimant. It's enough to make you crazy. But it's pretty obvious the guy can't quote the pamphlet at any length and you have to ask yourself how it is that a person is prepared to risk his skin, literally his skin, because those Guards love to flay the skin right off your back. How is it that a person can risk his skin passing out a piece of paper but can't tell you what the paper says? Does that make any sense? You'd think he'd be able to quote chapter and verse.

And asking about the party's objectives doesn't get you anywhere. You get the same answer as the pamphlet. "We want the freedom and democracy so the people can decide. We want the human rights and freedom of speech so the people are not afraid and everybody equal." After that the political analysis gets a little thin. And the party structure? Forget it. He knows the revolutionary hero at the top along with a few advisors and the rest is secret.

Like you try to break it down, right? Like if he's involved, he has to get orders from someone. Someone has to tell him where and when to get the pamphlets. But all you get is "My friend Barzun," who's some older guy who supposedly got him involved in the first place. Of course Barzun is a guy who's been busted, so he's not exactly available as a witness. If the story were true, which I don't believe for a minute, good old Barzun is hanging in chains off some wall in the equivalent of Evin.

But how would you know? Ordinarily, one of the ways you can check on credibility is to ask a lot of questions about the event that happened. If it's a personal experience, like if you tell me that someone beat you up yesterday and robbed you, I can ask a lot of questions about where it happened, how often you were hit, what the crook looked like. A lot of little details come out that can give me some idea about whether it happened or not. But in a case like this, you get nothing, zip, nada. Like, "My friend, Nezir, came to my work and told me don't go home, that my mother had told him the Pasdaran came to the house looking for me. So I went to hide in the home of my friend. The next day I am told Barzun has been arrested and I run away to the home of my mother's friend in Shiraz where they cannot find me."

What do you do with that? He doesn't speak directly with his mother, Barzun, or anyone. It's Barzun who's supposedly screaming his guts out giving up every name he knows. So what can you ask to check if it's true? So I ask him what he was thinking when he found out the Pasdaran were looking for him. "I was afraid." What's he going to say? Dumb question, dumb answer.

If I ask what the friend of his mother looks like, he could say anything. Who knows what she looks like? Actually his answer

cracked us up. He said she was short with a moustache. Old Fogarty's snorting like a stoat behind his hand. Fogarty's hearing the case
with me. I can tell you that didn't help. Good thing laughter does-
n't show up on the transcript.

Describe Shiraz, I say. So he does. "It's bigger than my town, there
is a big market, my mother's friend lives near the mosque, I do not
know the name of the mosque." But it's a loser question anyway. His
ability to describe it doesn't mean he was actually hiding out there.
He could have visited the place for a dozen reasons. Besides, *we* don't
know what Shiraz looks like. One of the problems with these cases
is we know so little about the country. Like if you tell me you ran
away to Ottawa from Toronto, then you tell me the trip took five
days by car, I'll know you're yanking my chain. But these countries
on the backside of the globe? We know squat. We could look at a
map but it doesn't tell us a hell of a lot. We've got no idea whether
there's an autoroute or a donkey trail between the two towns. And
it's not like we're sitting on our butts, not trying. We hear claims from
over a hundred countries. That's a lot of donkey trails.

And nobody seems to have a phone. So how do they communicate? It's all so bloody vague. I ask him how he found out Barzun
was still missing. "A friend of my mother brought a note." Like
there's nothing to hang any facts on to figure out if it's true, and this
goes on for two or three hours in the hearing room, me, the lawyer,
the Refugee Claim Officer, all asking questions and suddenly the
hearing's over and I, the almighty member, am supposed to decide
if this little pisser is telling the truth or if it's a crock.

Documents? You mean does he have papers, like ID and stuff?
Are you kidding? Sure he has papers. He's got a phoney passport.
How else would he get out of the country? He sure as hell couldn't
walk into the passport office. They've got very tight exit controls.
You need an exit visa just to leave the country. Can you imagine
that here? You have to get a visa from the Canadian government to
go see a Bills game in Buffalo? It's like a different world over there.
Except you can buy any document you need if you've got the
money. Which is another thing that bugs me, like only the rich can
get out. You need bread, some serious moola.

That's a good one. You need lots of moola to escape the mullahs.
I like it. Anyway, I figure if you're rich, there's less chance you're a

real refugee, like you can't be suffering too much harassment if you're able to accumulate all that wealth. Although this guy is supposed to be broke. He says his uncle came up with the money for the smuggler. There's always an uncle or a cousin who's well off, or the whole family chips in. There are always a dozen aunts and uncles, which is what supposedly happened here. Pass the turban. Sorry, bad joke, they don't wear turbans. Basically they hire a smuggler who does the whole package: comes up with a passport and exit stamp to get him out of the country and once he's in Turkey, they give him a Greek passport, which is valid except for the photo switch, and at the hearing I ask what name was in the passport and he doesn't know because it was written in Greek and the smuggler, who was travelling with him, held onto it until they landed in Venezuela and when the smuggler puts him on the plane to Canada, he gives him the passport right at the airport and tells him to tear it up and flush it down the toilet before he lands in Montreal.

The courier is protecting his own ass. He doesn't want the document traced. So he scares the shit out of the guy and says if you don't tear it up, the big bad Immigration will send you back to Iran soon as you land. So he tears it up and he has, as I said, squat for documents, except for a birth certificate that his uncle has sent by mail from Iran. Of course a birth certificate has no security features at all. No photo. Could be anyone or it could be a phoney, printed by some local press in Tehran. Your only clue is it's written in Farsi. After that it's a crapshoot. So forget the documents. And no ID card from the revolutionary party either. Even I can accept that membership cards aren't too practical if the security police kill, maim, torture, and generally squeeze the crap out of any party member they can catch. I once had a case where the guy produces a party ID card saying he's a loyal and upstanding member of the Blah-blah party. Nice little card, three-colour printing, cute little logo in the corner, like the ink was still wet. If only they were all that stupid. All of which puts me back at square one. No valid ID and no way of knowing if he's telling the truth or scamming me.

Tracking their route to Canada doesn't help either. Like this guy. He barely reads Farsi, which has its own alphabet and a completely different script, not even Arabic letters, so he doesn't recognize names in English, Spanish, or Hebrew for that matter. He knows he was in Turkey since the couriers parked him for a month in Istanbul until they came up with the Greek passport. After that, he says they changed planes in three airports but he doesn't know where. Doesn't know the language, can't read the signs. He just followed the smuggler, did what he was told. His plane into Montreal came from Caracas. Before that, who knows? Is he lying about that? And if he is, so what? His flight pattern doesn't really relate to his reasons for fearing persecution. Unless, of course, he's been living illegally in the US or Saudi Arabia for the past ten years. So you wonder, if he's lying because the courier told him to, would he lie about the rest of the story?

It reminds me of this nightmare I used to have. Still do, come to think of it. One of those dreams that come back every few years, like you have it and remember that you've had it before. It's not really a nightmare, no waking up screaming or anything. I'm in this foreign town, at night, little narrow streets, not even streets really, a car couldn't go down some of them, not a Western car anyway, and it's like a maze and I'm trying to get back to the hotel, which is Western, flush toilets and everything, and just when I think I'm about to find my way out, I end up where I started. Like I said, it's not really a nightmare, no panic or terror, no one's going to kill me. I just can't get back to the hotel. There's maybe a sense of danger because it's nighttime and foreign as hell and the streets are dark and narrow and wet like fog or after a rain, but it's mainly frustration at the repetition and getting nowhere. Civil servant's nightmare, I guess. Well, hearing these cases is sort of like that. Except there's no danger, not for me anyway.

So how did I decide this case? Well, there was this one little hitch in his story. Which is what you have to look for, one little fact that doesn't quite fit, something you can pick away at, like a label that's glued real tight except for one corner that's a little loose, and if you can just get that corner lifted you might be able to peel back the whole thing.

And what was that one little thing? You ready for this? Military service. That's right, military conscription. All Iranian men have to do their time when they turn eighteen. It's a big deal, everybody has to make the sacrifice for Allah, Country, and the Revolution. I think it's left over from the Iran-Iraq war when they were piling up the

bodies like bricks. Somehow the opportunity to become a holy mar-
tyr for the Revolution wasn't as big a selling point as the government hoped.

And that was my loose corner to pick away at, because this guy
had done his military service. They all say they were drivers or medical corps or something. No one admits to carrying a gun. This guy
was a driver, supposedly because of being a mechanic. You never
know about that stuff but how are you going to find out? I asked
one claimant once what kind of jeeps the army used, just to test
him, and you know what he said? A Mercedes! Can you believe it?
A bloody Mercedes. I just about crapped. Then he explained that
the Iranian army used a lot of Mercedes trucks, diesel engines,
'cause they're cheap on gas. I guess they don't use jeeps. Although,
truth to tell, how would I know? It's not like we've got a manual
on Iranian army vehicles. There's no way we can get into that level
of detail. You have to ask the questions sometimes, even if you don't
know the answer, and just bluff them, pretend you know and look
for their response. Is it spontaneous? Is it reasonable? So the Mercedes guy got by on that one. Although he slipped up on something
else, some horse manure about a lost passport that didn't make any
sense, so he got the old heave-ho anyway.

So back to our loose corner, I'm getting off track here. Got to
stay on track. You want another beer? Last one, I promise. Hey
Miss! Two more over here.

I didn't care what the guy did in the army, it was the fact that he
went in. I know what you're thinking. Like so what? Everyone has
to do the military service, right? Except this guy hated the regime
from day one. They'd killed one of his older brothers years before
and another one skipped the country, both of them supposedly
political dissidents. The second brother's in Canada, been here for
years.

So here's the question. Why didn't he leave before he was eligible for military duty? He'd already been kicked out of high school
because of being a shit disturber. Why not split right away if he
hated the regime so much?

And here's where I was served two slices of cow-plop pie. First
he says he couldn't leave without a passport and you can't get a
passport in Iran until you've done your army time. That part's true,

except after his army duty he tries to sneak out of the country without a passport. Said they wouldn't give him a passport because of his dissident brothers. You'd think he would have found that out earlier before doing the army time. Don't you think? That's two years of his life he supposedly just threw away. Does that sound reasonable? I don't think so.

And second, he meets his friend Barzun just after he gets out of the army. Barzun's also just been released but somehow he's politically hip, met some Iranian war veterans who it turns out are all pissed off because half of them are shell-shocked or wounded from the Iran-Iraq war and the government's stingy as hell with the pension money. Apparently only dead martyrs enjoy the state's appreciation, flowers on the grave, money for the widows but nothing for the vets. So Barzun supposedly gets in his ear and persuades him that he should work against the government rather than just splitting from the country. So he stays. That's his story.

How does it not make sense? Well it just doesn't hang together. Here on one hand he decides to become some kind of underground revolutionary except he still applies for the passport. And when he doesn't get the passport, he tries to escape on a ship, which he could've done any time, before his military service. Turns out the boat, which is overloaded with illegal emigrants, gets stuck on some rocks and they all end up doing six months in jail. When he's released, he's more pissed off than ever and rededicates himself to Barzun's little revolutionary group and decides to stay. The whole thing is too complicated. It sounds like it's made up.

So what was the so-called political activity? I told you, not much. They passed out pamphlets at night. "Khomeini didn't tell the truth." "Party members get preferential treatment" Not exactly the *Communist Manifesto*, but I suppose it got the mullahs excited. So these guys skulk around at night, secret meetings in some garden, and then Barzun gets caught.

Why couldn't it be true? Well I suppose it could, but, frankly, for me, it just has too many holes. The whole thing doesn't feel right. The case law says I have to believe the guy on a balance of probabilities. That's more than fifty percent. It's a question of probability. Is it likely that these events occurred? No. Sorry. It's maybe forty percent possible. Sure, the story's not totally out to lunch. But I just don't happen to think it happened, not all of it, anyway. And I get to make the call. Sorry. He doesn't get my vote.

What happens to him? God knows. That's not my job. I decide if he's a refugee or not. After that he's someone else's responsibility. If he finds a good lawyer and can afford him, he can hang around during the appeal. A smart lawyer can tie the thing up in court for years. Sometimes they even get the decision quashed. That always pisses me off. These pompous judges who don't know squat about refugees come up with this crap about "not listening to all the evidence" or "drawing unreasonable inferences." Truth is they just have a different opinion on the evidence but they come up with some bullshit about "error of law" to make it sound good. Anyway, the lawyer at the hearing was a lazy fuck, just going through the motions. Most of the lawyers make me puke, frankly. They're either too smart or too lazy. This guy was the latter. There are a few good ones around but you'd have to be lucky to find one. There's no money in refugee law, so how many of the good ones are going to stick with it? You know the old saying, ninety percent of lawyers give the other ten percent a bad reputation.

Besides, they wouldn't deport him right away. Immigration takes its own sweet time, especially with places like Iran and Somalia. Personally, I think they're a bunch of chickenshits. They've got a removal rate of about fifteen percent. Here we do the dirty work and say the guy isn't a refugee and has to go back, then they fart around for years before actually sending him back. It's a travesty! Some of them go underground, like the so-called Caribbean refugees and the former East Europeans, but not the Iranians, come to think of it. They may go kicking and screaming, saying they'll be killed, but they don't run and hide, which is kind of peculiar. You could take that two ways: either they're law-abiding people who let themselves be sent back to hell or they don't really have anything to fear back there.

What? No, I don't know what happens to them. How the fuck would I know that? It's a totalitarian state for fuck's sake. Look, I already said they don't allow human rights agencies into the country, so there's no way of finding out. Whatever happens, happens.

And yes, it's true. I'd never know. If they hang this guy on a wall in Evin for forty fucking years or rip his fingernails out, I'd never know. It's true. I'd never know I made a mistake. I just would not know. But what the fuck am I supposed to do about that? Let them all in? I don't think so. No way. I hear the story, I make the call. It's a balance of probabilities. That's not me, that's the law. That's the system. Now lighten up and order another round. It's your turn to pay.

7

ETHNIC IDENTITIES

THIS IS A STORY OF TWO WOMEN, and it is the face of the second that haunts me even now, years later, and yet if you had asked me before their hearings which of the two was the refugee, I would have immediately said the first. On paper, both cases were quite straightforward and pointed in opposite directions.

But please, let me first light my pipe before responding. You have asked a good question that deserves a thorough answer. What was the difference between these two women?

To answer I must begin with the personal information form, we call it the PIF, you can learn so much from it. It is a very long thirteen-page form that asks everything about the claimant, and I used to disparage it as dry tombstone data, typical of our Western fixation on so-called objective facts. But I have discovered that between the lines, there are many signs and indications intimating truth or falsity. Some files shriek credibility, where the narrative is completely consistent with everything you know about the country and it all makes sense. The story itself appears true and the only thing you need to know is whether or not it matches the claimant. In other words, is this the claimant's own story or did they make it all up or borrow it from someone else? We expedite such claims, granting the claimant a half-hour interview, quite informal, simply to be assured that they are who they say they are, and Presto! They are accepted. It is a gentler way to treat genuine refugees and of course it is also much more efficient, a saving of Board resources.

If the person does not fit the story, they are sent to a full hearing. I mention this because of the first woman who, according to her PIF, was a Tutsi claimant from Rwanda who had survived the genocide of 1994 and had lost more than any person could be expected to in a most horrible manner. Under such circumstances, I expected the interview would be a mere formality, an opportunity to speak with the claimant, to confirm her story in the hope that a brief and sympathetic interview would not be another obstacle on her long road back to normality.

This was a claimant who did not need to be bludgeoned with questions or made to re-enter that hell of eviscerated children – as though the bland dry walls of the hearing room or the equally bland, pale faces of the questioners could provide any reassurance or security against reawakened demons. We are not exorcists and we must at least take some care before we poke our sticks into the embers of hell. It is an impossible task, really. There are no good ways to ask the questions. It is like having to touch a burn victim for whom even the lightest touch is painful. All we hope to do is not seize them in a rough and awkward manner. It is a modest ambition and sometimes quite difficult.

The person who appeared for the interview surprised me with her appearance and manner. She was a short wide-faced angry woman with deep furrows in a low brow, truculent, unwilling to answer questions. Who wouldn't be after such trauma? And why be concerned about physical appearance anyway?

For too many years, I have heard two supposedly informed, sincere, and contradictory opinions. You can tell a Hutu from a Tutsi at a glance. The Tutsis are tall and slim, with narrow heads and faces, smooth features, lighter skin, and smaller noses. The Hutus are shorter, darker, and heavier, with wider heads, shorter brows, and bigger noses. You can tell the difference. You just know. I should add that this is the majority opinion and not just from Tutsis, although the Hutus seldom mention the larger nose.

However there is a strong minority opinion that asserts that the distinction between Tutsi and Hutu is more one of class than of tribe, that at one time in the Grand Lac region of Lake Tanganyika, which includes Rwanda, Burundi, parts of the Congo, Uganda, and Tanzania, the Tutsis were the tall cattle herders, dominating the shorter, more numerous, agrarian Hutus. But it all ended with the arrival of the Germans and then the Belgians, who heard about these Tutsis, the wealthy ruling tribe, who recognized a valuable managerial class when they saw it and so chose the men of wealth, anyone owning ten head of cattle regardless of tribe, and declared them overlords and officially Tutsi, with a modern magical identity card confirming their official tribal identity. A wonderful Western syllogism: Tutsis are wealthy, you are wealthy, therefore you are Tutsi.

Few wealthy Hutus objected to their new status and with intermarriage in succeeding generations, a trained geneticist could not distinguish between Hutu and Tutsi, and differences in appearance are more folklore than fact; certainly a person meeting a stranger in the street could never tell one from the other, at least not with any certainty. Miscegenation obscured the bloodlines but not the class distinctions. The Tutsis were the monied minority feeding off the carcass of the imperialist European slaughter. This was the more intellectual view, often held by educated moderates who urgently wished that their people might move beyond the nets of tribal hatreds that have held them in bondage for too long.

I must unfortunately say that although both opinions have some merit, the first holds three-quarters of the truth. There are observable differences between these peoples and of course it is not all in the size of the nose or the shortness of the forehead, but the Tutsi do tend to have the slimmer heads and finer features, though it is at once more subtle than that and readily apparent to the untutored eye of a white North American. With exceptions of course, always with exceptions. But it is certainly more obvious than the much-proclaimed Eastern European distinctions between Slavs and Jews, big noses, swarthy skins, and bushy eyebrows that have spawned the breaking of doors and bones, the burning of houses, barely decipherable death threats stuffed in the mail box, Dirty Kike face get out! And all this over a land through which endless migrational tides have swept, slanty-eyed Mongols, bushy-browed Greeks and Scythians, blond Goths, red-haired Vikings, short skinny French, all having their go over a land that still boasts dozens of little-known tribes: Kumyks, Udmurts, Yakuts, Tatars, Komi, Mari, Dagistanis, tribal detritus within the modern metamorphic mass formed from the sedimentary layers of migrating peoples clinging to distinctions in shapes of noses, foreheads, cheekbones, chins, skin pigment, hair, height, weight, shape, strength, intelligence, combativeness, commercial acumen, sexual proclivity.

Thus it is sad in a different way when a young Tutsi woman sitting before me with her soft manner, fine features, and very slim and narrow head, exquisitely shaped, who has escaped the rape and slaughter that overtook her sisters, is manifestly, irredeemably Tutsi, as is her brother, sitting next to her, who has escaped most but not all of the same hell. I can only offer the solace of safety in a cold northern land where they already speak one of our official languages, a gift from their colonial masters.

Can you understand this sadness? Not for the horror or the wounds, physical or psychological, which are manifest. No. I am saddened that her appearance, and that of her brother, fit like a glove into their own stereotypes and those of their Hutu neighbours.

How much more difficult when confronted with a dark wide-headed angry woman, testifying that she is also Tutsi and a victim of genocide with a similar litany of death and fear. Certainly appearance can never, never, never be the reason for saying no. Quite rightly, the Federal Court has struck down decisions where Board members have foolishly stated that claimants did not possess an appearance typical of their ethnicity. I almost laugh while saying this, remembering the blond-haired blue-eyed white-skinned fellow who claimed to be an Algerian Arab from the dry and barren hills beyond Marrakesh, and who spoke Arabic in a strange accent that may have been German, though the interpreter had neither the knowledge nor confidence to say with any certainty.

But I was telling you about the differences between paper and hearing-room realities, which, in the case of this small angry woman from Rwanda, included far more than appearance. She did not contain the unquenchable grief found in so many of the Tutsi claimants, at least the ones who had been caught in the undertow of the genocide and had somehow been tossed clear rather than swallowed like their aunts, uncles, parents, husbands, or children. So much of the post-genocide literature speaks of the amazing passivity of the victims, the compliance, the failure to flee, the acceptance of the machete. Even amongst the claimants sitting in refugee hearing rooms in Canada, who clearly did act, did flee, there is an internal quiet that is both disconcerting and discouraging. There is a quietness, no, a deadness, in the eye and voice, untouchable, on the far side of a chasm so deep with no apparent way back. A more spiritual person might speak of an injured soul.

Again, in this woman there was no quiet, no sense of damage. Which is why I speak of anger. Though you may well ask, is this not also a legitimate emotion, this anger? Have you not rejected this poor woman for her physical appearance and her legitimate emotional reaction simply because they do not conform to your expectations, which are based on exactly what? White man.

And I would agree, truly, with as much humility as I could muster, if that were my only evidence. But I hasten to assure you there was more, a dozen small facts, subtleties, nuances that in themselves prove nothing but as a whole weave a fabric with a very different pattern. It is the tone of voice, the toss of the head while delivering certain remarks, too often striking the wrong chord. She knew the names of places and people but there was no affection or sense of identity when she spoke of particular Tutsis and no alienation or anger when she pronounced the names of local Hutu genocidaires. I am sorry I must use the French word, we have no English equivalent. In this business, it is a very useful and effective word. Often it is the French that is less direct, that employs the roundabout expression, but not in this instance. Similarly, her list of grievances against the Hutu was exactly that, a list, read off as though memorized, without passion or differentiation.

Almost every Tutsi speaks of the pervasive sense of fear of being surrounded by potential and real hostility, of being such a small minority. Rwanda was about eighty-five percent Hutu, fourteen percent Tutsi, and one percent Twa, the so-called forest pygmies, everyone's victim. Most Tutsis believe they must always be on guard, although they will also speak of times and places where there was peace between themselves and the Hutu. In a way, they remind me of the Israelis surviving in their Arab sea.

This woman said nothing of her fear or its context. "They do not like us. We do not like them."

She was confrontational, almost dismissive, expressing something more like the blunt Hutu justification for the genocide, a fact of life, different peoples who do not like each other. When asked about the summer of 1994, the events of the genocide, she spoke in the third person. It was all they and them or the "Tutsis." Never "I" or "we," never a sense of personal involvement in the fear and flight.

So what? you say. She is a middle-aged woman, clearly from Rwanda. So what is the problem? Isn't this where you grant your famous benefit of the doubt? Surely. To such a woman, enduring so much. What if you are wrong? How could you dare make a mistake with so much suffering? If you accept her erroneously, you have let in someone from an impoverished country who is lying. Is that so terrible?

Ah, if it were only so. But the genocide in Rwanda was unusual in that way. It was not the German holocaust where the slaughter was hidden away in camps and perpetrated by the few, where most German citizens were fearful ostriches. In Rwanda, the common people, Hutu neighbours and friends, were the agents of persecution. Yes, there were the Hutu militia, the Interahamwe, the indoctrinated ruthless young men, but this holocaust was unique. Men, women, children, priests, and teachers wielded machetes, hacked their neighbours, betrayed students, parishioners, colleagues. This was killing by the people and some of the worst killers were women. If this woman is not Tutsi, there can be no presumption of harmlessness. If she is Hutu, why is she fleeing so far and what kind of person would have the means and ambition to flee so far when the innocent Hutu peasants, and there were thousands of innocents, were languishing in refugee camps outside Rwanda?

Lastly I should mention that the claimant had a document, a ration card, which showed that she had been in North Kivu, in what was then Zaire and now the Democratic Republic of the Congo, which was the primary refuge of the Hutus. The camps were controlled by the Interahamwe and former Rwandan army who had fled in advance of the Rwandan Patriotic Front, the army of Tutsi expatriates who reclaimed the country. Although not impossible, for nothing is impossible amidst such human chaos, it is still most improbable that a Tutsi woman entered and escaped the Hutu camps to come to Canada.

It is a complicated tale, and in the end I am left with her angry face and too many inconsistencies to believe this woman, but I am fortunate. It is not my job to refuse her but to simply not expedite her. She will now go to a full hearing before two Board members, neither of whom, thankfully, will be me.

Yes. Please. Take some brandy. You don't mind the pipe? You have heard only half the story, for hers is not the face that haunts me. I must remind you that the purpose of this too-lengthy discourse is to contrast two claims that on their surfaces seem so clear and straightforward, until they run off in opposite directions.

The second claimant was younger, about twenty-two, Romanian, not Rwandan, and everything about her claim appeared resoundingly false. Apart from the mentally deranged American claimants who believed that the FBI had placed monitoring devices in their molars and skulls, I cannot recall a claim with poorer prospects.

She was allegedly Roma, a people more commonly known as "Gypsies," but that is a term too closely associated with the historical oppression of these people for me to use, although it still enjoys popular coinage amongst the Roma themselves. I am sure you know in a general way that the Roma, along with the Jews, have been a European whipping boy for a very long time. No one knows how many died in the Nazi death camps, more than half a million.

They have responded differently than the Jews to the legacy of European hatred, remaining nomadic in spirit and in fact, excluding themselves from power and prosperity. More isolationist, they avoided education and thereby assimilation. The Jews, when permitted to do so, excelled at education and entered all available bastions of European commerce and culture. Precisely because they prospered, they were perceived as more of a threat than the Roma in the eyes of Western and Eastern European nationalists – tribalists is the more accurate word – and thus became more of a target.

The Roma remained on the outskirts, literally. Even today, many camp in their own shantytowns on the edges of great cities, where they are viewed more as a minor pestilence than a threat, accused of minor crimes and debauchery, scorned rather than feared – although bad times in a Romanian town can still result in the burning of a few Roma homes, and no Roma in Poland likes to walk alone on the offchance that he might turn a corner to find a few young toughs looking for an alternative to boredom.

Most of the postwar Communist governments forced the Roma from their nomadic ways, often with good intentions. It was easy to do, with a system of residence permits. They could live, work, go to school, and get state benefits only in their city of assigned residence. Even today, there are too many stories of discrimination at school. Little Georgi sits at the back of the class with one other Roma child. The teacher on occasion sneers, lowers his grade, ignores his complaints that his lunches are being stolen and that he is subjected to beatings in the schoolyard, ignores the protesting parents, passes them on to a disinterested supervisor, so that the children drop out early, often in grade three or four. They rarely go on to high school, although you wonder why, when the alternative is landing at the lowest end of the labour pool: garbage collection, tanning factories, jobs for the unskilled and uneducated. And still the beatings happen, the exile and the beatings, the name-calling, human vermin, unwelcome in cafés, lunchrooms, and most certainly marriage beds, despite dark good looks.

Against all this is the luminous face of a young woman claimant from Romania. It is difficult to say why her face should haunt me in ways that the hundreds of other faces that endured similar sufferings, and many far worse, do not. Perhaps because it was her sole piece of credible evidence, contradicting everything she wrote and said, yet telling a truth more piercing than ten human rights reports. Perhaps it was the way it hovered over the well-padded shoulder of her Canadian lover, who testified on behalf of this young woman with the beautiful broken face.

But I am getting ahead of myself. I was telling you about the PIF, the paper surface of the claim that shouted deception and deceit. There were so many holes in her story. She had come to Canada in three different ways, depending on whether you believed her PIF, her interview with the immigration officer, or her subsequent interview with the RCMP. Pick a story, any story. And understand, it was a time when there had been a flood of young Romanian claimants tumbling out of container ships into Halifax, Saint John, and Montreal. Men and women, mostly in their early twenties, your classic economic migrant with nothing to eat and nothing to lose.

They had poured out of post-Communist Romania in their tight jeans and black leather jackets following the Pied Piper of Western

democracy, freedom, jobs, cars, jazz, and education and found themselves, after jumping the fence, crammed into sealed containers at
night by dockside entrepreneurs in Calais and Rotterdam for one
hundred German marks or francs or whatever they had, and here's
this iron bar to break the container seal once you're out of port, otherwise you suffocate and here are three cans of water. You can piss
in the first one after it's empty and it's ten days to Canada. Bring
some food. For the women, pissing into a small container within a
large container in the dark with eight male strangers, only one a
friend, could be taken as strong evidence of a fear of something, if
not persecution. She was clearly running away from something, as
were her companions with their chipped teeth and flawed dreams.

Most of their claims failed, because of a Change of Circumstances; their broken noses and smashed knees were old news from
the Ceaucescu regime or from the miner's demonstrations of 1990-
91 and were no longer redeemable. Unemployment is not persecution and sorry Bucko, back to your own country. Most of their lies
were transparent, pathetic attempts to update past injuries, obvious
add-ons, embellishments. The Securitat still has my arrest record
and yes, after five years they came around looking for me and beat
up my father when he said I wasn't there and it's the same policemen as in Ceaucescu's time, you know. Which is half true, but the
story is still concocted and we have to say no. Except for the Roma
claims. If you were Roma, there was a chance of asylum.

Here I am waxing poetic and losing the thread once again. Hard
to believe people like me were trained to stick to the point, to carefully walk the line of the relevant and irrelevant, keep everyone else
on track. So here we are. I read this young woman's story against
this background of failed Romanian claims, thinking there is no
way, just no way that this is anything but the biggest piece of nonsense. She had three different reasons for fearing persecution and
each one appeared more dubious than the last.

She first said that she feared persecution because of being Roma.
Fair enough. Most of the Romanian Roma claims were successful
because of the quite horrible things the Romanians still do to Roma.
It's the worst of the Eastern European countries in that way and the
central question for the panel is whether or not the claimant is a
genuine Roma. That question is easily answered if the claimant

speaks Romany, since few non-Roma would know the language. However, many Roma do not speak Romany fluently, often due to oppression, not being allowed to speak it in school, getting beat up if they speak it in the street, that sort of thing. But they will always know some words, gleaned from parents, friends, et cetera. They will also know something of Roma culture. As I said, the Roma are quite insular, so there are a lot of unique aspects to their dress, food, weddings, funerals, that sort of thing. No matter how assimilated the family, there are always little cultural fragments to be found in their lives, gifts from uncles, stories from grandparents. It is a rich culture. And if there aren't any, they are almost certainly not Roma.

But this young woman trumped us, a pre-emptive strike, so to speak. She's a Roma but was orphaned at birth to be raised by Romanian parents in another town. She did not learn that she was a Roma until she was thirteen. Her adopted parents finally told her after she had been called names at school. Very suspicious. There would be absolutely nothing, no language, culture, nothing to prove – or disprove – the Roma connection. Except appearance of course, and I will come to that.

Without being too tedious, I will get on with it. Shortly after this discovery about her true ethnicity, the claimant was victimized by her older adoptive brother, sexual advances, although she was vague about the consummation. The narrative suggests that disclosure of her Roma identity somehow provoked the brother to view her in a different, more enticing light. What nonsense. After a few years of fending off the brother, the claimant realized that she is attracted to women rather than boys. Again, there is this questionable suggestion that the two events are linked, as though the brother's fumblings caused a sexual reorientation. And so we are faced with this prospect of a young sexually abused lesbian Roma who fears three different types of persecution. Domestic abuse cases and sexual orientation cases are always very difficult because there is rarely any objective evidence outside of the claimant's personal history.

There are no documents saying you are a lesbian or domestically abused. Rarely are there medical reports. Potential witnesses are most often in the home country and I assure you, a hand-written letter from a friend or an official is useless. Even hospital and medical reports can be falsified. On the one hand, you could say that it was a difficult case to prove. On the other hand, from our view, it was a difficult case to disprove. How convenient, or inconvenient, that she was an orphan without a scintilla of Roma cultural knowledge and the abusive brother and one lesbian lover were both inaccessible in Romania. Perhaps I sound like a battle-worn sceptic but I would not have given you three figs for the possibility of a positive decision.

Humility is a useful virtue in this business. It is a world of subtleties and surprises. One of the truisms of the refugee business is that you never know what might walk through the hearing-room door. Opinions dissolve and shatter easily. Best not cling to them too tightly, there are just too many possibilities for misperception and miscommunication. Pinter would say – do you know the plays of Pinter? – Pinter would say that all of social intercourse is like that, each of us trapped on our own little island, bound in by lies and fears, but it's a very bleak view and I am talking about something quite different, something far more optimistic, actually. Despite all of the differences in language, perception, and all that, I believe there is always the possibility of truth. A very relative truth, mind you, but truth all the same.

So my first surprise was meeting the young woman in the elevator on the way up to the hearing rooms in Montreal. One glance and I knew it was her. There were others in the elevator but it was obviously her, in the corner, alone. Black leather jacket, black hair, rich black hair, curling to the shoulder, sallow skin. Sallow is a negative word but that was the hue of her skin, which at the same time was lovely, a darkened cream. Funny, really, all of the features, the heavy eyebrows, the colouring, the clothes, the jewellery, everything shouted Roma. I almost suspected her of wearing a costume, part of an elaborate hoax. I actually followed her out of the elevator knowing we would be walking by the hall windows. I wanted to see that hair in natural light to see if it was dyed or was possibly a wig. It did not appear to be, although I have no expertise in such matters.

I needn't go on about the hearing. Her testimony was a disaster. Filled with the kinds of contradictions that are ordinarily our most reliable grounds for rejecting a witness. They are the easiest means of challenging the credibility of a claimant. She was inconsistent about times, places, even her motivation for quitting school and coming to Canada. And yet through all the confusion and contradiction, there was an emotional continuity as though she were struggling to tell the truth as best she could, as though she did not have all the information.

Now let me say, for fear of sounding too sentimental, that most of us have seen too many tears in the hearing room, both true and false. We have all heard serial liars who are able to go from one story to another with complete belief in their veracity although they are manifestly false. There are certain countries, which I cannot name due to the forces of political correctness, where the storytelling tradition is so strong that claimants nimbly leap from absurdity to absurdity with no sense of chagrin or shame, telling each tale with equal sincerity. But this was nothing like that.

Despite all the contradictions, I believed *something* had happened to her. Although jumbled, her testimony was obviously delivered from some private hell. However, I needed more cogent reasons than my own gut feeling to grant a positive decision. So the outcome might well have been reluctantly negative but for the testimony of an unexpected witness, her Canadian lover, a large jolly woman who had also been her ESL instructor – excuse me: English as a second language. The witness obviously cared for the claimant and had been a comfort and a mentor long before becoming a lover.

It is easier to discern truth than falsity in this business, an axiom ignored by most of my colleagues, and this case was a wonderful example of that principle. There were a dozen tiny moments when it was so obvious that these women had a full and loving relationship, and I say that, I trust, without a hint of prudery. The witness recounted how she had first noticed Maria at the back of her class, her eye caught by a torn and haunted face, which proved to be quite effective testimony since Maria's face was in my own line of view as she sat at the back of the room, hovering like a pale and gibbous moon just over the left shoulder of her lover. It was quite an extraordinary contrast between this very direct and lively Canadian woman and the muted porcelain face of the claimant, listening to her own story. Of course, these are not the kinds of observations one can mention in the formal reasons for the decision, but they are often more persuasive.

The witness, I cannot recall her name and shouldn't tell you in any event, was able to tell me, with great indignation, what the claimant couldn't. Maria had endured far more than the sketchy outline of sufferings in her narrative. The brother had brutally abused her for years while constantly affirming that it was her Roma identity that justified his actions – some sort of twisted logic that Roma women invite this sort of thing and also *like* it since it perverts good Romanian men like himself. And of course, her beauty only made it worse, a beautiful Gypsy, all part of the seduction. It's really no different than the logic that men have used in all societies, raping and seducing women and then somehow passing on the blame, the evil temptress, the beautiful witch. It's been going on since Eve I suppose. It simply seems more shocking when you see it so vividly played out in the hearing room like some repertory drama, using the metaphors of ethnic identity and sexual orientation. Except the damage is very real.

In the end it all seemed so simple, once I understood that we had been listening to a claimant who had been abused from age thirteen, had been vilified by classmates and that all of this confused and contradictory testimony was coming from a shattered psyche. So my usual analytic tools were useless; inconsistency and contradiction did not, in this case, indicate falsity.

Thank God for the witness who was so credible. A breath of fresh air, really. Of course it always helps to hear a witness directly in English. You lose so much through the interpreter, the meaning of the words is out of synch with the witness's expression and body language. And in this case, the witness was exceptional, a wonderfully unvarnished, forthright manner, an open demeanour, all the pauses and hesitations in all the right places. We could have been talking over coffee and doughnuts at Tim Horton's.

It is frightening to think that there have been other negative decisions, other dubious testimony filled with contradictions that may have been saved by such a witness who knew the claimant's story to be true. But I am wandering. I was telling you about first perceptions of cases and how much the documents can reveal and how, occasionally, the true story is quite the opposite of what it seems.

So the Hutu lady is God knows where, for I am quite sure she was Hutu and the claim will have been decided by now, and the young Romanian woman is probably somewhere in Montreal and in counselling I hope, building a new life in Canada. With so many cases, they come at you day after day, you know, it's quite unceasing and the details tend to dissolve or get jumbled together. But there are a few indelible moments and certainly that was one. I shall never forget that face, quite haunting, such a sad and beautiful moon. It has never left me. We do such terrible things to one another.

8

WADSWORTH'S EXCUSE

A TALL, SLIM WOMAN IS STANDING before a wall-length mirror in what is obviously a public washroom. The room is long, narrow, and immaculately clean. The tiles sparkle. The woman is dressed in a light wool suit that is somehow the perfect shade of grey. She is scrutinizing her face in the washroom mirror when the door bangs open with considerable force.

"Oh, he is such a stupid bastard!"

The woman entering is shorter and younger. She also wears a wool suit of a more ambiguous colour that appears tight across the shoulders.

"Who? Wadsworth?"

The younger woman walks to the end of the washroom and turns to face her colleague. Her arms crossed, she leans back against the wall. "Who else?"

The older woman still faces the mirror. "It could have been Madame, except for the gender. She's almost as bad."

"She isn't today. Just now, not five minutes ago, he told a seventy-two-year-old woman that he couldn't see any reason why she shouldn't go back to Somalia since the principal threat to single, unprotected women is rape, which would obviously not be a problem for her."

The older woman turns to face the younger. "I suppose I should act surprised, but I'm not. Not really. That's worse than stupid. It's so unfeeling. Its … it's … sorry, can't think of a word for it. It's just so bloody awful."

"We're talking about Somalia, right? He forgot to mention disease, pestilence, looting, and all-round tribal testosterone-driven violence. Most of those nasty little buggers are under eighteen, kids really, roaring around in those trucks they call technicals, shooting at anything or anyone who belongs to another tribe. No mother, no home, no morals. It's ludicrous. One might assume an elderly woman with no family might have just a few problems wandering around the countryside."

"Did he do that differentiated risk thing? You know, 'You're all in the same boat, you are no more at risk than anyone else.'"

"No, he's stopped doing that since he was slapped on the wrist by the Federal Court last month, for about the umpteenth time. Someone from Legal Services finally talked to him, explained that it's not the law. I think maybe B.J. had a talk with him. Told him it's an embarrassment to the Board. If some refugee lawyer was clever enough and pissed off enough to do a computer search of Federal Court judgments, well, the fact that he's had about ten decisions overturned in the past year just might catch the interest of some newspaper. That got his attention, however briefly. He's arrogant in the hearing room when it's all confidential but he sure doesn't want to be held up to public scrutiny as the King of Overturned Decisions. Oh no. Not he."

"Can they do that?"

"Do what?"

"Do a computer search for Board member names in Federal Court decisions."

"Probably not. Most court decisions don't mention the name of the Board member. Did you ever notice that? Even when they quash the decision, even when they slam it, the court rarely names the individual Board member who made the decision. A few judges name names but they're the exception. It's a conspiracy, really, when you think about it. Why shouldn't the Board member be held accountable? He's sitting there with the power to send some poor claimant back to hell. If he's wrong, that is. We all know it's an awesome power. If he doesn't use it well, why shouldn't the world know it? Judges are publicly accountable, why not Board members?"

"Probably an unconscious conspiracy. Instinctively they don't want to embarrass the system. What is the expression you lawyers use, 'bring the administration of justice into disrepute'?"

"Well if justice is disreputable because of shoddy reasoning or blinding stupidity, then the public bloody well should know it. They *should* know it if Wadsworth treats an elderly woman the way he did that woman. God! I'm still angry. I'm really not ready to go back in there."

"How long do you have?"

"Wadsworth called the mid-morning break. That means at least half an hour. He always goes down for a cigarette and coffee with whoever is in the coffee shop."

"So you have time for a coffee. Let's go next door to Java Hut. My treat. They have low-fat cranberry muffins."

"No, really, it's fine. I don't know why I'm so irritated by it. It's not as though I haven't heard worse. Don't you have a hearing too?"

"Not any more. Madame adjourned for the rest of the morning to 'review the evidence.' What evidence? We barely got started. Come on. Really. I can use the break and I can tell you why Madame is actually worse than Wadsworth. Indifference trumps stupidity. That's my argument."

"No way! You haven't got a chance but I really want to hear this. Loser pays."

A few minutes later, the women are seated at a small table near the window of the coffee shop. There is a blue vase with a single rose, remarkably fresh, sitting on the table along with two cups and one muffin.

"Do you think there's a relation between slovenly appearance and slovenly thinking?"

"I don't know. I never thought about it. Maybe lawyers. Definitely not artists. What prompted the idea?"

"Well, did you notice Wadsworth on the way in? He was standing across the street at smoker's corner."

"No, I didn't notice. Did he see us? Not that it matters. Wait. I see where this is going."

"Well, it is a thought. You don't notice it quite so much when he's sitting behind the bench and you only see the top half, but it just struck me. He's standing there in baggy unpressed pants. He's oblivious to the fact that his stomach hangs three inches over his belt. You can't see the grease stain on his tie but it's there. I saw it this morning. He wears a big, wide Windsor knot to hide the unbuttoned collar because of his big fat neck. So the argument is that he is a slob because he thinks like a slob. He doesn't notice the issues or the evidence because he doesn't notice anything."

"I get the impression that you really don't like the man."

"It's nothing personal. I just can't stand to see what he does to people in the hearing room. I'm never sure whether he's being stupid or mean."

"Then what about Madame? Now there's a European appearance. Great perfume. Great skin. Great clothes. She was her typical self this morning, wanting to know why the claimant hadn't entered his nickname on the personal information form. Terribly relevant, that."

"You mean the question about alternative names or identities?"

"That's it. The one for people with multiple identities. Not that they'd ever tell us. And you probably know the whole Somali nickname thing where they have this custom of giving people nicknames based on some unattractive characteristic, like this very important general named 'Tur,' which means Big Ears. Except somehow it's not an insult once it becomes common usage. I suppose it's like calling someone 'Shorty' or 'Stumpy.' We don't do that much anymore, do we? Anyway, to come back to the point, my mind's wandering just like Madame's, this poor fellow mentions during his testimony that he's known as 'Kor' which I suppose is the equivalent of 'gimp' in English, which seems very cruel but he didn't seem to take it that way and Madame suddenly becomes very animated, saying this is new information going directly to the issue of identity and why didn't the claimant disclose this before the hearing and on and on and she had to adjourn to 'consider the implications.'"

"Does he limp?"

"Limp? Oh, the claimant. You know, I believe he does. How silly! I should have thought to look. But I'm sure he does, a slight limp, on his left side."

"Not that it matters. It's irrelevant. The nickname's got nothing to do with his identity or his fear of persecution. You have a point, I do concede that. She can be very obtuse. And cold. I suppose Wadsworth isn't really mean. He's ignorant. Thick as a T-bone steak. But it's usually not deliberate. He just doesn't see alternative points of view. But Madame, Westmount born and bred – I detest the way she looks down her nose at claimants!"

"Well she was at her immaculate best today. This poor little fellow is a member of the Darood clan. Typical story, father shot in the street by soldiers after the Hawiye takeover, the claimant flees Mogadishu in a truck with his mother and two sisters. There's another brother lost somewhere. One of the sisters gets sick and is left behind in Kismayo. Three years in a refugee camp in Kenya until an uncle sends money from Saudi Arabia. So can you guess what Madame asked about?"

"The money. She wanted to know where the uncle got the money."

"You peeked. No fair. She has a wonderful instinct for the irrelevant. And of course, terribly bothered by the fact that he wasn't really the claimant's uncle. His maternal aunt's brother-in-law, I think, if I got it right. Excuse me? How many years have we been hearing Somali claims? And she still hasn't figured out that an 'uncle' or an 'aunt' can mean just about anyone up to third cousin. What a stupid waste of time and emotion putting him through all those questions. And you can imagine the claimant's answers."

"I don't know."

"Exactly. This is too predictable. He was twelve when the family fled Mogadishu, fifteen when he came to Canada. You know the family doesn't consult. The uncles and aunts decide. He's told where he's going."

"I had a Somali case last week, almost identical facts except the claimant was a woman, early thirties, about eight children, only three with her in Canada. But typical, right? No education, raised to bear children and feed the family. She didn't know where she was going when she got on the plane in Nairobi. The deal was completely between the uncle and the hired courier who gets the false documents, gets the tickets, and takes her to the airport. She only knows that she and three of the kids are going. The rest stay behind with an aunt. The uncle doesn't have enough money for more tickets or they can't find enough phoney documents with US visas. Who knows? She certainly doesn't. They don't tell her and she doesn't ask. Like it's not her role to ask, she's not part of the conversation. She's just the cargo to be moved. She was in a car leaving New York before finding out that she was going to Canada. Except Hooper was hearing the claim. She wasted less than five minutes on the false travel documents. She'd already established tribal identity and the claimant was very credible on the incidents of persecution. So what's the point?

"It's not like we haven't been hearing these stories for years. But Madame plows the same ground over and over. She probably thinks she's being judicial, 'scrupulously scrutinizing the facts of each case.' It's so unnecessary. And scary for the claimants This little fellow this morning was so frightened. He knew he wasn't giving the right answers. You know how Madame's voice gets sharp and irritated when she's not happy with the answer? This little guy kept saying he didn't know, his uncle got the tickets, et cetera, and she kept asking how much money the uncle made and where was the other uncle in Saudi Arabia who sent money and what was his job and I'm sitting there thinking, please, please, make this end. Because you know what happens. They start to lie. They know the member's unhappy and will say anything to make her happy. Tell them what they want to hear. And then she clobbers them with inconsistent answers. 'I thought you said you didn't know. Now you are telling us that … blah, blah, blah.' Finally, her lawyer asked for a break. I hope she will talk to her client and calm him down, tell him it's okay that he doesn't know the answer and for God's sake don't lie."

"Barbara Goulet's the lawyer? She's okay. She'll cool him out. But it's not fair, you're making Wadsworth sound good by comparison. Can you imagine the two of them on the same panel? How did she get appointed anyway?"

"Who knows. Friends in high places. It certainly wasn't based on her professional credentials. I think she worked in public relations and did some fund raising for some cabinet minister in Montreal. Or maybe her husband did. You never get the complete story. Cabinet secrecy. It all takes place behind Cabinet's curtain of silence. I call it the *rideau* on the Rideau."

"Oh my! Bilingual puns."

"Well she's a gem, wherever they found her. And I did sit with her and Wadsworth together. A full week of Sikh cases with the two of them last year in Calgary. Lucky me! The dream team. I would have called in sick except all of the other RCOs would've been instantly sick. They would never have forgiven me. Are you okay for time?"

"I'm fine. Wadsworth's still out there. I can see him if I lean a little. Besides I want to hear the story. I have never been with the two of them together except you better not make Madame sound worse."

"Well, it's a close call. This one case, a young woman, grassroots political activist, about four or five arrests and beatings, a smart, smart woman, she knew everything about Punjabi politics, completely credible. Wadsworth keeps asking why a married woman with a child would put herself and her family at risk. The implication being that only men are entitled to put their families at risk for political principles. Madame, on the other hand, thought the claimant would be safe in New Delhi as long as she wore a different style of sari to hide her Punjabi identity. It was so embarrassing, I couldn't look her counsel in the eye. And all of this drivel is coming through an interpreter who speaks Urdu instead of Punjabi, which he assures us is 'almost the same thing.' I don't know about his Urdu but he sure as hell couldn't speak English. 'I were asking about the situation to resolved.' Whatever that means. They should have adjourned the hearing for a decent interpreter.

"The poor claimant must have thought she'd landed on Mars. Can you imagine? It would be sort of like someone from the Deep South who didn't understand a word of Chinese, making a claim in China with a Scottish interpreter with a heavy burr they can't understand, and their lawyer telling them the guy's barely comprehensible in Chinese. Unbelievable."

"It's like that party game we played as kids, Broken Telephone. We say something, 'I'm a peanut,' it goes through five other kids and comes back as 'Amy is a pee-pee hole.' Sometimes I think it's that bad. Actually, sometimes it's worse. So her claim was refused?"

"No! That's the irony. After seven hours of mainly pointless testimony, they went positive and gave her the 'benefit of the doubt.' Basically because they couldn't figure out how to write a negative.

Thank God. This woman would have been scooped the minute she landed at the Delhi airport. I think what turned it was the lawyer. He speaks fluent Punjabi. He kept correcting the interpreter, which Wadsworth didn't like but he couldn't do much about it because the lawyer was always right. The interpreter kept apologizing. 'Oh, so sorry. Yes, I think that is maybe the correct word. Urdu is almost the same but a little bit different. Veddy sorry.' Anyway, counsel submitted this report about ten refugee claimants who had been refused by Canada and arrested upon their arrival at the New Delhi airport. I think that scared both of them. The report didn't name the members who had given the negative decisions but you could see that thought going through their minds. They hate the idea that one of their decisions might boomerang back on them in the press. But this woman was so credible. Every little detail about the food program she set up, her arrest, and her father having to sell half his land to buy her release from the police. It was all there, without exaggerations."

"Last week Wadsworth turned down an Ethiopian claim that should have been open and shut. It was one of those cases where the credibility of the claimant was totally clear but the members just didn't see it. It drives me crazy. The poor man became so upset he lifted his shirt to show us the burn scars on his abdomen. Of course, it didn't help that his counsel didn't have a medical report. I don't think he even knew about the scars. So Wadsworth goes negative on change of circumstances. The essential logic being there's a new gang of human rights abusers running the place and you haven't yet been tortured by them although I'll bet you five bucks to one birr that he will be after he's sent back."

"Enough! I surrender. Wadsworth's worse. Now let's talk about something pleasant. How about Hooper? I'm with her for the rest of the week. You know, she's a dream. Prepares the file, listens to the testimony, doesn't get fooled, doesn't get excited, doesn't argue with counsel, gives a clear logical decision. She makes it look easy."

"And did you know that she might not be reappointed?"

"No! Don't say it. I don't want to hear it. Tell me it isn't so. How do you know? When is she up?"

"In about four weeks. She hasn't heard a thing. I remember when the members didn't find out about the reappointment until their term ran out. Now they're supposed to let them know two months in advance. Except they don't. Especially when they are not going to reappoint."

"I don't believe it! Wadsworth was just reappointed. How could they reappoint him and let her go? I mean, there's a limit. I cling to this notion that they really do care. I know it's all politics and ignorance but surely, surely, underneath it all I really do think they care. The government talks about humanitarian legislation and protecting genuine refugees. How could they do that?"

"Wadsworth also has friends in high places, very high places, so they say. He's been a party fundraiser for years. His locker at the Athletic Club is right next to a certain minister's. He brags about it. Your original backroom boy. God knows what he does at the Athletic Club. I suppose they have a bar."

"Fine. So take Wadsworth. Well, not fine. But okay, we're stuck with him. But why dump Hooper? Why get rid of the best? Don't they know how hard this job is? Do they have the faintest idea how difficult it is to figure out who's lying and who isn't when you don't speak the same language, live the same culture, have the same history, the same world view? I can't stand it! I really can't."

"Me neither, but there's no point getting our knickers in a knot. Not for Wadsworth, anyway. Hooper's okay. She can always go back to the university. It's the poor bloody refugees who end up with Wadsworth and Madame. And us. Don't forget we're stuck with them too."

"I hate it. And not all the members have a fallback like Hooper. I hear Guy Brisson is still at home twiddling his thumbs. It's been more than a year since his appointment wasn't renewed. He was a good member but after ten years at the Board, what's he got to go back to? He's out of the work stream and there's not really a big demand for specialists in human rights abuses in sub-Saharan Africa."

"At least we have jobs. Half the pay, but we do have jobs."

Is that the good news? I suppose it is. Maybe I'll go on language training. Six months without Wadsworth or Madame and I could come back to French hearings with Lalonde and Cartier. She's great and he's okay. How does that sound? I think it's a plan."

"It's a wonderful plan except for your mangled French. Do you really think you could do French hearings?"

"Probably not. I'd probably sound like that Punjabi interpreter.

Definitely not a good idea from the claimants' view. Well, I could always become management. They always need people with passable Public Service French. I know how to say, 'With additional resources, we are confident that we can meet the current challenges confronting the program.' 'Avec des ressources supplementaires,' See? It's easy."

"How do you say, 'Let's get back to the hearing?' I just saw Wadsworth crossing the street."

"I'm okay. He'll now go to the washroom. But I'd better get back first. Wadsworth is never eager to go back but he loves it when the RCO is late. It gives him an excuse. And I am officially looking for another job. The thought of being Wadsworth's excuse just did it for me. I will go back in, I will smile, I will ask the obvious questions, I will await the not-so-obvious answers, I will hope for the obvious decision, and I will go home to my cat. Until tomorrow."

"Now that sounds like a plan. You've convinced me. Wadsworth is worse than Madame. It was neck and neck there for a while, but you're right. He's worse. Stupidity and bias trump indifference and bias. But it's a close call. The bad members make it so bloody hard to remember that it's not like that most of the time. I have to remind myself constantly that these are people's lives and I can make a difference. I am not just making ineffectual noises. We do our job, file the relevant evidence, ask the right questions, help the good members, limit the damage with the lousy members, and sleep at night. That's not so bad."

"You're right. You're right. It's not so bad. I'm having an off week. Just too much Somalia, too much Wadsworth. I'll stop whining. My cat hates it. Besides, next week I'm in Saint John with Hooper and Lalonde and all the Cuban fishermen who can't go back to Cuba because they jumped off government fishing boats and Fidel is a mean SOB behind that beard and cigar. They have such beautiful old faces and none of them know how to lie. Better yet, Hooper knows all the good places to eat and Lalonde is funny when she's on the road, away from the Board."

"See? Life after Wadsworth. So shall we be getting back? I'd hate for you to truly be Wadworth's excuse."

9

CIRCUMCISING MUTILATION

"FINGERNAILS. THAT'S HOW THEY DO IT IN GUINEA. Well, not all of Guinea. It is a custom unique to one particular tribe. Other tribes will use a knife, a razor, something sharp. But for this one particular tribe, I forget the name, an older woman, usually a relative, grows her nails long and strong enough to pinch off the clitoris, no anaesthetic, no antiseptic. Then again, it's only the clitoris. Across the continent in East Africa some people practise full infibulation. A lovely word, that ... until you realize that it means the full removal of the external sexual organs of a woman, the clitoris, the labia minora, the labia majora, all the equipment God has given women for sexual pleasure. The vaginal opening is then sewn up, leaving a small opening for urination and menstruation. The operation is most commonly performed between age seven and twelve. The girl is restrained by female relatives while the operation, I use the word loosely, is performed by an older woman with a razor, without anaesthetic."

The speaker was a big man with a large heavy head and a face to match. He flung out one arm in a wide, authorative gesture to emphasize his final remark concerning the lack of anaesthetic. Without pausing at the end of its arc, his hand grasped a wine glass which he raised to his lips with surprising delicacy.

"Young girls die from the practice. Excessive bleeding, infection, rusty razors. The great majority of the women survive, although many have long-term health problems, chronic infections. Traditionally the husband removes the stitches on the marriage night –

cuts her open, is a more direct way of saying it. Sometimes a trusted female relative of the husband will do the dirty work for the more sensitive grooms who aren't up to the task, although they do want the assurance that good old Hymen is hiding intact in the closeted cave within. This is all about property, remember. Chattel. The new owner requires evidence that he has not contracted for damaged goods. Ironic notion, don't you think? Damaged goods. What the hell does he think they already did to her? Of course, it's also about the maintenance of property. He wants assurances that his wife, his cow, won't stray into other pastures. Removal of any possibility of sexual pleasure certainly takes care of that. Talk about cutting off your nose to spite your face. Silly buggers."

"He's drunk."

Two women were seated together some distance from the two men who were lounging around a dinner table set outside on a wide stone-walled patio. Both men were dressed in formal evening wear, now slightly askew, suggesting they had already attended some more auspicious function. A heavy linen tablecloth and candlesticks had been moved outside for the occasion. It was a warm summer night. A three-quarter moon hovered over the treeline of the substantial gardens below the patio.

"He seldom gets like this. It's those damn refugee cases. I wish he wouldn't hear them. It gets him so upset. And he doesn't have to, you know. He's a senior judge. He could ask for tax cases, unemployment, airports, aboriginals, that sort of thing. He could leave the refugees for the junior judges, but he won't. He's so darn stubborn that way."

Across the patio, the judge resumed. "And don't give me any of that cultural relativism crap." His companion remained silent.

"Western democratic notions, imposing cultural values on other less-prosperous peoples. Nonesense! Ask the women. First give them a choice, then ask them. And I don't mean the self-serving spokeswomen. Every nation is cursed with its Margaret Thatchers, conservative battleaxes who have prospered in a male regime. Ask the women, the ones who are cut."

"And what do you think, fifty-fifty?" Unlike the judge, the second speaker had not loosened his tie. He leaned forward to tap the ash of his cigarette onto the edge of a heavy crystal ashtray. A dapper man, his every motion and utterance appeared ironic, almost a parody of itself.

"You're a cynic, Robert. I said give them a real choice. Most don't have a sense of alternative. It's something that's done to them, a rite of passage, unquestioned, inevitable. But you know it's changing and very quickly. It's a shrinking planet, they're finding out that it doesn't happen to other women in other cultures. They are starting to ask questions. I say it's wonderful. Give them all the radio, television, magazines they can get their eyes and ears on. Give them birth control, give them education, give them a job, give them a bloody choice and they'll take it, every time."

"Interesting choice of words, Henry. You're outdoing yourself tonight."

"Oh, don't be so damn sardonic, Robert. Bring it home. Think if it were Jessica. How would you feel if it were being done to her?"

"Well, she's already mutilated herself. Pierced ears, pierced navel. She is now talking about a tongue ring. Not quite the same thing, I grant you, but it's moving in that direction. Certainly the clitoris has not been overlooked by the young as one of the pierceable parts of the anatomy. I hear in Berlin some of the more radical youth, the cutting edge, so to speak, are using facial implants. Surgically slitting the skin to slide various silicon objects underneath to achieve a kind of Star Trek Ferrengi look, or one of those exotic aliens. All quite temporary of course, change your look every Saturday night. So I wouldn't beat the Western breast too hard, my friend. Mutilation has been with us for a while."

"Not the same thing and you know it. Firstly, it's self-mutilation, voluntary. In addition, it's temporary and cosmetic. I can't imagine those kids doing anything to detract from their own sexual pleasure. And they're dilettantes. They damn well know the rings are removable." He waves his hand dismissively, unconsciously the superior court judge even amongst his friends." Besides, it's primarily magazine culture, glamorizing a desperate fringe element amongst our young people."

"Easy for you to say with Brennan in law school and Meaghan looking down the right end of an electron microscope. Lucky you.

My kids live at the mall. Out of boredom, they identify with that fringe element, or at least their image of it."

The judge appeared oblivious to these asides. "The women do it to themselves. In a way, that's the most bothersome. They do it for the men, but they do it themselves. The mother or the maternal aunts decide when it will happen. Often the aunts are the ones to restrain the girls. You would think they'd be the most sympathetic."

"Not so strange, really. And I don't think we're all that different. Don't you remember that great lunk of a fellow at school, Chummy MacNaughton? The one who made our lives miserable in our first year? Nasty bugger. Do you recall how he got that way? When he was new, a bunch of seniors made him take off his pants in a dark room, then turned on the lights with half a sorority present. Passed around the photos if I remember rightly. He took such delight in hazing the hell out of us. Human psychology, I'm afraid. Do unto others as was done unto you. Sorry chum. Fifty-fifty are pretty good odds when it comes to man's inhumanity to woman. Or vice versa."

"Why doesn't Robert take a judicial appointment?" Beth finished her coffee. "He's well connected and Henry would speak for him."

"Not enough money, my dear. Robert's quite happy at Bunnington, Reach. Look at him. He's a senior partner without a grey hair on his head. The bank is his only client. He has platoons of eager young lawyers to hurl at any problem. Robert says his litigation strategy most resembles that of General MacArthur, waves of marines hitting the beach after a barrage of long-distance shelling and bombing. Frankly, he can't afford to be a judge."

Friends from childhood, the two women had surrendered potential careers to marry and raise their families. Paired with successful husbands, they have borne the greater share of parenting and loved their children, now grown and departed, fiercely. They continued to manage their households and support their husbands with patience and intelligence. They have both passed into middle age with as much grace as money and determination would allow. Occasionally, they chafed at the borders of their world of reading groups, charitable committees, obligatory social events, and too-brief three-star holidays. Both have invested in an art gallery that continued to lose money. Occasionally, they reminded one another that their marriages were intact and that their husbands doted.

Henry was leaning against the stone parapet overlooking the garden. His shoulders were hunched forward as though too heavy for his torso, an unconscious posture adapted over a lifetime of adjusting his height to shorter people. His thick heavy hair, worn too long, was streaked with grey. He turned suddenly to face the two women.

"What would you do? Can you conceive of mutilating your daughters in that fashion? Is there any form of social duress that could compel you?"

Both women moved to the men's table, joining the conversation while Henry remained standing.

"Well, Henry, your mother loved you dearly and she permitted your circumcision." Bobbi smiled at Beth. "I'm making assumptions, of course. I speak not from experience."

Henry also moved to the table, reaching for the wine decanter. "Bobbi, you are as cynical as your husband and I suppose I'm being a bore. Circumcision it is not. That's what it was called for so many years in the literature, female circumcision. A charming little euphemism. God, dare we say 'mutilate'? It is the cutting away of significant amounts of flesh. Perhaps 'operate,' like sucking out cellulite after an incision. We can't dignify it with 'surgery,' not with those rusty razor blades and fingernails. Possibly 'amputate' is the correct word, although the labias, minora and majora, cannot be called a limb. They are probably as large as an ear and one can certainly talk of an amputated ear, can't one?"

Beth watched her husband refill his glass. "Henry, now you're playing the cynic. We all think it's terrible. I think for poor Robert, humour is an antidote. We all feel so helpless. There's really little we can do. We are talking of the culture of another people. And it's not just a matter of cultural imperialism. We can't just go swaggering in playing the offended modern European to the poor Fuzzy-Wuzzy to raise him, or her, from their primitive state. You know it's just not on."

Amongst their friends, Beth was famous for being able to tame her husband's more eccentric proclamations. Henry's head had sunk towards his chest, his chin nearly resting against the starched shirt front. Slowly he raised it. The candlelight emphasized the creases running from his nose to the corners of his mouth and the deep vertical lines carved into the long cheeks with the precision of scarification markings, perhaps from the tribe of judges.

"This case. Today. This woman has endured quite horrible things. Numerous beatings, not only by her husband but other members of his family. Beatings, imprisonment, complete ostracism from her tribe. She had nowhere to go."

All three unconsciously turned to Henry, anticipating the story. Bobbi was the first to speak. "I thought you said they circumcised, sorry, mutilated, I'll never be comfortable with that word. I thought you said that girls are cut between age seven and twelve."

"They are. She'd been mutilated many years before. She described it quite graphically during the testimony. I won't ruin the remainder of the evening with the details. But I will say that it was worse than the documentary evidence. She said she has never forgotten how this one aunt who had been particularly kind to her had held her so forcefully during the pain. She has never forgotten the unrelenting power of those hands on her shoulders. She was particularly young when it happened, only six, and no one had explained anything. She was simply taken one morning from her bed along with two older girls and led to a hut where it happened. She could not walk for two weeks from pain and loss of blood. One of the other girls died. On her marriage night, her husband insisted on cutting away the stitches himself, many of them grown into the flesh."

"Henry! You said no details! Bobbi, I will take some of that cognac."

Robert's interest was piqued. "I still don't understand, Henry. If the mutilation already occurred, why is she here claiming refugee status? You've told me a dozen times that asylum is only granted to prevent future persecution, not to acknowledge past persecution."

"Yes, of course, I'm sorry, I forgot to mention. She has daughters, two daughters, now aged twelve and eight. She has three sons as well but they don't have the same concerns, obviously."

"But I thought you said the mother had the right to decide."

"Sorry, Bobbi. I suppose Robert would call it the first right of refusal if it were a contracts case. The mother gets to decide *when* but not *if*. The mother, her name was Hawa, sorry, is Hawa, didn't want her eldest daughter mutilated and stalled as long as she could. Her mother-in-law had been badgering her about it for years. In Hawa's tribe, a wife lives with or near her husband's family. But she was fortunate, her husband was indulgent and respected her wishes for a time. The daughter, Nimo, was somewhat sickly. Hawa said she was waiting for her health to improve. It was really the coming of age of the younger sister, Miriam, that caused the problem. The whole family wanted the sisters done at the same time."

"You see! You said, 'done.' We all avoid the ugliness of the word. It's understandable. It's human. We use language to muffle the harshness of the world." Robert waved his cigarette as he spoke, as though conducting a silent symphony. Henry continued, ignoring the interruption.

"They beat her. First the husband, then the mother-in-law. Really beat her. Sometimes so badly she couldn't walk for a week. The husband even locked her up in a small hut for several days during the summer heat. Finally this quite vicious paternal aunt had a go. It was never clear to me what her involvement was other than the love of inflicting pain."

"I suppose from the point of view of the husband and mother-in-law, Hawa was acting in a quite aberrant manner," Robert mused, watching the thin line of cigarette smoke drift up into the night.

"Precisely. In their eyes, she had gone crazy. The mutilation rate in the tribe was very high, over ninety-five percent. You can bet that extra five percent were wealthy urbanites who had a lot of Western contact. Daughters of businessmen and ambassadors, that sort of thing. It is correct that in their eyes, she had cracked up. She was acting against her own daughters' interests. Without 'circumcision,' the daughters were not marriageable. For young women, the goal in life is to marry and have a family. Of course, they also bring in a dowry for their father."

"So Hawa is a crazy person who is upsetting the norms and structures of the society, threatening the social stability of the tribe and probably embarrassing the hell out of the husband's family?"

"True. That is undeniable. At that point, she had become a social misfit. I suppose one of the most compelling aspects of the case is the claustrophobia." He paused, searching for the right words.

"Claustrophobia? You mean when she's imprisoned in the hut?"

"No, in a wider sense. She had nowhere to go, she was a prisoner of the village. Here she is being beaten, legs so bruised she can barely walk, locked away in this little tin hut in ninety-degree heat and there's no alternative, nothing she can do to save her children. Quite horrible, really. But she wouldn't give in. That's the amazing thing. The whole village against her, a creature of shame. Possibly her own daughters, certainly the older one, also ashamed of her. And she wouldn't give in! It's astonishing. She had her truth. She knew it was wrong to mutilate and wouldn't surrender. A mother's courage, I suppose."

"Surely she could go back to her own family! I take it they lived in a different village?"

"Yes, they did and no, she couldn't. She tried. They sent her back. 'Be a better wife. Listen to your husband. Why are you shaming us?'" He shrugged. "Who knows what they said? They didn't want her back. After all, these were the same people who had mutilated her. Her refusal was an implicit criticism of them."

Bobbi stood abruptly as though to leave, then turned to face Henry. "Are you saying she had nowhere to turn, nowhere at all? It's hard to imagine such estrangement, such suffering. I can't imagine hearing such cases on a daily basis."

"Well, remember that I don't actually hear the live testimony. I only hear the appeals of the Refugee Board decisions. It all comes to me on paper. I do read the transcript of the hearings but I don't speak directly to the claimants. I do sometimes wonder how the Board members manage to hear these cases day in, day out, to see the anguish of these people. I suppose it's no different from working in the emergency room of a hospital or a mental institution or anywhere else where you deal with human suffering on a daily basis. They either develop calluses or burn out."

"Well, it certainly seems too much to me." To relieve her anxiety, Bobbi had begun to clear glasses from the table. She now held up the cognac. "Would anyone like something stronger?"

Beth nodded, holding out the glass. Henry did not acknowledge her offer. "I do not deny that the transcripts are unsettling. However, I deal principally with the law, whether the decision was made fairly, in accordance with natural justice."

Robert interrupted. "You haven't let him finish his story. What happened to this woman? Clearly she escaped. How did she do it and did she save her daughters?"

"Again a yes-and-no answer. Well, possibly a yes-yes. That is still to be decided." He paused to reach for the wine decanter, pouring for himself and Robert.

"The husband's family decided to mutilate the girls without her. It was only the husband's indulgence that had delayed the matter for so long. And then Hawa did something extraordinary. She fled with the daughters. Which may seem the obvious thing to do but really required an amazing act of imagination. I say this now, but I only know it from the transcript of the hearing. This was a woman who had never been more than ten kilometres from her village. Her life, her world, was the village. She had no formal education. She'd been raised to do one thing, bear children and raise a family. There was a lengthy civil war smouldering in her country although her only sense of it was the occasional appearance of soldiers with guns. Twice in the previous years, all of the village had fled into the hills. She had no understanding of the politics or the parties involved in the war. She knew about trucks and radios. She had never seen an office building, a TV, or electric appliances and she set off across the desert with her two daughters, leaving her three sons whom she loved as dearly as the daughters, fully expecting to be caught and killed.

"There was an unusual amount of evidence on this point, her lawyer did a good job. I could almost see this woman setting off barefoot across quite arid terrain, very dry, very mountainous, they'd had two severe droughts in the past ten years, so it's not as though her tribe and family hadn't been suffering other problems. God knows how far she thought she'd get. She'd taken as much food and water as she could carry but how far would the children be able to walk? They were too big to carry, although she ended up with the youngest on her back near the end. I haven't seen her, of course, but I have the impression she's quite a frail woman."

"Lord, even when Meaghan was two I had trouble carrying her. The thought of carrying a seven-year-old across a desert, I can't imagine. So how long did it take her and where did she end up?" Beth was leaning forward as she spoke, now fully absorbed in the story.

Bobbi appeared distracted. "I'm sorry, does anyone want coffee, anything else?"

"Let him continue, dear. He has us in the palm of his hand." Robert was clearly captivated.

"I don't know how long she walked. One of the things you learn early is that these people have no sense of time. You simply can't pin them down and you can waste a lot of hearing time trying to do so. Certainly it was a matter of many days and possibly two or three weeks. She stumbled across a village of nomadic camel herders who gave her food and water. She was fortunate that it was a neighbouring but friendly tribe, they still have slavery in those regions. It was quite an odyssey. She and her eldest daughter were nearly raped by a band of roving militia, her daughter was badly cut, they were saved by some commander, or at least that's what she said. Half the time women don't admit to rape even if it does further their claim. The stigma is enormous. In any case, they eventually got a ride in a truck and ended up in a squatters' camp on the edge of the capital city of a neighbouring country."

"We really have no idea do we? I can't imagine what that would be like, two children, no resources. How did she survive? Were there social service agencies to assist her?" Bobbi was moving around the table as she spoke, absent-mindedly rearranging the coffee service as though wanting to put her house in order.

"Social service agencies? Certainly not the way we know them. Sometimes the International Red Cross or other NGO's provide some minimal support. But there were distant relatives, members of her tribe from other villages, a small expatriate community sheltering from the civil war. Of course, they were all dirt poor in a country plagued with its own unemployment and poverty. But their resilience is extraordinary. She was allowed to live in the home of a family. One room, dirt floor, twelve people. She had to scrounge for her own food. The family didn't have enough to share. Somehow she managed to sell vegetables in the marketplace. Who's buying these vegetables? Other poor people. How is that enough to live on?"

"And how did she get from the slums of wherever to Canada? Don't tell me she saved money peddling vegetables." Robert had reverted to his habitual scepticism.

"She got here the way most African claimants do, someone gave her money. After a year or so a second or third cousin working in Yemen heard about her plight. They had played together as children, apparently. He made all the arrangements through a smuggler – airline tickets, false passport, and US visa, the whole nine yards. From the slums of nowhere, she suddenly finds herself flying into Toronto, not speaking a word of English. Amazing."

"Henry, I'm curious about one thing. How did you get involved in the case? Surely the refugee tribunal, whatever it's called, didn't refuse the claim?"

"Ah Beth, as usual, you're looking at the wider picture. And once again there is a yes-and-no answer. It seems to happen a lot in the refugee business." He was enough of a showman to pause and keep his attentive audience waiting.

"The Board accepted the two daughters as refugees. Legally it wasn't a difficult case. Genital mutilation is now recognized as persecution. That was a legal issue a few years ago, some Board members viewed it as a customary law of general application and therefore not discriminatory, but that battle has been won. In fact, Canada leads the world on the issue. As well, the lawyer did her job, she provided medical reports stating that neither girl had been cut and Hawa was found to be credible in her opposition to the mutilation."

"So what was the problem? Surely they didn't reject Hawa?" Beth was sitting very erect, facing her husband.

"I'm afraid they did, on the dubious logic that she had already been mutilated and therefore had nothing to fear. As Robert has said, the refugee definition is future oriented."

"Henry, that's ridiculous! She's their mother! Who are these people? What kind of logic is that? Surely they wouldn't send her back?"

"Well, theoretically they could, but the Immigration department does a humanitarian review before it deports anyone and I am sure that in a case like this, they would never remove the mother."

"And what about your role in all this? Surely you don't agree with these Board people? Can't you overrule them?"

Henry laughed for the first time that evening. "I haven't even decided yet and my private court of appeal is overruling me!" He reached across the table to take his wife's hand. "Are you interested in hearing the issues before you pass judgment, Madame Justice?"

"Don't patronize me and don't give me any of your judicial mumbo-jumbo. There is no law in this land to justify separating that mother from her children and I don't understand why there is any hesitation. I am sorry, Henry, it's simply unacceptable."

Robert was clearly enjoying the interplay between wife and husband. "Well, Henry? Your Honour? You've heard the intervener's forceful submissions. What's your response?"

Henry had withdrawn his hand from the table and was now leaning back in his chair looking defensive. "The two of you should know it's seldom that simple in matters of law."

"The three of us. I also am a simplistic thinker who can't understand how anyone could talk of separating Hawa and her children." Bobbi had stopped rearranging the table to join the discussion.

"Bobbi, could I please have a small glass of that excellent cognac? I can see I'm not going to escape without some explanation and I admit to requiring fortification." The judge stood up and walked the few feet to the parapet, unconsciously seeking height and distance from his inquisitors.

"Let me first say that I shouldn't even be talking about the case since it hasn't been decided. It was indiscreet and, come to think of it, unethical. I admit to being bothered by the horrible facts of the case and the plight of this woman. And that's an excuse, not a reason."

"Henry, don't be a sop. We talk about your cases all the time, decided or not. And these are your best friends in the entire world. And don't tell me you've never consulted Robert on a difficult case."

"Actually, he never has, Beth. That's one of the many objectionable traits of your husband. He does play by the rules, always has. He has occasionally spoken about a case after it was decided but never before." Robert was pouring himself a cognac as he spoke, carefully measuring out the amber liquid. "So I for one say that you needn't answer if you do not wish to." He raised his glass towards Henry. "Cheers."

Beth was not to be put off so easily. "Well, I would like to hear the profound legal analysis that leads to such a perverse result. Sorry, perhaps that's a bit harsh. Bizarre result, how is that? What legal logic leads to such a conclusion that this woman, even in theory, could be separated from her children?"

Her husband stepped forward a pace, as though accepting the challenge. "You already know of the first principle, that each refugee case is decided on its own merits, each claimant must establish their own fear of persecution. That's the law. I cannot change that."

The judge raised his hand as his wife was about to speak. "But that leads to a corollary principle, which states there is no such thing as indirect persecution. In other words, if I fear arrest and torture, that's persecution, but although you, as my wife, may suffer some anguish while I'm detained, that is not persecution." Again he raised his hand to stave off his wife's intervention.

"I know for some that may be a dubious proposition, but for the moment, let us accept it to complete the analysis. In Hawa's case, given that the children are granted asylum, she doesn't have to be concerned with their mutilation."

"But what about separation of mother and child, isn't that persecution? That's the worst thing that could happen to her!" This outburst came from Bobbi, who was now seated beside Beth.

"Unfortunately, that is not persecution, not because it might not be a painful experience but because it does not come about as a result of action by her home state. If anything, the action is by the Canadian government. But please. I am only stating one analysis, I am not saying I accept it, only that it is an issue to be dealt with."

Robert was drawn into the debate. "But surely, if an event is a foreseeable consequence of a state's action, wouldn't that also be seen as persecution? Surely if a torture victim later suffers psychological problems, that would be considered to be a consequence of the persecution."

"Well, I suppose, but this isn't tort law, Robert. We are not trying to measure the amount of damage to the victim. That has already been decided. But the liability to harm does not extend to other victims."

Beth joined in. "But you're ignoring another whole area. The husband and relatives beat Hawa. You even said if she were caught they might kill her. Isn't that persecution?"

"That's what I was thinking too. Why isn't that persecution? Hawa even said her own husband might kill her." Bobbi poured more cognac for the men.

"Well it is, and if she had to return to her village, her fear of persecution would be well founded. But the Board considered that and felt she would have an internal flight alternative within her country. Internal flight alternative, it's known as an IFA. In essence, they said she could go elsewhere in the country. She only feared harm in her village."

"But you said the country was impoverished and drought ridden and in the middle of a civil war. Where would she go?"

"There are several cities and towns where her tribal group is in the majority. The Board members concluded she would be safe there. That's their right and presumably they are knowledgeable about country conditions there. More so than I am, certainly."

"And let me guess, civil war and poverty aren't persecution. You've told me that before. So if she's indiscriminately killed as an accidental victim of the war or starves to death because there's a drought and no help for a stranger away from her village, that's not persecution, just bad luck. Do I have that right?"

"Beth, Henry doesn't get to make up the law, you know that after living around lawyers all these years. There are laws and legal principles and you work within the rules."

"Nonsense. I've lived around lawyers long enough to know that almost everything is a question of factual interpretation. That's the fascination and subtlety of law. It's so rarely black and white. You lawyers live in a world of greys and are constantly shifting and emphasizing certain facts to make things fit within the law. Besides, you have both said a dozen times that judges make their decisions and then find ways to make them fit within the law."

"She's right. Robert, how many times have I heard you say the law was a living thing?" Bobbi had sat down next to Beth again, across from her husband.

The debate was in danger of splitting along gender lines. Sensing this, the judge intervened, complaining that he had not been given the chance to complete his legal analysis. "I suppose I've become spoiled. I'm not used to interruptions. Normally I can be as slow and ponderous as I wish while counsel waits respectfully. Today I am in a more trying court." He chuckled at his own wit and took a sip of cognac.

"Beth, I was merely giving you the Board's analysis to show that there was some thinking behind it and that it was based on legal reasoning, not mean-mindedness. These things aren't always that easy."

His wife gave herself more cognac while he was speaking, pouring a generous portion into a waterglass. "Mumbo-jumbo. I like that word. Legal mumbo-jumbo. If it's so logical and rigid that it can't find the solution that decency and common sense demand, then what good is it?"

"Careful, Beth, you're entering onto battle-scarred ground here. All the brilliant legal thinkers have been arguing over that one for a long time. The traditional response is that some rigidity is the price of predictability in law and you need predictability, especially in a complex society like ours. People need to know the rules of the game to guide their actions. Otherwise there's chaos, everyone doing their own thing as we used to say many years ago. But rules are never perfect. There will be the occasional anomaly, leading to a particular injustice."

"Well, thank you for that Robert, but I'm not going down that road with you. Have you noticed that you and Henry never say what you think? That you hide your own opinions behind a stalking horse? You say 'the traditional response,' Henry talks of the 'Board's analysis.' Dammit, you're talking about separating a woman from her two children. A bloody brave woman. Why can't you at least say what you think?"

A wisp of hair had slipped from Beth's normally neat chignon. She impatiently brushed it off her cheek. Henry wondered if she was slightly tipsy, although she was not slurring her words. The two men glanced at one another, each silently inviting the other to respond first. The judge reached for his glass without taking a drink.

"Because it's not just a matter of personal opinion, Beth. We do operate within the law, at least if we're conscientious. We have to stay within the parameters set by the law. Factual interpretation only allows a certain latitude." Subtly, without noticing it, his voice had lowered, become slightly condescending. The women shared a private glance. He took a large swallow of cognac before continuing. "This case causes me great concern. That's why I raised it here tonight, although it's never been my practice to discuss incomplete decisions."

"Henry, I have always felt you were a tiger. Now I am watching a tiger pace within its cage. I didn't realize there was a cage." Beth took a long unapologetic drink, thinking how she normally took tiny multiple sips. There was a smear of lipstick on the glass which she didn't bother to wipe away.

Robert leaped to his friend's defence. "Unfair analogy, Beth. Good judges like Henry are pillars of society, in the literal sense. They support the social structure. It's rather like asking Atlas to dance a jig with the world on his shoulders. Frankly, anyone can run around and be a wild man. Without putting too large a shine on it, there is a certain amount of sacrifice in bearing the burden of a powerful office."

"Robert, no one is attacking Henry." Bobbi glanced at Beth. "Not really. But it is frustrating to see such a bad decision come from such apparently impeccable principles. If a scientist gets an incorrect conclusion, doesn't he," she paused to look at her husband, "or she, question the correctness of the principles? Surely you don't just accept the unacceptable conclusion?"

Robert loosened his tie and laughed. He was determined to be amused by any situation the world placed before him. By now all four had noticed that the women were sitting side by side facing the men across the table. Robert shifted his chair to face his friend. "Well, Henry. Is there a principle to be re-examined or altered? Is there a way out of this cul-de-sac with our scalps intact?"

"Well, that's what I was coming to before the Indians came over the hill. I think there is a solution and we don't yet need to circle the wagons." He looked at his wife and smiled. "Beth, please understand, I am limited by judicial review. This is not an appeal, I can't just overrule the Board decision unless the findings of fact are patently unreasonable or unless there is an error of law." He paused to sip his drink, recrossing his legs, feeling once more in control of the situation.

"Although I do not agree with the Board's finding that Hawa would be safe elsewhere in that godforsaken country, I can't say it is patently unreasonable." He paused to raise a finger in the air, as though testing the wind.

"However," the judge twirled his finger as a kind of salutation to an announcement. "However, the Board did not clearly state that it had applied the second wing of the test for a viable IFA, namely that, even if it is *safe,* is it also *reasonable* for the claimant to go to live in some other hellhole within the country? For this they must consider all of the claimant's personal circumstances and they did not do this. And that, ladies and gentlemen, is an error of law and a valid ground for quashing the decision, which I will do." He finished the announcement with a triumphant flourish.

"Ta-Da!" Robert spread his arms wide, playing the role of the magician's assistant who applauds his master's magic: See? The rabbit was in the hat all the time.

Henry smiled fondly at his wife. "You see, dear, it may be true that tigers are caged, but some of them know how to pick the lock."

His wife was not as appreciative as he had expected. "If you quash the decision, doesn't it go back to the Board for a rehearing? And couldn't a new set of members decide the same thing, this time putting in the part about the reasonability of living elsewhere? Wouldn't this woman have to run another lap around the track only to end up in the same place, with another refusal?"

"Well, it's a possibility, but it's unlikely. I can certainly put some language in my decision hinting at how unreasonable it would be to do that. I think they would get the point."

Beth looked carefully at her husband, who was obviously pleased with himself. Over his shoulder she saw a woman in a thin dress walking away over dry and barren ground, holding the hands of two young girls. The soles of her bare feet flashed out from beneath the hem of the dusty skirt with each retreating stride.

"It seems to me you could tell these Board members, or your brethren or someone, that watching your children being mutilated and being separated from your children are forms of persecution, pure and simple. Sorry, Henry, there's nothing indirect about it."

His wife stood up to help Bobbi clear away the glasses and empty decanters. The candle flames guttered in the rising night wind, drowning in their own wax. The judge was thinking that his wife had more of a drinking problem than he had realized and perhaps he should speak to someone about it. Robert looked off into the darkness of the garden, distracted by a night sound. Beth stepped easily though the patio doors balancing china and glasses, her back straight, hips swaying slightly, thinking perhaps that for her daughters, she could walk through deserts, her bare feet flapping in the dust.

10

CRAP TRAP

"CREDIBILITY IS NOT EIGHTY PERCENT of a claim. It is not ninety percent. It is one hundred percent. I hope that is clear. Credibility is everything. Does anyone dispute that?"

He turned his head slowly to canvas the reaction of the room with the authority of a searchlight swinging through the night sky, confident of our silence. He was not disappointed. We were in the last week of a three-week training course for RCO's. That's me, or about to be anyway, a Refugee Claim Officer for the Immigration and Refugee Board and thankful to be so. Forty-two thousand a year. Need I say more? Not bad for being three weeks out of university. The speaker was Ronald J. Brak, a large man with a heavy neck and a ton of attitude. The man makes a white shirt and tie look like a uniform. I wish I'd said that but I must confess it was Sonia's line.

"For two weeks you've been listening to theory about the refugee definition, the hearing process, the preparation of cases, how to analyse a claim. I don't want to tell you to throw all that out the window," Brak paused melodramatically to look around the room as if to assure himself that no senior Board officials were present. "But you may want to put a hold on the theory for a while. Let's just say it's time to get introduced to a little hearing-room reality."

Sonia gave me a sideways glance with one arched eyebrow which I correctly read as serious scepticism. Sonia was very hip and very quick. We barely qualified as acquaintances in school, we both went to UBC, but we've become pretty close as the only two trainees from the West. West coast refugees. We were so surprised to see one another on the first training day that we sort of fell into one another's arms. Sonia's maybe a little skinny, but nice hair and nice moves and it was all right with me if she wanted to get physical. I was more than pleased to see a familiar face, maybe not the prettiest on the block but lively, real lively, with a great smile. The kind of face you don't notice right away and later on you wonder why you didn't.

She says she got hired because she speaks about six languages. Her parents still speak Polish and Hungarian at home. They're Jewish and her parents or grandparents did the whole Holocaust thing and then took about ten years to get away from the communists after the war. They spent time in Santo Domingo before coming to Canada. Spanish was her first language, Yiddish her second, and English her fifth, which is a serious mind bender because she speaks it better than me. I, on the other hand, got hired speaking one language badly. But the qualifying exam had a lot of questions about countries, capitals, and ethnic groups. Piece of cake for a history and geography major with a decent memory. I never thought that knowing about places like Kinshasa and Bujumbura was actually going to get me a job, but here I am.

Maybe I should tell you a Refugee Claim Officer is the guy who prepares the case for the Board and is supposed to ask the questions in response to the claimant's lawyer during the hearing. We're also supposed to advise the Board members on the law but I'm not sure how that works since a lot of the members are old and have been here a long time. Some of them are even lawyers, so the legal advice thing is a little weird but hey! I'm here. It's forty-two thousand a year and I can live with it. We're also supposed to be neutral but we already know that's bullshit. Like the lawyer fights like hell for his client while we're supposed to be this even-handed nicey-nicey advisor to the members. Get real. Brak says the main thing we have to do is "pierce the veil of collusion and confusion which hides the truth of the refugee's story." Whatever that means. Actually, I have a pretty good idea. It means nail them to the wall.

Sonia seems to know a lot more about the Board than I do. She says that Brak is a senior RCO who has this heavy-duty rep and I have to say he looks the part. He has these big bulbous eyes that look twice as big behind these thick glasses. Sonia says that whenever he's really clobbered some witness, he always takes off the glasses to polish them with his tie before delivering the *coup de grâce*. He's famous as a first-class jerk. The lawyers hate him. Personally I've decided to reserve judgment. I mean the guy has been hearing refugee cases for umpteen years, so I think he deserves a little respect. And they put him in charge of the training on interrogation, which has to say something for him, despite the haircut. He could get rid of the buzz cut any time.

"You are going to hear a lot of crap about cross-cultural communication. And that's just what it is, crap. Take it in one ear et cetera. The average claimant has a lawyer, has the money to fly to Canada, and has had more than a year to think up a good story, often with the help of umpteen brothers, sisters, cousins and they all say they're cousins. Even if the story is true, and some of them are, I don't want you thinking they're all liars, some of them are genuine refugees, but even the genuine ones have had a long time to think about it, so this horse manure you will hear about the confused and misunderstood claimant is just that."

Knowing he had his audience, he put one foot up on the chair and leaned forward as though to disclose an intimacy. "Let me put it this way, they've had twelve to twenty months to rehearse their story while you are averaging eight cases a week from any one of twenty to thirty countries with barely enough time to review the file and remember the name of the current president of some little republic. Now, I ask you, who has the advantage? I wouldn't feel too sorry for the claimant."

"I'm feeling sorry for Brak's wife."

Sonia said it out of the corner of her mouth for my ears only, but Brak had heard something. His head swung around with the smoothness of a howitzer. The searchlight thing again; except this time it came to rest on me. "Is there a question over here?"

I admit I stammered. Not because I was really intimidated but because I was trying to think of something to say without passing the buck to Sonia. "Sorry. Didn't mean to interrupt. I was just saying that made sense to me."

Brak's expression resolved into something resembling mollification. Clearly he liked people who agreed with him. "Well, I appreciate the vote of confidence, but next time speak up so we all can hear. This class is just like Revenue Canada, all contributions are gratefully received."

That remark earned a half-hearted titter it didn't deserve. Sonia turned to give me a wide-eyed look of innocence, which I returned in kind. Hey, the deception game is not a problem. I'm a university graduate. Geography is not the most intellectually demanding subject but I still pulled down a B plus average with a thirty-hour-a-week job and virtually no studying just by barfing back the prof's notes. A lot of memorization, a little deference. Whatever works. Hell, I have a degree, a job, and fewer debts than any of my friends. Except for Sonia who's debt free, but she lived at home. Now she's busting to get her own place in Vancouver, which is cool.

Brak was passing out a sample case history for a practice round of questioning. We were to break into groups of four and question one another. I went with Sonia and two guys from Montreal. It was funny how the outsiders tended to clump together. Most of the class is from Toronto. One of the Montreal guys could barely speak English. Sylvain. He was a nice guy who was trying hard but I could only understand half of what he said. It seemed crazy that he was doing the course in Toronto. He said he missed the French course in Montreal because his "wife was having the baby." Neat guy. The other one, though, Jean-Pierre, took about trois secondes to mix it up with Sonia. She had just corrected something Sylvain said, but she did it in a really nice way. Like she's a language student and it's no big deal, and this guy gets uptight and says something in French, then says she shouldn't be correcting anyone if she's not bilingual herself. Sonia came right back at him saying she's not bilingual, she's quintilingual, but none of the five happen to be French. Then she says something in Spanish, which does not sound like a compliment to his mother. I got to play peacemaker by pointing out that Brak was about to descend and we hadn't even started.

The practice story was pretty skimpy, just the outline. Brak said we could make up the rest and the four women in the class could switch from being a soldier in the army to a nurse in a hospital. It was about a Jewish guy from Moldova who had a miserable childhood, always getting beaten up by the other kids and made to sit in the back of the class, getting beaten up again during his military service and finally leaving Moldova after receiving threats from Moldovan nationalists. The only real details are about this one incident where he's beaten up by Moldovan nationalists on the stairs inside his own apartment building. That part sounds real because the guy's glasses are broken and he can't see but he doesn't want to call his parents because he's afraid the nationalists will beat up his father too who has a bad heart. Brak says you can't go by how a story sounds in the PIF. That's Personal Information Form, PIF, rhymes with whiff.

"Remember these stories can come from anywhere. It may sound real because it actually happened but to someone else. Smugglers will take stories from successful claims and recycle them. Listen up, people: you cannot assume anything is true. Credibility is one hundred percent of the game."

He also said it was based on a real story and a pretty typical scenario. A lot of claimants coming from the breakaway republics of the former Soviet Union claimed to be Jews and a few of them were. "Let's face it, economically the place is falling apart. Everyone wants to get out." He said they used to come with original birth certificates that showed that the parents were Jewish, but a lot of them proved to be phonies. The RCMP forensic lab found the parents' nationality had been "chemically altered." We all liked that story. Brak showed us a sample lab report, "nationality at line 17 chemically altered and over-written." After the Board started sending all Soviet birth certificates to the forensic lab, most of the so-called Jewish claimants showed up with photocopies, which couldn't be checked, or no birth certificates at all, saying they'd been lost in the mail. We already knew before Brak's explanation that you couldn't deny a claim solely because of their inability to produce an original document.

"So that's your job. You have to break down their story, expose the contradictions, inconsistencies, and implausibilities. Some Jews are still persecuted in those places so you have two issues. You have to establish whether or not the claimant is Jewish, and if so, did they suffer the persecution described in their PIF?"

Everybody did their practice round and most of us were pretty terrible. You're supposed to ask open questions first to get the witness going, questions like, "What kinds of problems did you have at school?" or "Tell me what happened at school." And then, once you get on a roll and want to home in on a subject, you ask closed questions that don't allow the witness much room: "What was the name of the boy who hit you? Where was he standing when he hit you?"

It sounds easy but it isn't. Believe me. Poor Sylvain really had a hard time because of the language thing. Sonia was pretty gentle, giving him straight answers, no curve balls. But what are you going to do with "Tell me da name of da tree guy who hit you." It was pretty weak stuff.

I did my practice round with Jean-Pierre, Sonia refused to, and it was sort of like a wrestling match. I would try to pin him down with questions and he would slip away, which he did fairly easily. He had the advantage because he could make up the story as he went along. Brak says in real life you can nail them with the documentary evidence but we didn't have country documents for the scenario. I did catch him, though, by using the double-whammy geography bender. It was sort of neat. I did a paper on the Soviet breakup in second year so I knew some place names and locations. So after he ducked a dozen questions about Jewish religion about which I knew zero, I started him off with a closed question.

"You did your military service in the Ukraine, before perestroika and independence, is that right?"

"Yes, I did."

"Where in the Ukraine?" Puffball question to set him up.

"Uh. It was only a small military base in the country." Shifty, but I'm not letting him off the hook.

"What city was it near?" A closed question to keep him in the corner.

"Kiev. It was not too far from Kiev." The capital. I bet it's the only city he knows and now I shift ground to keep him guessing.

"And it says in the PIF that you were beaten so badly by other soldiers that you were in hospital for a week. Is that correct?"

"Yes, for approximately a week. It's been a long time." Smartass thinks I'm looking for details about the beating or his medical treatment. He's setting up his failing memory defence so I can't pin him on the details, but this is all diversion. I'm feinting high before going low.

"After the beating, when did you next return home to see your family in Kishinev?" Second feint. He's still thinking about the beating.

"Uh. Let me think. I believe it was Christmas time. Yes, definitely not before Christmas." Double feint, J-P, I got you thinking about time.

"How far is it from Kiev to Kishinev?" Boom! Gotcha!

"Pardon?" Ha! Lost his balance. He unconsciously uses the French pronunciation – Mr Bilingual.

"I asked you the distance from Kiev to Kishinev. It's a simple question. You've made the trip. You just told us that. So what is the distance?"

Two Tongue was going down. He was struggling for time, trying to grab for the ropes. "Well, it's been a long time. I've made many trips since then. Are you asking me how long the trip would take?"

Nice try but I'm not falling for it. Time is too elastic. He can say the trains were slow, he had to go by truck. It gives him lots of outs. "No, distance, in kilometres, which should be easier for you. How many kilometres is it from Kiev to Kishinev? Or if you prefer, Chisinau." Now I was showing off, I admit it. Not many people would know that Chisinau was the Romanian-Moldovan word for the capital city. The Russian-speaking Soviets said Kishinev. This was really just to keep him off balance and maybe intimidate him.

J-P knew he didn't have a choice. He would have to come up with a number. He might get lucky or I might be bluffing. Maybe I didn't know the distance.

"It's quite a way. As I recall it's about a thousand kilometres, maybe a bit more or less. I never really paid too much attention to distances." I didn't move, letting him dangle. "Maybe it was closer to twelve hundred. I think so."

"For a soldier with military training and a resident of Kishinev, it seems strange that you wouldn't know the distance was less than six hundred kilometres." I was enjoying this. Most people don't realize how squeezed in all those tiny Eastern European states really are. It's the central and eastern portions of Russia that are truly immense.

Jean-Pierre simply shrugged his shoulders. West Coast Wonder destroys Mr Bilingual. Yes! My smugness was somewhat deflated by the look on Sonia's face. She has very expressive brown eyes, which were now asking me a question. I thought she'd be cheering. She was the one who'd been mixing it up with old Two Tongue.

"Not bad! A crude but effective use of the trap. That's exactly what we need to do to test the credibility of the claimant." Brak was enthusiastic.

"People, pay attention. This is what you want to do. Our friend here, John? James, okay. James has given us an example of what I call the "trap." Actually, I call it the "crap trap" but that's just between us. You see, people, if you just let the witness run on and on, you get nowhere. You all had that experience this morning. The idea is that you need some factual fence or barrier of firm evidence so you can work the claimant up against it. In this case, the hard fact is the distance from Kiev to Kishinev. Now you need to ask a series of questions to manoeuver the witness into the trap. So James first confirms that Jean-Pierre here has supposedly made the trip to Kishinev. That's good. It prevents weaselling out. That's important. Don't spring the trap until you're sure there are no holes in the fence. Only thing is, James, you could be a lot more aggressive. I know the statute says *question* the witness, that the RCO is *neutral*, but those are lawyer's words. People, you *cross-examine* the witness. You probe, you dig, you find the holes in the story and you expose them. It's not easy. That's why a good RCO is worth about four Board members who are paid twice as much to do half as much."

Brak said he would do a cross-examination demo after lunch and I would be the witness since I obviously knew something about Moldova. Over lunch, I quickly reviewed my internal Moldova file: population, city names, ethnic groupings, that sort of thing. I wanted to be ready for Brak, maybe give him a surprise or two. Generally I recalled it was a small piece of Romania that had been gobbled up by the Soviet empire after the Second World War and was now a tiny moraine of a country left in the wake of the retreating Soviet ice age. The Moldovan nationalists wanted to rejoin Romania but one-third of the population were Russian speakers, detritus from the massive Stalinist relocations, who preferred independence or linkage to the new Russia. The country splintered further in 1992 during a brief civil war between the Russophiles and extremist Romanians, although most Moldovans wanted their own independent country.

Of course no one liked the Jews. One of the worst pogroms in European history had occurred in Kishinev, although I couldn't remember when. Dates didn't matter too much. I planned to play dumb to give Brak as few targets as possible. It was a little disappointing that Sonia had chosen to sit at another table with Sylvain and two other women. I tried to catch her eye several times but she seemed quite absorbed in her own group.

"Mr Shiner, what do you know about Judaism?"

That was his opening. I hadn't even settled into my chair and didn't respond at first. I forgot Shiner was the claimant's name. People started to giggle.

"Me? Oh, you mean me? We're starting now?" Brak didn't change expression.

"Mr Shiner, you state in your personal information form that you are a Jew. Please tell us what you know about Judaism." Ah yes, we are underway and Brak tries to body-slam me with an open question. Well, I'm ready.

"I am sorry I do not know about the Judaism. I am not growing in house with religion." It's not the best accent in the world, probably more Polish than Russian, but I can't help smiling at the audience. The look on Sonia's face is a warning. About what, I am not sure.

"Do you know anything at all about the Jewish religion?"

Better to play safe. "No. Not so much. My parents are not religion people."

"Did you know your grandparents, either paternal or maternal?" Now he's shifting ground; was the religion thing a feint?

"Uh, yes. I know grandparents from my mother. Other grandparents die in war." Pretty safe, a lot of Jews died. Maybe I should have killed them all off but that would seem suspicious, something he might attack.

"It says in your PIF that your mother was born in Kishinev, the same as you. I take it she lived there for most of her life?"

"I am sorry, please, what is this PIF?" Gotcha. Brak was the one who said we should use simple language to avoid unnecessary confusion. No slang. No acronyms. Brak was not pleased. He gave me a dirty look and I tried not to glance at Sonia.

"Your PIF is your personal information form, Mr Shiner. Is it correct that your mother was born and raised in Kishinev, the same as you?"

"Yes." I don't know where he's going, play safe, stay with the PIF.

"So you must have known your grandparents when you were growing up, you and your brothers and sisters, I see you have two of each."

"Yes." This is going too fast. He's setting something up but I can't tell what.

"What is the Yiddish word for grandmother?"

"I beg your pardon?" Where did that come from? Stall, stall for time.

"Mr Shiner, what is the Yiddish word for grandmother?"

"Grandmother? I don't know. My parents never spoke Yiddish." I haven't the faintest idea what languages Moldovan Jews spoke. Maybe they were deaf and dumb. Think of something.

"Mr Shiner, my specialized knowledge and the documentary evidence will show that Eastern European Jews virtually all spoke Yiddish during the first half of this century. As well, many of them were religious prior to the Communist takeover after the Second World War. Now you tell us that you don't know anything about the Jewish religion and you don't even know what you called your grandmother. What did she call you? Do you even know that?"

He barely paused for breath. I was speechless. "No, I can see you don't. Mr Shiner, or whatever you real name is, it's obvious to all that you are not Jewish. Why not admit it?"

He finished with a full sweeping look around the room as he was speaking, like a bullfighter giving that final swing of the cape after he has completely confused the bull, who is left standing, legs splayed, head down, tongue out, snot coming out of his nostrils, which is pretty well how I was feeling at the moment.

But it wasn't fair. Of course I didn't speak Yiddish. It was a cheap shot. Anyone could do the same number if they had special knowledge. Brak was a bully more interested in showing off than teaching us something. Maybe I had done the same thing to Jean-Pierre, but it was different. And I sure didn't do a twirl for the audience with my bulgy eyes. On the other hand, it was impressive. West Coast Wonder Boy just got body-slammed and pinned in one minute flat by Brak the Beast. He certainly could snap the old crap trap.

Brak wasn't resting on his laurels. "That really didn't give us much to look at, did it, although you can see the basis of the technique. Choose your factual barrier, in this case the ability to speak Yiddish and move your victim, sorry, I mean the witness, towards it." This time no one responded to the heavy-handed humour despite his accompanying chuckle.

"But remember, people, this technique does not harm the genuine refugee. Remember it is the *crap* trap. If the claimant is truly Jewish, they will know some Yiddish, sometimes not a lot, but something, and so you move on. And in case you are feeling sorry for poor old Mr Shiner here, ask yourself what kind of person would try and pass himself off as a Jew? My guess is he's probably an anti-Semite and good riddance. So save your sympathy for those who need it. Now, since our claimant didn't last too long, let's have another go. Who's next?"

There were no takers. Everyone had seen the speed of the carnage and no one was looking to be victim number two.

"Oh, come now, it's relatively painless. Remember, it's all in fun." No one believed that. Brak was obviously amused to see that the entire class was cowed by his first performance. He looked over the group, waiting, enjoying his power. Then a thin arm was raised from the second row. Sonia.

There was pleasure in Brak's eyes. I was sitting close and could see it. Victim was the correct word. This guy was Jabba the Hut and suddenly Sonia was looking like Princess Leia. I got up to offer her my chair, which she accepted, avoiding my inquiring gaze except for one swift meaningful glance, which suggested that Sonia had some reason for volunteering. I couldn't imagine what it was other than masochism.

Brak had moved his chair a little closer to hers, setting his wide body directly opposite Sonia, who was looking more vulnerable all the time. He was looking more and more like Jabba the Hut. I was just waiting to see a lizard tongue slither out of his mouth.

"Bubbi and Zeyda."

"Uh? Excuse me?" It was Sonia who had spoken first, looking directly at Brak. She had a nice clean way of speaking, good articulation. I suppose that was part of her talent for languages.

"Bubbi and Zeyda. It's Yiddish for Grandma and Grandpa. I thought I would save you some time." She smiled sweetly. Brak looked confused. Princess Leia had just tweaked Jabba's nose while he was pondering what to do with her.

Brak shifted his weight to the other haunch. "Well, I guess we are underway then. So I take it then that you speak Yiddish, Miss Shiner?"

"Yes. My parents spoke it at home." She paused. "Never in the street of course. It was too dangerous." She actually looked frightened when she said it.

"Why was it dangerous?" Brak's response was automatic. Sonia had taken the initiative, he was following her.

"We were Jews, of course." She said it matter of factly, as though it explained everything. I could see that it also invited Brak further down the path that Sonia had already chosen.

"But why would being a Jew be dangerous? Lots of Jews live in Moldova. They aren't all afraid for their lives, surely." This was probably an attempt to regain control of the testimony.

"No, not everyone, not all the time. But people get attacked. It happens. You never know. Speaking Yiddish in public is an invitation to strangers, an unnecessary risk." Brak was about to follow with another question, he was drawing air to speak as Sonia continued. "And there are not so many Jews in Moldova. At one time there were many, but not now. Many left as soon as they were allowed to."

Brak hesitated. I could see she was leading him on, leaving a trail of bread crumbs. Surely he could see it. He had at least two directions to go in. Surprisingly, Brak picked up the new spoor.

"The documentary evidence shows that Jews were allowed to leave after independence in 1991, that the Moldovan government has been very cooperative with the emigration to Israel. If you were afraid, why didn't you leave at that time?"

It looked to me like Sonia had Brak off balance. He wasn't following his own advice to carefully work the claimant towards the barrier, closing all the loopholes. He was simply trying to ram her up against the fence without preparation.

"Bubbi." She appeared to be on the edge of tears. Brak didn't give her time to continue.

"I don't understand your answer. You were asked why you didn't go to Israel when you had the opportunity if you were so afraid." Brak's tone of voice had strengthened. He had decided to push harder, to shove her off balance.

"Because of my Bubbi. She refused to go without Zeyda who said he was too old. She said she would die where she was born. She could now go to synagogue and that was enough. My parents wouldn't leave without Bubbi and Zeyda and I couldn't leave without them. They were all I had."

Brak forged ahead. He still hadn't figured out that Sonia was leading him onto her home turf. "But you did leave, in 1998. So you did abandon them anyway. Why not do it earlier in 1992 or 1993? What's the difference?"

Sonia barely paused. Her eyes had already widened in surprise at the question. "Why because of the beating by the men at my apartment! It was horrible. It's all written in my information form if you read it. I was in the hospital for more than a week. My mother said I had to leave. I did not want to go without her but I was always afraid and did not want to go out of our apartment. Sometimes I would shake for hours and she said I must leave."

She looked as though she was going to start shaking right there on the spot. She wouldn't look at Brak or anyone else and her thin shoulders were suddenly looking thinner. I had to remind myself it was an act and she was doing a pretty good job on old Brak the Beast. The part about reading the PIF was clever, implying that he hadn't read it because anyone who had wouldn't ask such a stupid question about why she left. Suddenly Brak was looking clumsy instead of powerful. She was using judo instead of wrestling, using his power against him.

Brak realized he had to shift the line of attack. "You said your grandmother went to synagogue after independence and that's because the Jewish religion was permitted to be practised openly, isn't that correct?"

"Yes." Now Sonia was playing the waiting game, anticipating the next move.

"How far was the synagogue from your house?" Brak was setting something up, moving towards some kind of reality fence, but I couldn't see what.

"It was about half an hour away." Clever answer. She'd remembered my little tête-à-tête with Jean-Pierre. Time is more flexible than distance. Brak appeared unruffled.

"I assume that is by bus. Do you know how far that is in distance?"

"About four or five kilometres. The buses are slow."

"And you've been to the synagogue yourself?"

"Yes, of course."

"Did you go with your grandmother?"

"Sometimes, not every time. Sometimes my mother went with her."

For me it was still a wrestling match, they were circling each other, feinting, trying to upset one another's rhythm. Brak was looking for an opening and Sonia wasn't giving it to him.

"So I take it that either you or your mother, or maybe both, accompanied your grandmother to the synagogue. Is that right?"

"Yes." I was wondering where the grandfather and father were in all this but neither of them seemed interested in that angle.

"And it seems your grandmother was quite a religious woman, going to synagogue as soon as it became legal again. So it's reasonable to assume that she would have gone to synagogue every Saturday, is that correct?"

"Yes, except when she was sick, she went to *shul* regularly." Now Sonia was showing off a little, throwing in a little fancy footwork with that "shul" thing just to show she wasn't intimidated. This was like watching Muhammad Ali fighting some big mean flatfooted bruiser.

"Now everyone in town knows what the synagogue looks like, don't they? Everyone knows it's a Jewish synagogue." Brak was still moving forward, pushing her into the corner.

"Yes."

"And Saturday's a pretty busy day in Kishinev, isn't it? Market day, shopping day, everybody out in the street if they're not work-

ing, probably a lot of farmers and townspeople coming in from outside, that sort of thing?"

"Yes, I suppose. I didn't think about it much. For many people
it is not a work day. Maybe some stay at home." She wasn't going
to give him any extra leverage for his attack, whatever it was.

"Well, Miss Shiner, here is what I don't understand. On the one
hand you don't speak your mother tongue, Yiddish, on the street
because you don't want to be identified as a Jew by strangers. And
yet once a week, you or your mother traipse off to the synagogue
with your grandmother, by bus, on a busy day where all the world
will know that you are a Jew. Frankly, it doesn't make a lot of sense
and it's a little hard to believe."

Sonia straightened in her chair, levelling her gaze right at Brak.
"Mr Brak, are you suggesting that I am not Jewish?"

"No, not at all. I think it is fairly evident that you are Jewish, although that is for the Board members to decide." He turned to look
at us as though we were the Board members who were still reserv-
ing judgment. "What I *am* suggesting, however, is that you were not
particularly afraid. That you and your mother, who lived in the
same apartment, openly and regularly went to synagogue on a
public bus, announcing to all the world that you are Jews, and that
action is not exactly the act of someone with a genuine fear of persecution. *That* is what I am suggesting. Or are you going to tell me
that in a country like Moldova, people don't pay attention to who
goes to the synagogue and who has a Semitic appearance?"

Sonia's head was bowed. She didn't move, she did not answer.
When she finally looked up, she was pale. "It is true. Getting off the
bus would tell anyone we were Jewish and that is something everyone would notice. I was never comfortable going on the bus but for
my grandmother going to shul was everything. For her, it was freedom. And I could not ask my mother to take the risk all the time.
Besides she was often sick, she has an illness of the lung and I could
not refuse my grandmother. So I went despite my fear."

Again she paused, lowering her gaze then looking up just as Brak
was about to speak. "But I never went after the beating. Never.
Bubbi understood. When my mother was too weak to go, especially in winter, my grandmother pretended to be ill as well. She knew
I could not go."

Brak had missed a loophole, he hadn't closed off one escape route before springing his trap. He hadn't confirmed that the claimant had continued to go to synagogue until her departure. Brak was still in mid-thought, about to speak. I wondered if he was going to move on to a different attack or simply quit while he was behind. Suddenly, Sonia lashed out, almost spitting the words.

"Do you have any idea what it is like? Any idea? To walk in the street and avoid the eyes of everybody, especially the men. To be anxious to get home before it is dark because there is bad lighting in the street and somebody could be waiting in the shadows? Sometimes you only hear a voice, always a man's voice, in the dark,'Hey Jew! Dirty Kikeface! Go to your own country!' And you run, not knowing if more of them are waiting for you in the next alleyway. Or they touch you on the bus when it is crowded, knowing you cannot say anything, cannot draw attention to yourself. Do you know what it's like that you must be always vigilant, always pay attention? You cannot read a book on a bus because sometime you will look up and there is a man watching, he knows who you are and gets off at the same stop as you and follows. You cannot read a book in a park alone because there are suddenly four pairs of legs surrounding you, they came too close because you did not notice, you were careless and now you must threaten to scream and run before they touch you too much even in daylight, teenagers who should be in school."

She paused for breath and Brak tried to speak.

"I do not think you know these things. You are a big man. You live in a country with freedom and police to protect you and you are the right colour. You do not know what it feels like to have four men seize you in the darkness of the landing of your own building and be unable to call to your parents only a few feet away while they beat you and do terrible things while you can smell their tobacco and their hate. If you knew such things, you would not ask such questions."

Sonia sat there like a perfect china figurine, perfectly poised, perfectly still except for the slight quivering of her head and the light snapping from her eyes. Brak was transfixed, sitting straight, his chair now further away from hers. None of us had moved.

Brak's right hand reached up to remove his glasses, seeking some habitual gesture to return him to reality. He took a moment to clean his lenses on his tie.

"Well now, that was a dandy." He turned to us. "Well, you can see it's not always an easy job. Especially when you get a competent witness like this one." He turned to Sonia. "You're quite the little actress, young lady. And you figured out that offence can be a good defence."

Sonia stood up and nodded to him, as though taking a modest bow. Brak continued. "Of course, you had the advantage of being Jewish, that certainly gave you a leg up. But still, you did well. You should make a fine RCO."

Turning to us, he added. "You can see how tough it is if the witness knows the territory better than you do. You will have to deal with that all the time. The claimant will have superior knowledge of their country, culture, history. They may even be able to graphically describe circumstantial details about torture, rape, or prison, not because it happened to them but because they were there as a prison guard or torturer." He looked vaguely towards Sonia as he said this as though she were somehow complicit with all the lurking anti-Semites in the darkened doorways of Moldova.

"But that's enough for today. We'll break early and continue with submissions tomorrow. Everyone have a good night and get lots of sleep in those fancy hotel rooms the Board is paying for."

Walking out, I was thinking that psychologically speaking, the man had the hide of a bull elephant. Sonia had given him about three shots right between the eyes that would drop anyone and he was calmly climbing out of the ring shaking the mild buzz out of his head. I caught up with Sonia as she was heading for the hotel. We were the only two staying at the Sheraton. The Toronto people lived at home and the Montreal RCO's were in a different hotel. Originally I thought something might come of this cozy arrangement but so far it had been strictly business.

I told her she was great, she'd floored old Brak the Beast. She'd put him down for the full count and everyone knew it. He was such a phoney.

"James, sit down." We were crossing this little private park linked to the hotel. There were a few old-fashioned benches and a Japanese-style fountain, the sound of water over pebbles, very West Coast. Up close, I could see she was trembling.

"James, don't you get it? I wasn't faking. It wasn't an act."

"Hey! Easy now. Time out. What do you mean, it wasn't an act? Hello. Reality time, please. Sonia, you're not from Moldova and I don't think you've been beaten within an inch of your life."

"Not to me. To my mother, after the war, in Poland, not Moldova. But it happened. She never told me until three years ago. It wasn't an act because I know what it is to feel different, knowing there's always the possibility of danger, to know that if I'm not watchful, I could get hurt. I'm a Jew. It's in my blood. It's in my history."

"It's not just Jews. Anyone with a history of oppression. A lot of women know about it. You are so spoiled here in Canada. So spoiled. Most of you, especially the men, no offence, have no idea what it means to be physically vulnerable in a hostile society that can turn on you at anytime."

"And that's why you decided to take on Brak?"

"Not really. He's a jerk and a bully, and who cares. But when he said that thing about his little crap trap not hurting the innocent ones, the genuine refugees, I couldn't stand it. I looked around to see all these people sitting there, believing this man. I felt like I was in Torture School with the professor assuring us it wouldn't really hurt. It was so creepy."

I protested that some of us weren't buying his bunk. Just because people weren't saying anything, it didn't mean that they believed him.

"But no one said anything, no one spoke up. Don't you see, that's what happens? You don't need a lot of little Hitlers, maybe five percent Nazi boys and the majority remains silent. I'll bet in Moldova there's only five or ten percent who are real Jew haters. Everyone else is indifferent or moderate but passive. My mother was beaten in the hallway of her apartment building. Unlike Ms Shiner, she screamed, really screamed, and not a single doorway opened. Neighbours, friends even, who had watched her grow up, stayed behind their doors either because they didn't care if a Jewish girl was being beaten or because they knew who was doing the beating, everyone knew, and they didn't want trouble. You have no idea. The intolerance is so thick that no one is brave enough to challenge it. Jew-lover. That's what they would be called. They could be attacked."

"You're exaggerating. This is Canada. People speak up about that stuff."

"Sure, if it's obvious. No one can openly dump on Jews or Aboriginal people anymore. But tell me this, is Brak a creep?"

"Sure. Grade A, number one certified creep."

"And what about his little cross-examination crap trap routine?"

"Well, it's a tool. Maybe if a witness is lying his head off ..."

"But for every claimant, no matter how scared, is it a shotgun to be levelled at them?"

"Well, no I suppose not."

"But that's what he said. Credibility is the only issue. You don't question, you *cross-examine* and, and, don't forget, it doesn't hurt the innocent ones. He said that. Who are the innocent ones? The ones who have been badly beaten in hallways, the ones who have been abused all their lives, the ones who daren't go to the police in racist and totalitarian regimes, who don't trust any authority, who are afraid of being sent back to hell if the Board members don't believe them? Are these the ones he doesn't hurt with his crap trap?"

Sometimes a person has nowhere to hide. There are no rabbit holes to dive down and so you just stop and give up. I did that. No argument, no come back, just stop and listen.

"James, it's not just our little class, although the idea of twenty more RCOs being trained to grill victims is not too attractive. Even if half of them actually apply those techniques, it's too many. But don't you wonder why Brak is the trainer? Why Brak? We heard about his reputation, the man's a jackboot. Who made the decision that someone like that would train others? And how do those people view claimants? Do they see them as potentially genuine refugees to be given asylum, or as liars, cheats, someone jumping the queue, just like those clever, sneaky Jews? Who put Brak in control? Who allows him into the hearing room every day? And how many are silent about that decision?"

She was shivering now, shaking, her arms tight to her sides. It seemed natural to put an arm around her shoulders, feeling her head come against my chest, looking for its own refuge. We stayed there for a long while as the light faded, listening to the movement of water over pebbles. Slowly the shaking left her body and I admit that I began to wonder if tonight, I might finally get lucky.

11

RAYMOND

I THOUGHT I'D NEVER STOP LAUGHING. There she was, mouth open, eyes as big as saucers, when he told her. Told us all for that matter. I suppose my eyes were popping just as much but at least I started laughing. Oh my! How could you not? Well, except for Blanche. She'd never laughed in a hearing room and she wasn't going to start for someone as crazy as this character. He was something.

But I'm not going to tell you the punchline, not yet. It would spoil it. You have to understand that Blanche and I had been sitting together a lot, which wasn't the easiest thing for either of us, I suppose. Blanche was a terror, she'd never let anything go. If there was one little thing wrong with a claimant's story, the tiniest little detail that didn't fit, relevant, irrelevant, didn't matter, she'd be on it like a dog on a bone. And she'd work it and work it until she was satisfied, no matter if we were there all day or had to adjourn for a date four months away.

I was located in Halifax at the time and she was up in Ottawa so she didn't get down all that often. They'd rotate some of the members through to sit with me. Blanche came as often as she could. She had family there. She had a sister right in Halifax and a whole school of aunts and uncles up in Sydney. She's from Cape Breton Island, you know. A lot of people don't know that but it's true. Straight from the Island, a Caper, though you wouldn't know it from the accent. Been up there in Upper Canada too long I suppose.

But I'm not criticising. She had her style, same as me. A lot of people would say Jimmy Boutelier wasn't the easiest person to sit with either. Too lackadaisical, too easy, a former Member of Parliament just sitting on his arse chewing up his eighty-seven thousand dollars a year. I'm sure they say it. Rather say yes than have to write a negative decision. And the public would applaud them for saying it. Take the fellows down at the Schooner, they'd be cheering on someone like Blanche, say she's doin' the right thing, keeping out the foreigners. Course they wouldn't know a refugee from the local bank manager but they got their beer and their pogey and their problems, most of which can be neatly laid at the door of the government or the foreigners.

Don't get me wrong! I'm not knocking Maritimers. Not a bit. I know. I sat on that damn' Immigration Committee in the House for more years than I care to remember and I can say, God's truth, Maritimers are no different than the rest of Canada when it comes to immigrants, maybe even a bit better. If they know someone personal, they take them to their heart, give them the run of the house. But the *idea* of a refugee, now that's a different kettle of fish. They're all afraid of being taken advantage of, afraid their generosity is being abused. You'd see it all the time. The same people who would vote to keep out refugees and foreigners, taking all the jobs they'd say, why, you take those same people and have a little brown fellow crawl up on their shore at five in the morning and they'd be serving him tea, toast, and jam quicker'n you could blink. Taking a day off work to drive him into Halifax to make his refugee claim. Give him five dollars and take him to the Salvation Army.

But if they read about it in the papers, doesn't matter if it's the Halifax *Chronicle-Herald* or Toronto's own Globular Mail, they're all the same, if they read that our refugee acceptance rate is fifty percent and only twelve percent in France, why, then they're right hostile. And if they read that Jimmy Boutelier, retired MP, is now a member of the Immigration and Refugee Board, receiving eighty-seven thousand of their hard-earned dollars, why that doesn't do much for Mr Boutelier or for refugees. No matter that France has got its head up its chauvinistic arse, turning away the misery of the world. So they would love Blanche and her seventy percent negative decision rate and I fear what they would say about the case of Raymond Foxbury.

That was the fellow's name, Foxbury. Not your average refugee name. Not your average refugee colour either, not unless he's from

Refugee Sandwich | 146

Eastern Europe. But Raymond wasn't from Bulgaria, Moldova, Estonia, Latvia, or any of those ex-Soviet states ending in "a." Rather, he was the only Australian to claim Convention Refugee status in Canada. Only one at the time, anyway. I can't say as I've kept up since leavin' the Board.

Well, you can imagine, it was a bizarre case from the beginning. It's not like the Board hasn't had its steady diet of crazies. We have. But they're Americans, not bloody Aussies. You know the type: "The CIA drugged me and put a transmitter in the back of my brain. They follow me everywhere. They want to control my mind." The Board probably hears a dozen claims like that a year. They're all crazy as hoot owls but very clever, mind you, often very clever. Paranoid people can be extremely intelligent, keeping track of every detail. But that wasn't Raymond, not at all. He was loose as a goose, a dozen like him in any pub in the city. My God, the man was wonderfully indifferent to the details of his claim, frequently contradicting his own testimony. It was beyond bizarre, I can tell you.

His story was simple enough. He said the Australian government wanted him for certain obscure reasons. He and his mate were fishermen working out of Sydney when they seen some weird lights on the water at night, which wasn't normal at all and it was either aliens or some strange doings, so they reported it to the police. Next thing you know men in sunglasses were comin' around to his house asking strange questions like "What else did you see? Who are your friends?"

He said he didn't like their tone and they would only say they were from the government. Then his mate disappeared. Went for a walk and didn't come home, so Raymond took off. Didn't call the police or anything, just got a ticket and come to Canada. Didn't know what had happened to his mate and no, there was no family to call. Parents dead, no wife, no kids, not even a cousin.

Ordinarily you try to end the crazy cases as soon as possible because you're afraid they could go on forever. Get those people talking and they won't stop. They've got such complicated stories and it's all so circular, with layers and layers of detail. So you try to be real polite, ask enough questions to establish that one of the elements of the refugee definition is missing and you end it. Say thank you for your testimony today which has been most helpful, and we will consider it in light of the country documents and send you our decision in the mail as soon as possible and goodbye.

And we had that with Raymond. He hadn't sought state protection, didn't go to the police. Australia is a democratic state. There's a presumption that the state can protect its citizens. There's a christly great decision by the Supreme Court of Canada that says so and Bingo! We're out of there. We don't need to go into the details of what he fears exactly and who's going to do it to him and why. Irrelevant. And we could have done that and should have done that except for Blanche. She said it was his accent, said it didn't sound right. And I'm thinking, who cares? We're going negative! We don't need to put ribbons and bows on the damn decision. He's from bloody Australia, is what I'm thinking. But she kept asking questions: Where did he fish? What kind of fish? What did these strange lights look like? Where was his mate's family?

And I have to admit, the story did start to get interesting. Not that it made a lot of sense, Raymond kept tripping over himself, contradicting something he'd said ten minutes before and obviously not too concerned with the inconsistencies. It was all crazy but not crazy crazy, if you know what I mean. The fellow wasn't nuts, just kind of dumb and indifferent. So Blanche kept going, asking more questions. She wouldn't let it go. And I did everything but beg at the lunch break. Pointed out we had more than enough to go negative on the state protection, credibility, or any other damn thing she cared to suggest. And she said there was something strange going on and we hadn't got to the bottom of the story. She was one of those people who didn't acknowledge that some stories were bottomless, the facts just dribble off into a muddy bottom with no certainty whatsoever.

So we adjourned since we had an afternoon case, and I was fit to be tied. You have to understand, the bean counters at the Board were all over the Halifax office, wanting to close it and run the whole show from Ottawa. Fly in members once a month to hear cases. Sounded good but it didn't account for all the little things we did for claimants who don't understand the refugee system and were always coming in with questions. How could you deal with that stuff by mail when half of them were illiterate in their own language and changing addresses like underwear, since they're all living in rundown tenement housing?

Anyway, I'm carrying on about lost battles. Enough to say that I was worried about our case efficiency and Blanche wasn't helping, but there was no turning that woman off her course once she had her bearings. So we adjourned and continued the hearing about three months later when Blanche come back to town.

During the adjournment, Raymond had been told to get himself an identity document. He said he'd lost his passport. Well three months later he produces a driver's licence as proof of identity. Only problem is it's a Nova Scotia licence. And we have to say, "No, Mr Foxbury, an *Australian* identity document if you please," and he does have a foolish grin on his face when we say it, which also does not accord with the conduct of your average nut case, so Blanche keeps asking questions. And finally it comes out by mid-afternoon. We'd reserved a whole day for the case to avoid another adjournment and suddenly the real story pops out. You ready for this? He's not Australian.

So what, you say? The Board must hear lots of claims where the person lies about their nationality. And I would say to you that is true, but how many turn out to be Canadian? That's right, Canadian. Our Raymond was from Sydney all right, Sydney, Nova Scotia! He was a bloody Caper! And he was *hoping* to be refused. The silly bugger thought he would be deported back to Australia. He had heard there were good jobs in the mines there and was looking for a free airplane ticket.

So that was the end of it. Blanche got to the bottom of the story and Raymond went home to Sydney. We sent the file back to Immigration but I don't think they did a damn thing. There must be some sort of criminal charge dealing with attempted fraud, misuse of Canadian tribunals, etc., but there was no one smart or energetic enough to figure it out. So everyone was happy except me. Blanche was looking smug and there was no skin off of Raymond's nose. He withdrew his claim so it didn't even count as a completed case, and the Halifax office, after a day and half of testimony, was looking more inefficient than ever.

Now I can't claim as that one case sank my ship but it sure put a hole below the waterline. Dollars to doughnuts the government would not be reappointing Jimmy Boutelier, former MP, to the Emigration and Refugee Board. Ha! Now ain't that a hoot?

12

A CRACK IN THE MIRROR

SOMETIMES TRUTH IS UNDENIABLE. It is fresh, alive, a piece of ice on a hot stove, as some American poet said. I think he was American.

I practise immigration and criminal law, mostly refugee cases. I spend a lot of my professional life separating fact from fiction. At least I see it that way. The judges and Board members may have a different view. I'm often accused of trying to mix fact and fiction, muddy the waters so to speak, but I beg to differ. My task is to disclose the truth that is already there, to find some way for the Board members to see the same truth. And I try to have it come through the mouth of my client. They had the experience, it's their story, but it's not easy, especially with a schmuck like Hess.

We called him various names of comparable value: Goebbels, Himmler, even Göring, which I always thought the most inappropriate, since Hess is a small thin man, finely chiselled features, the nose a little too beaky, accentuated by those rimless glasses that leave a matched pair of red marks on either side of the beak. A repressed and weedy man, not at all like Göring who was large and robust, a man of appetites. I thought Hess a lot closer to the mark, myself, but you get the idea, we all agreed that he resembled someone in the Nazi pantheon of infamy.

The man had an obvious love of power, it oozed out of him like skin oil. He had this jeweller's loupe that he used to examine identity documents, slowly perusing the document while the claimant waited for his next question. It was all a power trip. He could have examined the documents before the hearing but he preferred to make the claimant sweat. The loupe was a prop. He'd start tapping it against the palm of his left hand whenever he was closing in for the kill, the claimant looking like some frightened rabbit caught in the headlights. This rhythmic tapping, as sinister as the ticktock of a clock in a Hitchcock movie. You could tell he was enjoying it, the soulless little prick. He didn't give a shit about the refugee claimant or what would happen to him if he were sent back home. It was all about winning, tripping up the claimants, trapping them in some way, exposing a falsehood, whether it was real or illusory.

I should explain the "we." I'm talking about the local immigration lawyers in town. There are about fifteen to twenty of us, depending on whether you count the part-timers. Some, like Doug Delaney, are criminal lawyers with immigration as a sideline. I mention Doug because he's the one who had the run-in with Grabowski. That's Hess's real name, Anthony Grabowski. There were other nicknames, Slippery, Snake-eyes. All very complimentary. But mostly, and for me always, it was Hess.

You might ask what qualities this man had that elicited such a large measure of personal dislike from a bunch of thick-skinned lawyers. After all, in our profession, it's a necessary virtue to ignore the failings of others. We see a lot of the dark side, from clients, cops, and colleagues. And to some degree, they're all the same. Everyone thinks they're a hotshot, like no one is onto their little scam, when in fact half the world sees through them. There's a lot of strutting, a lot of blind self-importance. Everyone loses track of the clients. It's about looking and sounding good. The lawyers are probably the worst. So why did we detest Hess so much?

He was hated because he had a small amount of power and liked to use it in the wrong way on the wrong people. I mean, the RCO, that's the Refugee Claim Officer, gets to ask questions, right? I'm assuming you already know about refugee hearings and all that, how they work and everything. The thing is, they're supposed to be *inquisitorial*, not adversarial. Now, I know that sounds worse in a way, inquisitorial, like Inquisition, right? But it's the opposite. The hearing's not adversarial, you're not supposed to win or lose, you're supposed to *inquire,* to ask questions to get at the truth. And that applies to everyone, the RCO, the lawyer, and the board member. Of course the lawyer cheats a little. He's got a client, so he *leans* a little, if you know what I mean, not a lot, just a little. But the RCO, he's supposed to be diamond-straight neutral. No games. No crap.

It's different in the courts, which are adversarial. There, it's a battle. That's the theory. Two people have a dispute. They hire gladiators and go to court and their guy is supposed to pound the crap out of the opposition, and if both sides hammer the other, supposedly the truth will out. Same theory as beating gold, you hammer it till you remove all the impurities and you're left with beaten gold.

Personally I think it's a crock. The adversarial system is a lousy method of discovering truth. I know that's heresy coming from a lawyer, but it's true. Look at the Zundel trial. The guy is charged in 1984 with spreading racial hatred. He's an anti-Semite and Holocaust denier. And what's his defense? The Holocaust didn't happen. What did it take, eight, ten months? To figure out that the Holocaust actually happened? Gimme a break. Think of it! An event that happens to millions of people within living memory and they take eight months to decide it actually happened. And for a while there was some uncertainty about the outcome. There was Zundel's lawyer, what's-his-name, the paladin for all right-wing causes with an open licence to have a go at all those old Jews with faulty memories and bad hearts who are trying to remember what happened when. And what does he do? Attack, attack. Are you sure that happened in July 1943? In your affidavit five months ago, you said you didn't arrive at Treblinka until August 1943. Now you are telling us that blah, blah, blah. It's nuts. Why don't they just read any of the Holocaust literature? First hand accounts by Primo Levi, Elie Wiesel. Or talk to a few of the Canadian soldiers who liberated Dachau? Nice goyishe white boys who have no reason to lie, not like the sneaky Jews.

So that's what really pissed us off about Hess. With the inquisitorial system, you're not supposed to hammer the witness. It says so right in the statute. *Especially* the RCO, who is this hired flunky who's there to *assist* the Board members. He's supposed to *question,* not cross-examine. No leading questions. None of the when-did-you-stop-beating-your-sister stuff. And it's a better system. I like it. Everybody lays their cards on the table. Doesn't mean the claimant isn't lying and the RCO sometimes has to ask the tough questions, but you don't trick, you don't intimidate.

I guess the other half of that whole issue, the other reason for being inquisitorial, is because of the nature of the witness. We're talking about refugees here. Most of them are terrible witnesses. They're scared silly. A lot of them already had some very bad things happen to them. They don't understand what's happening in the hearing. They don't speak English and half of the interpreters are faking it half the time. You couldn't have more vulnerable witnesses and they're really counting on the lawyers and the Board members to figure it out for them. And that's why inquisitorial is better and that's the second half of why Hess pissed us off.

Hess cross-examined. He'd set people up, he'd take advantage, he'd try to trip them. I had this Lebanese claimant once, a Shiite woman from one of the villages in the Bekaa Valley, grade three education. A lovely kind woman, not the greatest claim in the world but the militias had shot half her village and she had nowhere to go except her son in Vancouver. As I say, not the greatest claim, the militia weren't after her personally but there was no issue on credibility. Until Hess starting picking away at her, picking away at tiny little details on dates of personal history that happened fifteen years ago, challenging every inconsistency. My client couldn't remember. Hell, she barely understood what was in the PIF in the first place. By the time Hess was finished, she was so confused she would have agreed to anything. She kept contradicting herself. That was his method: scare 'em, confuse 'em, then clobber them. And as I said, he'd move in for the kill with that little jeweller's loupe tapping away.

So that claim went negative. I wanted to appeal but it's hard to get the court to quash a decision based on lack of credibility. Her son sent her back home to live with an uncle in another village and she's probably safe, miserable but safe. And maybe that was even the right decision, but not the *way* it happened. Not for the reasons the Board gave. And that's the third half of the problem, the hard-ass Board members loved Hess. They thought he was the expert who could break through the bullshit, get to the real truth. In their decision, they would sweep up the pieces of broken testimony, point out all the inconsistencies, and conclude she wasn't credible without ever engaging the real issues in the case. God, it pisses me off just to think about it.

This one time Doug Delaney had a client, I forget which country, somewhere in Central America, probably El Salvador, maybe Guatemala. Doesn't matter, the military did the same thing in both countries. The whole rape thing was more about power than sex, right? Insult the men of the family, dishonour the wife, make the daughters unmarriageable. Big macho game. Sometimes they'd do it right in the family home, bang down the door at night, knock the older kids around, especially if they couldn't find whoever they were looking for, the father, adult sons.

So Doug had one of those cases, middle-aged woman, raped in front of her kids, husband somewhere in the hills with the guerrillas, so she flees the country with the younger kids, afraid of the military coming back for round two. She's not an attractive woman and she bought a false passport to get out of her country. So what? So Hess is like a dog on a bone. Where'd she get the money for phoney documents and all the tiny little details of the soldiers coming at night, detail by detail. How many soldiers, where did they take her, exactly where were the kids while all this was happening? Doug objected, but with lousy Board members there's not much you can do. You protest too much and they think it's just an attempt to cover up. A lot of them don't like lawyers, don't like them and fear them. So they let cockroaches like Hess do the nasty work and sit back with clean hands. Only some of them, right? There are lots of good members who would never let it happen.

Anyway, it was ugly, the witness became completely distraught, asked for a break but Doug couldn't calm her down, she wouldn't talk to him. Just sat there in the waiting room, holding her daughter's hand. When the hearing resumed, she'd say whatever Hess wanted her to say. He kept leading her into contradictions and she kept agreeing. Doug said she gave up. That's how they get people to sign confessions in prison. Of course Doug should have had a psychiatric report saying she was fragile, suffering from post-traumatic stress, which Doug said was obvious, but not so obvious as it turns out. So he didn't have one. Legal aid won't pay for the things unless you beg, and who has the time? And there's a short list of psychologists who will do them for free. A very short list and it's getting shorter. So I can see myself in the same boat, you tend to skip the report unless you really think you need it.

So Hess won that round. And that's how he thinks of it. Winning. Doug swears he's going to introduce Hess to Fat Frank. Frank's one of his long-standing clients, lives somewhere up the valley around Mission. Huge guy, over three hundred pounds, big beard, always wears farmer jeans, long-time drug dealer, has a steel door on the front of his house. You do not mess with Frank. Killed a man with a two-by-four. Doug got the charges knocked down to manslaughter. A six-year sentence, out in two. Doug says Frank is very loyal to his friends. I don't think Doug would ever do it, but I know he's stopped taking refugee cases. Says he can't stand the hypocrisy. At least in criminal court it's open warfare. You're not supposed to check your gun at the door. In the hearing room you are.

Anyway, I don't agree with him. I still prefer refugee hearings. Partially because of the clients but also because it is a search for truth and when it works, it works well. Fair questions, straight answers, everybody moving in the same direction and getting to the same place. Even if it's a negative, it's a fair negative, not based on some warped misconstruction of the evidence. The claimant says the authorities haven't been looking for him for the past two years, the members decide he's no longer at risk, so be it.

Anyway, here's the story I was intending to tell. This is what got me started on the whole thing. This is where Hess gets handed his ass. He's like a hound, right? He starts sniffing up a trail, he keeps going until he finds something or the member calls him off. Some of the time he doesn't find anything, he doesn't confuse the claimant. Then he really is like a hound, just sort of snorts and starts off on another scent. He's relentless and he never gets stopped in his tracks. Except this one time.

My client's from Russia, the former Soviet Union. A wonderful woman, been through hell and survived, full of life, always doing something for someone else. Not that her case was simple, hell of a story. She suffered terribly during the Stalinist era but it's now post-perestroika, so there's this whole change of circumstances thing. Remember, the question isn't *were* you persecuted, it's *would* you be persecuted if you were sent back? And in this case, she probably wouldn't be. But let me tell you the story so it makes some sense.

Natasha's a kid during the Second World War living in southern Russia when she's captured by the Nazis, along with her mother. Her father's off fighting somewhere. She's separated from her mother and gets shipped off to a Nazi labour camp. Not treated too badly, just scared and lonely. After the war, she gets shipped to Murmansk with thousands of other ex-prisoners, assumes she's going home. By now she's in her late teens. Little does she know the Stalinist regime is totally paranoid about anyone coming back from the West. She could be a spy or full of weird capitalist ideas. Everyone's under suspicion and subject to interrogation before release. Still, she's nineteen and not full of anything except a compulsion to find her parents. Shouldn't be a problem. Except the KGB lieutenant interrogating her thinks she's good-looking and lets her know it. Makes her an offer she can't refuse, except she does. She didn't think he meant it but he did and the next day she's on a cattle car heading to the Gulag with a paper saying she's politically suspect. You've read Solzhenitsyn so I don't have to go into the details. It was as bad as he described it and she was pretty solid on the details.

Right away they put her to work on a construction site, working outside in cold horrible conditions, lousy food, no heat, people dying. After a couple of years, a two-storey wall falls on her, crushing her arm. She lies under the wall for a few hours until they haul her out and amputate the arm just above the elbow, without anaesthetic. She survives. I told you she was strong. Being kind and considerate communists, they send her to a different work camp, can't use one-armed people in construction. Nobody bothers to consider why she was sent to the Gulag in the first place. So she spends more time counting garments in some lice-infested hole until they finally release her.

She's now twenty-nine. They send her to Vladivostok, the ass end of Russia, with an identity document that classifies her as Section 49. I think it's Section 49. I can never remember numbers. Maybe it's sixty-one. Either way, she's a political undesirable, the mark of Cain. The Soviets used an internal passport system which was needed for everything, residence permit, employment, ration card, police surveillance. It was very efficient.

She was left in this totalitarian purgatory, no longer in hell but no hope of heaven or redemption. They stuck her in some factory as a low-grade technician. Natasha was brilliant, could have a been a wonderful scientist or doctor. And of course, she was devastated to learn that both her parents had died. She had no right to travel to her former home near the Black Sea and there were no graves to visit. So she had her job and her weekly visits to the KGB for company. The Soviets must have had hundreds of thousands of KGB, they kept such close tabs on so many people.

They were pleasant visits, mind you. "How are you, Natasha? Any politically incorrect thoughts this week?" A few put-downs, a few leers, off-colour remarks. No fondling, just a little pressure from the State Thumb, pushing you down a little, a small reminder that you are nothing and can be sent back to hell whenever any apparatchik chooses to do so.

Naturally by this time she was having a ton of politically impure thoughts. She detested the Communist state. She'd seen the underbelly of totalitarianism and didn't have a lot of positive comments. Then, just to make her life a little more interesting, she married a Jew. She tells a very funny story about her KGB interview. The visits were monthly by this time. They knew she was going to marry of course. And here's Agent Boris, "So why are you marrying a Jew?" And she says, "For love. What else? I am already a Section 49. How low can I go?"

Her fiancé tells her he also has been called in by the local political officer, every factory and work unit had one. "So why are you marrying a Section 49? Don't you realize she is a political undesirable?" She'd been lucky in one way, she'd found a classy guy. He tells the officer that he loves her. Besides, he's a Jew. How low can he go? They both thought it was very funny. Reminds me of that book, by Richard Farina, from the sixties, *Been Down So Long It Looks Like Up to Me*.

And so she lived a life, had a daughter, her husband died after a good marriage, she retires after thirty years in the factory, the KGB never completely go away although she's only called in occasionally, still with the Thumb business. Perestroika happens, Gorbachev, glasnost, and she and her daughter, Olga, get the hell out of the country as soon as they can. She had an old friend living in Canada who helped her because Natasha had bupkes. Sorry, that's Yiddish for "squat." It wasn't just her of course, Olga, now an adult, was legally a Jew and had her own problems. Ethnic identity was noted in the Soviet internal passport. By law, with mixed marriages, the children could choose their registered ethnicity at age sixteen, but the registration clerk didn't give Olga a choice. Under nationality, he had already entered the word Jew. She asked about it, said her mother was Russian. The clerk barely bothered to respond. Told her, "We know who you are."

So they come to Canada and claim refugee status. The Vancouver office is accepting most Russian Jewish claims so Olga's okay, but Natasha's claim is a problem. She's not Jewish, married to a Jew but he's been dead a long time. Change of circumstances, the new Russia, they're no longer persecuting anti-communists, it's been more than thirty years since she was in the Gulag, yadda yadda yadda. And they've got a point, although Natasha is not convinced. She's saying, "You don't know these people, it's still the same KGB under a different name, the KGB schmuck who gave me a hard time is now a major in the new security police."

And there's no way I'm going to convince her that it's ever going to be safe. She keeps saying, "You don't know, you weren't there."

But I'm being a good guy. Remember I was saying about the non-adversarial system, right? So, I'm being straight, and I'm saying to the Board, look, my client may not be convinced but I concede she may not have a valid fear of future persecution now. So let's not waste our time, let's look at compelling reasons.

There's this special provision in the Immigration Act, it's built right into the definition, that says that where there's a change of circumstances, there still may be compelling reasons for not sending a person back where there has been previous persecution. The courts have said that the past persecution has to be atrocious, nice long Latin word. Basically the compelling reasons exception says that if you have been hurt very, very badly, been so severely damaged that you can't stand your country, then you don't have to go back, even if there's been a change of government. It's a humanitarian cripple rule and it's pretty narrowly applied.

But I figure Natasha falls right square in the middle of the rule. It was designed for people like her. That's why I say you can't convince her the government has truly changed. She would always fear the police, always be afraid they're going to do something to her or her daughter. She even gave testimony to the Memorial Society, this group that was collecting stories about Gulag abuses, and that made her even more afraid when her story was included in a television program.

So we're set for the hearing and I assume there will be some questions. Like, are her reasons for fearing the old Soviet regime really compelling since the really bad stuff happened thirty-five years ago, and isn't there an awful lot of water under the bridge? And I'll be saying, look, they did such terrible things to her for more than ten years that she will never forget something like that. She lost her arm, for God's sake. She lost her parents. And furthermore, the persecution continued. Being hauled in on a weekly, monthly, yearly basis by the KGB. It didn't matter, she was always labelled, always made to feel small, always reminded she could be sent back to the Gulag. They held all the power, she was nothing. So for her, hell was always fresh. We're talking about permanent damage here. I figured the issues were obvious. The testimony would be fairly brief, we'd both put forward our arguments and the members would decide. Except I didn't know about Hess.

There's another RCO on the case so it's a surprise when Hess pops up at the last minute. He has a reputation for snatching cases he has an interest in, so I am definitely feeling paranoid when he walks into the hearing room, although I'm wondering, why this case? He usually goes after credibility and there's Natasha with her prosthetic arm and medical report. What does he want? I never did get the answer, although his logic was probably along the lines of "Just another Russian grandma playing the phoney Jewish card. Physical injury is not necessarily evidence of persecution. The woman could have lost her arm in a dozen ways."

I'm only guessing. I couldn't be bothered trying to follow the twisted reasoning. When you're dealing with a kinky mind like that, you can get lost in the labyrinth real easy and it's probably not worth the trip. If you do check it out, I'd take a ball of twine to find your way back. Something that doesn't dissolve in acid or faeces.

My questions for Natasha are fairly brief. The facts really aren't in dispute. She's a very credible witness. The real issue is atrocious persecution and continuing fear. Her written narrative already describes the ten years of Gulag hell. There's the missing arm and she's had chronic pain her whole life, a serious neck problem because of the prosthesis. I've filed a medical report. So I focus her testimony on the badgering by the KGB, the repeated threats. And I mix in a little of the Jewish stuff since the family was always getting nasty notes in the mail, even after the husband died. Marrying a Jew is almost as bad as being a Jew. In some ways, it's worse. I don't remember who the panel was, a couple of zeros who were going to let Hess do whatever he wanted.

Then it was Hess's turn. To my great surprise, he didn't even touch the postperestroika stuff, or maybe he planned to later. I don't know because he never got there. I wasn't too worried about Natasha. Despite what I said before about vulnerable witnesses, Natasha was the exception. Compared to the KGB, Hess was pretty small potatoes. He wasn't going to intimidate her but he might use her strength against her. If she easily stood up to his challenges, he might reverse the logic: "See, this is a powerful woman. She's not fearful of anything. There are no compelling reasons for her to stay in Canada. She'll do just fine in the new Russia." I said he was sneaky.

Turns out he was on a different tack altogether. For some reason, he went directly after the credibility of her early life. Asked all kinds of questions about her capture by the Nazis, the labour camp in Norway, getting shipped to Murmansk. Her answers were right on, I could almost smell the vomit when she described the cattle-car journey to the Gulag. I don't know what Hess was thinking. I thought perhaps he was trying to retraumatize her, break her down by reliving the bad times.

Maybe he just didn't believe her, which is astounding, but maybe it's that simple. It has always been a puzzle to me when members and RCOs just don't get it. Lots of testimony can be pretty ragged, especially with a lousy interpreter. The claimant is scared, tightens up, or doesn't understand the questions. Sure, there's some doubt even if the story's true, but sometimes … I have to tell you, there are times when the testimony is screaming credibility. You know it's true, so many little details, so vivid, the claimant would have to be a graduate of Lee Strasberg's School of Method Acting to be faking it.

And the Board members sit there like lumps, still looking for more. It makes you crazy. What the hell do they want? A video? There's this old *New Yorker* cartoon where a claimant in rags is standing in front of the desk of this immigration officer, handing him a paper and saying, "Here is this document from my government, Sir, stating that I have a well-founded fear of persecution." You feel like nothing will satisfy them.

So by now, Hess is asking questions about the Gulag camp and construction work during the winter. He's taken out his jeweller's loupe and he's tapping it into his fist and I still don't know where he's going with his questions until he finally asks, "And what did it feel like when the wall allegedly fell on you?"

He looks over at the Board members with this meaningful look. I don't know what he expected and I can't imagine what answer he thought he would get that would undermine Natasha's credibility. Given that it happened over forty years ago and she had a ton of wall on top of her, it would be amazing if she were able to give any account of her thoughts or feelings. I swear I don't know where they find these Board members. Here they are dutifully leaning forward, looking interested as though she were going to say something that would suggest she had not lain under a wall in the freezing cold with a crushed arm some forty years before.

And Natasha fools them. Fooled me too. "Oh, it was wonderful," she says, her face glowing. "I felt like I was floating in clouds in a beautiful field and there were so many flowers and a beautiful light and I knew I was going to see my mother and father." She went on for quite a while and I'm sitting there watching Hess's mouth open and close, slowly, like a fish, close then open, making a small round O, and he's put his loupe down, he's just listening.

When Natasha stopped talking, he didn't say anything for a minute. He didn't look at the members. He did glance over at me and for once I was smart enough to shut up and wait. Finally he thanked her for her testimony and said he had no more questions.

And this from a man who would burrow into the most painful human experience like a dentist drilling into a cavity. But this one blew his mind. In some wacky way, Natasha's unexpected response threw him off balance, leaving him suddenly uncertain, a moment of vulnerability in which he must have really listened, catching a genuine glimpse of the incredible hardships this woman had suffered. The case ended quickly after that. Hess made nominal submissions. I tried to keep my submissions clear and simple and the panel returned a positive decision before I could buy and drink a coffee.

There's nothing like a glimpse of truth to alter a person's view of the world. It is depressing to think that Hess had spent years in hearing rooms, grilling witnesses, playing his little win-lose games, caught in the nets of credibility assessment without ever once looking beyond the witness, beyond the story, to actually empathize with their experience. I know we all do that more than we think. "Gosh, that's too bad. I know how you feel," when we don't have the faintest notion and haven't really bothered to think about it at all. I see judges do it all the time. "Prison will not be a pleasant experience for you."

As though His Honour would know, never having visited the place. Mentally he's schtupping his secretary while he's blathering away. Sure, we all do it. But there are usually a few chinks in our armour. Some fresh air gets in. We stop and look around. Even judges. You see them suddenly look at a witness, really look. Like you can see them for an instant, putting themselves in the other person's shoes, thinking, what would that feel like?

I don't think Hess ever did that. Not until Natasha anyway. I like to think that he now has a permanent crack in his mirror, that he can't return to the role of the desensitized, invulnerable inquisitor. I like to think that, but I don't know. Shortly after the hearing, he transferred to Montreal and I never saw him again. It's not like I think he's joined Care Canada or anything. The man will always be a gatekeeper, but is it too much to hope that occasionally, hearing something wacky or inconsistent from a claimant, he will pause to wonder about the experience behind the words? Only now and again, just like the rest of us.

13

THE GO-BETWEEN

YOU SEE, IT IS NOT MY JOB to say if it is true or not. I am
the interpreter. I will tell you if the words are correct or not, in my
language or in English. But the truth? That is not the same thing.
The truth is for others, it is not for me to say. And yes, sometimes
it is difficult for me. There is so much misunderstanding and I try
not to think about that. Sometimes the communication goes very
badly. They do not understand each other but what can I do? I am
the interpreter, not the translator. There is a difference, you know.
Did you know?

You are an English speaker, an educated English speaker. You
should know there is a difference. An interpreter works with the
spoken word, the translator with the written. And that leads to
other differences, more subtle because the craft, the place of work,
are different. Do you say "is" or "are" different? You see there is
no end to the effort of mastering a language that is not the mother
tongue. There are always small imprecisions that do not easily fit
together. And that is the advantage of the translator, he has time to
tinker. The interpreter must work quickly, standing between or beside the speakers. Oh yes, you are correct, sometimes in a booth at
the back of the room, very far from the speakers, but still, meta-
phorically, I would assert, between them, between their minds. The
words come so quickly. We must provide near instantaneous con-
version from one language to another. Of necessity, we must focus
on the literal meaning of the word and the phrase.

Translators have more freedom. They can turn a phrase over in
their minds, play with it, attempt several combinations, smooth and

bevel the edges of the phrasing and, of course, be less literal, more metaphoric, to convey the essence, the sense of it in ways we interpreters could never hope to. In some ways, I envy them, although I confess I find translation boring. Perhaps it is the difference between live theatre and film, such a metaphor conveys the excitement and demand of our work but possibly not the rigidity that we suffer under. We are bound more strictly to the literal meaning of the words in order to remain faithful to the meaning. I suppose a translator would say that we do hasty work. Perhaps, to continue the exalted metaphor, I might say that we work rapidly in fresco while the translator has the luxury of oils.

But if you think this work is not difficult, my friend, I must tell you that I have seen people sent to their deaths and have been unable to intervene, unable to assist, although if I had reached out, I might have saved them and I did not. I could not. I am the interpreter. There is a line, you see. A line drawn by law. There are rules. I am the interpreter. I am the go-between. I deliver the message. I do not tamper with it or comment on it, no matter how absurd or wrong-headed it is. I interpret, I do not intervene and yes, this is not good for the soul.

I will tell you a story by way of illustration. It is the worst but there were many where meaning went awry, fell between the cracks. You Canadians like to say "between the cracks." I must tell you, they are sometimes very large cracks for we are talking about the gaps between languages. Perhaps it is similar to different computer programs that are built on different concepts. I am the program between programs to allow them to talk. Oh, this is not such a good comparison. I am too ignorant of computers. But the concept is correct. Languages are based on different concepts, different perceptions of reality. I am sorry to be so banal. This is all so obvious yet we ignore it every day. We have the same human experience but our peoples have formed social and linguistic realities that are so very different. So those cracks can become such deep crevasses and that is a very good analogy. I have climbed in the mountains of my home country, stepped over the innocent cracks of crevasses that reach down hundreds of feet into the glacier, such a brilliant green, the ice. The crevasses open with the shifts in temperature between day and night and they are suddenly not so easy to cross and a misstep leads to disaster. You cross at your peril.

At other times, I think of languages floating like untethered islands on the surface of human existence with nothing below but black undefined space. It is so easy to lose your way crossing from one language to the other, to sink into confusion and misunderstanding. The interpreter is the go-between, the boatman, to take you from one island to the other.

So you see I have taken you from mountain to ocean in the blink of a metaphor. You may think that I exaggerate, but let me tell my story. Meaning, or lack of meaning, has consequences. Oh it does, it does. I have interpreted for ministers of government at affairs of state where the words are polished stones carefully laid upon the table and I suppose there could be a misstep, but it is all so carefully calculated and recalculated that it usually results in tedium. If there are crevasses there, they are ones of attitude, political will, but rarely linguistic miscommunication. No I am speaking of the refugee hearings. You knew that much of my work at one time was at the Refugee Board? I interpreted the testimony of refugee claimants during their hearings. For an interpreter, this is, what is the expression? Grunt work? Yes, grunt work.

You sit alone next to the claimant, without an alternate, not like the government or United Nations where you change seats with a partner every twenty minutes. The hearings can last all day and there are few breaks. It is exhausting, really, work for a young man, although I know several older men and women who take the work out of desperation. They are not linguists, they are immigrants in need of work. Of course their English is not the best and I cannot help but wonder about the results.

You might think the work would be easier since the language lacks the precision of diplomatic exchanges, but this is precisely the problem. Yes, that was a small linguist's joke. It is my amusement to put the same word into the same sentence as different parts of speech. I find it more interesting than puns. Noun-adverb is one of the easier combinations.

If I may continue, it is the sloppiness of the language that presents the challenge. Often the claimant is uneducated or from a town or village, speaking a dialect with no sense of doing so. Although I must say that many of the Board officials are almost as bad. Their carelessness with language is unforgivable. They bandy about acronyms like bureaucrats. "That's not what you said in your PIF." What is a PIF? Are these people idiots?

Excuse me, I become incensed too easily over such matters, which is why I had to leave refugee work. So many of the Board members, they are the decisionmakers, seem to have no sense of their language, of the precision required when crossing the crevasses. For me, it was like working in a medical clinic where the surgeons were too casual about sterilizing their instruments. They knew about bacteria, they knew the effects, but they were not careful about their equipment. To be fair, the more accurate analogy would be to a field hospital in a war zone. The volume of refugee hearings is immense and perhaps fatigue and burnout were partial causes. However, as with hospitals, we are talking about human lives. Incorrect decisions send people back to death and torture.

Please, no, I am fine. I must tell the story. The doctor has encouraged me to speak of it and I do not. And now I will, with you. But it was not that one claim alone, it was the accumulation, the frustration of seeing too often the meanings go astray and being unable to prevent it. This one, the final one, was merely the culmination of the accumulation, although certainly the worst. So please, if you have patience for this patient, let me begin.

The claim was not a difficult one, quite ordinary really. The claimant, a young woman, spoke with a strong accent, typical of the northern regions of my country. She was educated, having studied for a time at the university, interrupted by the events that caused her to flee. The people of her region often invert their sentences to suggest doubt or uncertainty. They rarely employ the subjunctive. They also have their argot, as with most regions, where the language has stewed in its own juices for many generations. But none of this presented a serious challenge. I travelled in the region as a youth and was familiar with the regional nuances. It was not a true dialect, more of a heavily accented vernacular.

Ironically, that became one of the issues in the case, whether or not the woman was from the north. It was so obvious, not worth a moment's thought. If they had only asked me. But of course I am the interpreter. I am not a witness. There is a line and it cannot be crossed. I accept that the law requires certain immutable formalities. Still, in the more obvious cases, there should be a way to lift a finger, raise a small message flag, to warn the members, to tell them. That is the wrong road, it leads nowhere. Do not waste your time. This is a woman of the north.

But I could not and did not. Besides, the issue only emerged later in the testimony when the member exposed the depth of his doubt and disbelief and, if I may say so, his ignorance. Early in the hearing, there was no warning of future hazards on the path. The case was proceeding in a most predictable manner. In the previous few years, since the uprising, the Board had granted refuge to many political dissidents from that region. I interpreted many, many cases. The government repressions had been unusually harsh. It was often rumoured that the president resented the northern ethnicities, although his wife was from that region. The human rights documents thoroughly documented the excesses of the government. It was the usual sort of thing: arbitrary arrest, indeterminate incarceration in conditions inconsistent with international norms, execution without due judicial process. It is all such sanitized language to describe the breaking of human bodies and spirits. I suppose it is necessary to avoid appearances of bias, to serve as a neutral international authority. Still, the documentary evidence was quite clear. The police and security services were quite ruthless in suppressing any suspected political activity.

And this woman had done that, or said she had. Her name is unimportant. She was a robust woman, attractive in a large-bodied way, with a vigorous manner. She even laughed in response to one question, an open full-throated laugh, and there is very little laughter, understandably, in the hearing rooms of the Refugee Board.

She had the features of the north, a prominent nose, a certain cast to the skin, dark unruly hair, and a confident, near brazen manner. I have seen a dozen of her sisters in the market places of the northern towns. Her manner may well have been her undoing. I believe the member found her to be too confident, too lively. After the things that had been done to her, he was expecting a more diminished person, more damaged, I suppose. He did not say anything to suggest this view, but I have interpreted often for this member. He is a rather obvious person, lacking subtlety, although he attempts to hide his feelings. If he had looked more closely, he might have noticed the dark circles under her eyes and certain moments during the hearing, not when she was testifying, when she appeared distracted and inattentive.

Her story had its anomalies, of course, they always do. It was unusual for a woman of poverty to attend the university. Most of the students were men, or daughters of the urban professional classes. Her father was a small landholder. Here you would say a subsistence farmer but the historical connotation would be somewhat different in my country. Her father would have been a man without education, born onto the land in the same manner as his father and countless generations before him. The Great Emancipation of the peasant class occurred less than a century ago, although little changed in the lives of these people who were famous for their fortitude and stubbornness. They lived a hard independent life.

Despite her background, as I say, the woman attended the university, studying agronomy, again an exception for a woman, although not inconsistent with the interests of her district which was famous for its orchards and flowers. I remember a near intoxication as a young man walking the district roads in the evening, the overpowering scent of jasmine and violet, as the heat rose from the land. The air was thick with the perfumes of the fields and orchards and the sound of cicadas.

"What would you smell if you rode through the Valley of X_____ on a summer evening?" One question, if the member had doubts about her origins, one question could have answered all. It would have been so simple. No person of the district could have answered anything else. Jasmine and violet. In spring, the fruit trees, but in summer, the flowers overwhelm. I could have told him.

But the member was already building his doubts in another direction. The country documents said that only the leaders and activists within the student movement were liable for arrest, as well as those caught during the more violent demonstrations. Another document said that politics were dominated by men. All of the prominent leaders were men, both in the student movement and the separatist party. There were women who were active, but in the

background. The revolutionary movements, like the government itself, had a man's face.

I confess that my view, if I had been asked, would have been different from the member's. It was possible to see this woman as an
activist. She had a power and a confidence that communicated itself to others. She was not afraid. But I was not asked, of course.
That was not my role.

If I may point out, however, she was placed in an impossible position. In the study of psychology it is called a double bind. I believe
you would say a "no-win situation." Because of the horrendous torture, and I have not come to that yet, the member expected a diminished and defeated person and she was not that. She was too
spirited and confident for him. Yet if she had appeared as a diffident, non-aggressive person, possibly because of torture, then he
would have found her incapable of being a strong articulate political activist. But it is impossible. If she were more outspoken, she
would be less credible as a torture victim and if she were more beat-
en down, she would be less credible as a political leader. It is possible that she was both and he saw her as neither.

I suppose the root of the problem is this process of pigeonholes.
The members know so little about the countries of the claimants.
They rely on categorizations, objective knowledge, learning the names
of places and politicians, reading about social customs and practices. It is all a mass of generalizations and, of course, in a country
as large as mine, or any country, I suppose, exceptions abound. Too
often the member is putting the square-peg claimant in his round
pigeonhole. He is trying to identify someone from a cartoon, a minimal, stereotypical sketch. And now you tell me that I have become
an expert witness, instead of an interpreter. And you are correct,
naturally. It is not only the misunderstanding of language that takes
me to the edge of sanity, it is the misunderstanding of my culture,
my history, my people.

It is impossible for the member to know so much about my country. I have learned these things with my mother's milk. He hears
claims from thirty countries, none his home country.

But he relies on his book-learned information as though it were
the only measure of credibility. He has no understanding of how

little he knows. Here, I have a stark example, but first I must tell more of this woman's story. Please excuse my digressions.

She was in her second year of studies, a good student, quiet, without money or relatives. She lived at first alone and then later, in a house with other students. One of them was a leader in the student movement. He became her lover. She joined the movement, distributed pamphlets, attended meetings, became part of the executive committee. The police came looking for him after a series of unusually violent riots. They found her, not him, and took her. I will not tell you of the horrible things they did. There was a medical report, a psychologist's, not a medical doctor. I know because the lawyer asked me to interpret the report to the claimant prior to the hearing. The scars are psychological, not physical. Why is this so difficult to believe?

It is not. But it is if you view her situation through pigeonholes. Her background and gender are not correct for the university or her field of study. The sociology is wrong. Young women from the country do not live alone or in houses with men. They live with parents or other relatives. Young women are not seen alone with men. They do not take lovers. They do not join executive committees of revolutionary movements. Perhaps they would covertly distribute pamphlets. I suspect the member even believed that agronomy students do not become involved in politics. My close friend said that agronomists study cow shit instead of the horseshit of politics. He is a very clever and profane man and I apologize.

This square woman did not fit into any of the member's round pigeonholes. Unfortunately, her story was true. I am quite certain. You have an expression in English, "The exception proves the rule." Her story proved several rules.

Halfway through her testimony, it was becoming clear that the member had doubts. He began to interrupt her lawyer to ask his own questions. I observed this with some misgivings because it was already clear to me that her story was true. She was testifying about her first year at the university. Suddenly the member interrupted to ask how could she afford to go to university. I remember his question, which was most informative about his views.

"But your father is a farmer with a rather small farm. In your country, do farmers earn enough money to send their daughters to the university?"

It was a very rude question, of course, and I am sure that the member had read that the children of the wealthy and urban professional classes attended the universities, which in most cases was correct.

She replied that her father was a landholder. I used this word "landholder" for I could think of no other in English. I found it impossible to convey the sense of the word that she used. The word is peculiar to her region. It refers to a man who has a small landholding that belongs to him alone. The word came into use some hundred years ago at a time when the large estates of the north were broken up by punitive taxes and state decree. For the first time, tenant farmers, commoners without nobility, were able to own and till their own land. It is a word that grew from the blood and soil of the north. It was a powerful word that said everything about the ambition of the northern peasants to own and control their own land and, ultimately, their own destinies.

"Landholder" was a pale and tepid substitute but I could think of no other. To this day, I can think of no other. But the member was solely concerned with the size of the land, its modest dimensions and inability to support a family, let alone subsidize an education. He pursued this line of questioning for some time, focusing solely on her father's limited income and lack of education. Finally he asked, if there was only money for one, why she, instead of her older brother, had been sent to the university. Again, I am sure that he was thinking of her gender.

Her answer was striking. She said, "My father preferred me." This is, admittedly, a non-answer that she stubbornly clung to, without elaboration. It was impossible to divine the family secret that lay beneath it. Was there a disability? A family shame? It seemed obvious that she was protecting some family privacy whatever the cost. The people of the north are famous for being difficult.

These are small matters, but I mention them because they were also paths by which the member reached his conclusions. It was obvious that the member was inclined to walk in a particular direction regardless of her responses.

He was bothered by her poverty. He was bothered by her gender. He doubted that she had been a student or, if a student, a political one. I am quite certain that he saw her as a child of the urban middle class, probably from the city. Of course, this scepticism only emerged in the written decision. There were no documents proving that she was a student. The political underground had smuggled her out of the country with a false passport and a plane ticket to Canada. She had fled the country upon her interim release, without a passport, fearing rearrest. She assumed the student house had been rifled by security police. She never went back to find out. All of her roommates were in hiding or in prison. It was rumoured that her lover had fled the country. No one knew for certain.

The university was a state institution. It would not provide information about her to a foreign agency if she were truly a political dissident. Her lawyer had sent two letters without receiving a response. She had a smuggled letter from her parents that spoke of her being a student. The member pointed out that "anyone could write a letter." It had been mailed from outside of her country. Of course, for her parents, it would have been too dangerous to mail it from within the country. Everybody would know this. The human rights reports expressly mention that mail is routinely opened by the authorities. Her lawyer failed to point this out to the member.

Still, at the conclusion of her testimony, I thought there was some hope. The claimant had given a simple yet vivid description of her arrest. Perhaps my imagination is too active. During her description, I could hear the breaking of the front door below. She said it was a series of heavy muffled sounds followed by a loud bang. She was in her bedroom on the third floor, although her door was ajar. I could hear the shouts and pounding of the boots of the security police upon the stairs. There were violent sounds of breakage from the kitchen on the second floor. She heard the shout of someone below, another student, and then a scream followed by violent sounds of breakage, possibly a window.

She said her room had no window, it was a small garret room. There were loose boards in a short wall built under the roof. Her lover had spoken of converting it into an escape hatch, leading under the roof. It was one of many things he spoke of but did not do. She described her panic, of feeling trapped and hiding under her bed, of realizing it was a stupid hiding place as more shouts and screams came from below, of tearing her fingernails as she scrabbled at the loose boards to make an opening and feeling a flash of hope as she pulled a board free just before two men banged into the room. Something struck the back of her head and her next memory was in the prison.

During his cross-examination, the member asked her what the student had shouted from below and she replied, two words, "Police, run!" And to my regret, "police" is the word that I used and it was incorrect. She had used a vernacular word, probably popular with students although I have been away from my country for some time and cannot say for sure. I had thought of using the word "cops" but it did not sound right, so I said "police" and wanted to pull the word back as soon as it was out of my mouth. I had considered and rejected the word "fuzz." It has become an old-fashioned word in English. In the 1960s, they would have said "Pigs," which is a closer connotation, suggesting the social alienation of youth, but it is still not correct. "Pigs" implies uniformed policemen. The word she used refers to all police, regular and security police. In my country, security agents in civilian clothes were far more pervasive and far more feared than the regular police. These may seem to be minor nuances but they can be important, indeed, even fatal. They create unnoticed assumptions that send the questioner off in the wrong direction.

I was more satisfied with the word "run." The literal translation is "flee" but "Police, flee!" would have sounded awkward. In my language, the word is used exactly in these circumstances, it is an imperative, telling someone to escape immediately or there will be disastrous consequences. It is a word that young people would use.

Unfortunately, the member fixated on the word "police," asking if the men breaking into her room wore uniforms. The woman said that they did not. Then how did she know they were police? She became confused. I had been careful to use the same word that had been shouted from below. Now I saw that it confused her. The question did not make sense to her. I thought of explaining the ambiguity to the member. But I hesitated. It was not my role. How to explain that the member took the word "police" to imply solely uniformed police? Perhaps I could say it was a technicality of our language, not a misperception of the evidence. I was uncertain.

Before I could formulate an explanation, the member was asking another question. Why was she then so certain that the men in the room were police at all and why had the housemate from down below shouted "police" when he could not possibly know if they were police or not? How did he know they were police? She became more confused and said that she did not know.

I had hoped to explain the confusion to her in our language but the member's questions were so quick and short, there was little opportunity to add an explanation. Again, I hesitated. This is not the role of the interpreter. It is definitely against the rules. I am not supposed to add extra information in my own language. The Board member would think I was coaching her. But if I could explain to her or even to the member, explain how the secret police function and are feared in my country. It was so simple. There was no need for this confusion. And I hesitated, most understandably and unforgivably, knowing what happened. It was too late.

I thought perhaps the lawyer would understand and would clarify the evidence later. He would have an opportunity to ask more questions. The member is a stupid impatient man. Who else kicks down the door and puts you in prison besides the police? But he believed his question was more subtle – how did she and the roommate below know they were the police in that first instant of breaking in?

And the answer was because the word "police" includes, even, in these circumstances, implies, security agents in civilian clothes, and I could not, I did not, find a way to say this. In my country, the uniformed police direct the traffic. The secret police kick down the doors.

Even later I might have saved the situation, spoken to the lawyer during the coffee break. This is a violation of the rules as well. No evidence is to be discussed outside of the hearing room. But surely truth and justice were more important. Unfortunately, the lawyer had disappeared by the time I left the hearing room and he returned at the last minute, looking quite distracted. I might have spoken to the Refugee Claim Officer, asked her to speak to the member, to explain. But she was an abrupt imperious woman, unapproachable, and I did not approach. In the end, I hoped for the best, assuring myself it was a minor issue that might still be resolved.

In his written reasons, the member wrote that the woman's arrest was central to her claim and her account of the arrest was not credible. When confronted with the "blatant contradiction" of how she and her unknown housemate had assumed that strangers were "policemen" with "no other evidence than their forced entry," the claimant had given no reasonable explanation. The inevitable conclusion was "that the story had been concocted."

In an earlier part of the reasons, the member had already rejected much of the claimant's story as being "inconsistent with the country information." He did not accept that her father, "purportedly a poor farmer without obvious means," had scrimped and saved to send a daughter to the university when the average education for women was five years and "men were given preference in education and economic opportunity." He also did not accept that a young woman from the "traditional, rural regions of the country" would "act in a manner that was completely inconsistent with the social mores of the time and place." The member was careful to point out that he was making no judgment about her moral conduct, other than to note its inconsistency with "known information about her society." In conclusion, he said that "she had not satisfied the burden of proof on a balance of possibilities that she was a person who had a well-founded fear of persecution due to her political activities." Such formal and impressive language to mask such stupidities.

It is not for me to criticize our refugee system, I am only an interpreter, but I must observe that now only one member decides each claim and I wonder who will soften the views of the members who do not listen well. At one time, two members decided refugee claims. I noticed that small misunderstandings would frequently occur during the testimony on the part of one member or the other. Sometimes, the second member, not caught within the same set of false assumptions, would offer a different point of view before the misunderstanding snowballed into something larger. Often this occurred where one of the members had fixed opinions or did not listen carefully to the evidence.

I do not wish to avoid my share of the blame. I accept it, but the outcome might well have been different if a second member had been there to avoid this foolishness about policemen with or without uniforms.

Ordinarily, I would know none of this. My responsibilities end with the hearing. The final decision, unless it is given orally in the hearing room, and those are normally only the happier positive decisions, is delivered in writing weeks later. It is only for the eyes and ears of the claimant and her counsel. The interpreter rarely sees the conclusion of the play.

More than a year later, I was seated in a small café over a hot tea, sheltering from a cold and rainy November day. There was a young man sitting in a nearby booth who seemed familiar, a pale featureless face except for the oversized glasses. Ah yes, it was the young lawyer who had represented the woman and after some hesitation, I could not prevent myself from approaching to ask him about the outcome of the case. Yes, he remembered me. Yes, of course he remembered the case. He seemed curiously eager to have me join him. I was most eager myself, although fearful of the outcome.

A diffident man, more intelligent and compassionate than I had first supposed, he approached our common subject with caution. He said it had been one of his first refugee cases and his most painful. He had since gone into another area of law. Solicitor's work was more to his liking. From this I inferred bad news. I admit my hands began to tremble. He said yes, it had been a negative decision. The member had believed very little of her story, saying that she had not been a credible witness. He himself, his name was Nathan Crisco, still believed her, although he conceded that he was being perhaps a little naive. The member was very experienced.

I hastened to assure him that I too thought that she had been telling the truth, although it was not my role to draw conclusions. Her story was completely consistent with everything that I knew about the northern people. I told him there was no doubt that she was a woman of the north and I was certain that a few skilful questions could have easily confirmed that she was the daughter of a farmer and an agronomy student at the university. That part was obvious. He looked at me reproachfully. Yes, how silly of me. It was his responsibility to ask such questions. He looked away, misery overwhelming his eyes. I assured him that probably nothing could have dissuaded the member, his course was already set. It would not help this man to tell him about the confusion in interpretation. I asked if he had any recent news of her and he grew even paler, looking more miserable.

I said that it was not my place to ask but he insisted on telling me. His client had been shocked by the decision. She had cried in his office, repeatedly asking why and how it was possible. She could not understand how the member could not know that she was a student from the north of her country. She had described the arrest. He had seen her medical report.

A friend had come along to interpret and appeared equally distraught. Her own English was weak and she had difficulty understanding much of the decision. The claimant returned to his office two days later without her friend, despondent and distracted, speaking without emotion in badly broken English. He suggested an appeal. She appeared disinterested. He would represent her for free at his own expense. She reluctantly agreed but then did not appear for her appointment to review the evidence. She had no telephone. He drove by her rooming house to ask about her, but no one had seen her. Her landlord said the rent had been paid; he minded his own business. The lawyer left a note. He passed by her home twice more before the notice period for the appeal expired. Finally he decided there was nothing further that he could do.

He did not hear from his client and assumed that she had drifted into the underground economy. He had been told that the Immigration department rarely removed failed claimants, at least not for years. However, just two months ago, he had received a letter from the department saying that his client would be removed within ten days. The postmark was two weeks old. He had changed law firms and the letter had lain around for several days before a secretary had sent it on. He called the Immigration enforcement office to find that she had been put on a plane to her country two days before.

The immigration officer said the removal had been "one of the simple ones." She had not changed residence and was working for a local janitorial service. Attempting to be kind, he told Nathan that she had made no objection to her removal, that she appeared disinterested. In his experience, that was a sign that it "had been a phoney claim from the start."

Nathan rummaged around in his briefcase before pulling out a notepad. Here, he said, I still have it. I wrote down his words. They were probably said with the best of intentions, he said bitterly. Here is what he wrote.

"They go kicking and screaming if there is a ghost of a chance of being persecuted. This one was a piece of cake. Don't worry about it. Besides, she was such a quiet, mousy thing. You just can't see her as some political radical. Believe me. I read the file. This one was a no-brainer."

He said with some bitterness, "Quiet and mousy, he found her to be quiet and mousy."

There was little I could say. I wanted to confess, to share my own burden, possibly ease his guilt. It would not have been a kindness. I half-heartedly repeated my earlier assurance that little would have dissuaded the member, knowing it to be a half-truth. I soon mumbled my goodbyes, pleading another engagement. Nathan offered to send me a copy of the member's reasons and I felt compelled to accept, although I knew the reading would be unpleasant. We exchanged business cards, promising to inform the other if we heard any news. I received the reasons within a few days but have not seen him since.

The reasons became an obsession. I pored over every word. They were written with a cool legalistic logic that would be impermeable to judicial review unless one understood the gross misinterpretation of the evidence. It all sounded so reasonable. The passion of the young woman, her brave manner, her strong hands, the smell of jasmine and violets, her broken fingernails, they had all evaporated. These were not the facts upon which the legal conclusions had been based.

For some time after that, I slept badly, constantly waking from a dream, a nightmare really. I was sitting next to the young woman in a dark room. There was someone else in the room, a dark presence, unseen, something cold and indifferent but not hostile, not threatening. The young woman is looking at me expectantly. I am opening my mouth but nothing is coming out, my mouth moves without words and the woman is looking at me sorrowfully as she fades back into the darkness.

These symptoms did not last for too long a period. Time is the great imperfect healer. I took more exercise and the occasional sleeping tablet. I stopped taking refugee cases. My career had already evolved to more prestigious work and I soon accepted a full-time position with the Department of Foreign Affairs. I travelled a great deal and thought of her rarely.

And then two years ago, I was assigned to accompany the Minister to my home country, a place I had not visited in nearly twenty years. I felt some trepidation, having originally left to avoid my own uncomfortable relations with the security police. But my country had changed in the past dozen years. The state was less coercive and more respectful of human rights, at least in law and appearance, if not in practice. And I was travelling with a Canadian diplomatic mission so there were few concerns for my safety.

The diplomatic mission included a conference in the largest city in the north, less than a hundred kilometres from the Valley of X_____. It was also the home of the state university. After the conference, I unexpectedly received a free day. The Minister would be staying at the home of an old friend and colleague who spoke fluent English. I took the morning to visit the registrar's office at the university. I knew and feared what I might do. It was something more than impulse. I said that I was looking for the niece of a friend who had once been a student. An abrupt indifferent clerk instructed me to write the name on a piece of paper along with additional academic information, if known. Twice I almost left, fearing that the clerk, or her superior, would call the security police. This was still not a country of significant freedoms. My arrest would cause a small diplomatic stir but I was also a citizen of this country. Under their law, they still owned me, despite my Canadian citizenship.

Suddenly the clerk gestured for me to come to the counter. The walls of the registry office were bare except for a faded photograph of the president. She read from scribbled notes that she was careful not to show me. The woman had attended the university as an agronomy student. She did not complete her second year. Addresses were only available to state authorities. I thanked her for her trouble and left.

Now acting on pure impulse, although I knew there was little choice, I rented a car, which was a great extravagance in that country, even allowing for the devalued currency. It was my intention to drive to the Valley of X_____ to learn what I could of the woman's family. Perhaps the first flowers would be in bloom but it proved to be a chilly day in early spring. The buds on the branches of the trees and bushes were hard and tight, without a hint of opening. There was no perfume in the air. A woman in a roadside shop explained that it was a late spring, as she directed me to the far end of the valley where people of the woman's family name lived.

The sideroads were unpaved but dry. It would not be unusual to stop and ask my way of roadside pedestrians. Asking the local police would be unwise for me and possibly the woman, if she was alive. Despite my fluency, my accent marked me as a man of the south, a man with a shiny new car and Western clothes.

Twice I was misdirected to the wrong road but I made progress, moving to the upper slopes of the north end of the valley, the poorer land, where the houses were not so well kept and the parcels of land were smaller, divided by low stone walls, stones pulled from the fields by human hands over many generations. Finally, I stopped beside a woman leading a cow who seemed pleased to pause and rest. The cow began to graze on the sparse grass in the ditch. Yes, she knew all of the families in the area. She had lived all of her life on her land. She gave me a sharp, inquisitive look when I told her the name of the family before she pointed to a dilapidated house partway up the slope. That was the family home she said, but it is now abandoned.

For how long? I asked. For some time now. She used an expression that would have been rude in the city, suggesting that it was none of my business. I knew that here it simply expressed an inherent suspicion of strangers. Still, she seemed to be uncomfortable with my questions. Finally, I asked about the claimant directly. What of her? Was she with the family? The woman shot me a more direct and suspicious look. She knew nothing of these things. These were private matters. As she spoke she was already taking up the rope halter of the cow, prodding it out of the ditch with her walking stick. Our interview was terminated.

After a few metres, she turned to say that the family was no longer in the region and these were not questions to be asked by strangers. She turned and moved on as the cow raised her tail to propel a stream of green excrement onto the road, and I thought of my friend and the difference between cow manure and horse manure. I watched the steam rise from the warm green puddle, heavy with its own odour, watched it rise and dissipate into the cool odourless spring air of this valley of flowers, and I suddenly experienced the most desolate, unbearable sadness for this young confident woman with the unruly hair who had been broken and destroyed, not only by them but by us, by me. I looked up to the abandoned family home with its sagging roof and broken tiles and knew there was no point in going further.

So you see, I am no longer a go-between. I cannot convey the messages, cannot bear the weight of misunderstanding, and I desperately wish for a world with better endings. But I must of course earn a living, so I still do translations. Here is my card. I charge fifty dollars a page, which I believe is quite a modest fee.

14

LOOKING FOR THE LITTLE THINGS

For Lisa Gilad

IT WAS A COLD RAIN. Too cold for early November in the opinion of Hester Laframboise. Her opinions usually counted for something but not in this case. The wind was pulling her umbrella off to the side as she hurried across the street. It was difficult to manage the umbrella, her briefcase, and the armful of books. The books all pertained to homosexuality, a topic that had consumed her interest for the entire weekend. The wind cut through her thin cloth coat and she acknowledged with her usual clarity that she had misjudged the season.

Thank God the building superintendent was more attuned to the time of year. Or maybe it was the building computer, whatever, she appreciated the warm office that awaited her on the ninth floor of the Immigration and Refugee Board. She was met by her secretary, France, who should now be referred to as a Case Management Officer, a CMO. It was not an attractive acronym, but she would work on it. All in all she approved of the change. The class and gender undertones of "secretary" could not be ignored. A perfectly good word in its original sense, someone who could share a secret, an educated person who could write your personal letters while maintaining a discrete confidentiality; all of that ruined by the technology of the typewriter and the office abuses of the twentieth century. Case Management Officer was functional, although inelegant. The real secret of her preference lay in the quiet disappearance of the possessive pronoun. *My* secretary had become *the* CMO. Hester had never liked possessive adjectives used in reference to other people, except for family – that was different. Usually she bypassed all that nonsense by using first names and demanding them in response. She was the only Board member to be called by her first name. It was one of her many secret vanities.

"Good morning, France."

"Good morning, Hester. The *Globe* is on your desk but I'm afraid it's wet. Here, let me take some of those books." She was used to seeing Hester overburdened with armloads of books and documents. "The Earl will be here in two minutes."

The Earl was Earl Grey tea, one of the many private jokes that France shared with Hester. In a way she was a secret sharer. Hester immediately began to scan the front page of the *Globe* while taking off her coat. Yesterday's news from Eastern Europe or the Middle East might shift the possibilities of persecution in any one of a dozen refugee claims on her docket. The majority of Board members relied on the documentary information filed by the Refugee Claim Officer or the claimant's lawyer. If the lawyer couldn't be bothered to find the information, why should they? As with many issues, Hester held a contrary view. If the refugee definition required her to assess the likelihood of the claimant's being persecuted upon his return to his home country, then today's news was relevant to that determination. As John Morton once noted to many guffaws in her absence, only logic was on her side.

John Morton arrived with the Earl, following France through her office door. "Hester, don't you realize that it is politically incorrect to be served coffee by your CMO?" Morton was a fellow Board member, an endlessly jocular man. He claimed that he seldom said what he meant and never meant what he said. Hester suspected the comment was warmed-over Oscar Wilde. She found Morton to be facetious and superficial, qualities attractive in a dinner companion but lethal for a Board member.

"France is not *my* CMO, she is her own CMO. Besides, it's tea, not coffee, and it's friendship, not service." France gave her a conspiratorial smile and departed without making any offers of service or friendship to Morton, who plunked himself down heavily in Hester's large leather visitor's chair. She had brought it from home; she liked her visitors to be relaxed. The men visitors in particular liked to sink back into the deep leather cushioning, failing either to notice or care about the vulnerable position it left them in. She found them to be less alert and less aggressive in semirecline, and more manageable.

As usual she got right to the point. "Have you read the documents for today's case?"

Morton was rarely intimidated by her directness, although others were. "Not really, I glanced through the obviously relevant ones but I didn't bother to go through all of the nonsense about the parliament. It changes on a daily basis. The same for economic conditions, Mother Russia's cupboard is bare and Yeltsin doesn't have any answers. It's old news and bad news for Jews. The Semite as scapegoat. But of course that's not relevant to today's case." He hastily added the last comment as assurance that he had at least read the claimant's personal information form. This was not a Jewish claim.

Hester was careful not to give any sign of impatience; indeed she felt little. She no longer expected all of her colleagues to do their homework, especially Morton, and she didn't mind as long as they deferred to her better-informed opinion.

"Well, this is a little different than the typical anti-Semitism case. We still don't have a lot of documentary material on sexual orientation in post-Soviet Russia yet, just that affidavit from the woman in San Francisco, the Pink Book, and the Helsinki Watch material."

"I can't help noting that there isn't a whisper from Amnesty International. It tends to make one wonder. If Amnesty hasn't perceived any abuses, perhaps things aren't so bad for the gays as this woman makes out in her affidavit. After all, she's gay herself. Perhaps a medium-sized grain of salt is in order."

As usual her first impulse was to squash the inanities that littered the minds of too many of her colleagues. Yes of course the expert was gay. Who else was doing anything on the persecution of homosexuals? Who did the first detailed reporting on anti-Semitism as the Iron Curtain rusted and fell? The American Jewish Congress, B'nai Brith, Bill Cohen's group out of Colorado. No one challenged the reports of persecution of Christians from the various Christian churches in China. How was it different? She did wonder why Amnesty hadn't mentioned the persecution of gays; certainly there was no doubt about the horrific abuses of gay prisoners, but then again, she knew that Amnesty had its hobby horses and blind spots just like any other organization. They weren't the be-all and end-all.

"Tell you what. Let's hear the testimony and see if it accords with the documentary information we do have. The few sources sound authorative and do confirm some level of discrimination against homosexuals. Besides, we haven't tested the credibility of his story. There were a lot of beatings. Let's start with some of the key incidents, like the first big incident in the school, to see if he's credible. Then we could go to the sexual orientation or have the RCO test some of the weak points in the story. I'm really bothered by the fact that he made a complaint to the police, knowing what could happen to him. Are you comfortable with that as a starting point?"

"Impeccably, fearless leader. You are the Great Navigator and I shall follow modestly in your wake."

As the presiding member, it was Hester's job to define the issues and preside over the hearing. She would also have to write the decision if it were negative. Behind the veils of verbiage, John Morton always understood where his self-interest lay and would seldom pursue a disagreement with a colleague unless he were pushed. Dissenting decisions had to be written by both members, so there were few dissents when John was the second member. Hester thought him affable and lazy.

The rain was driving harder now against the office window. She thought of offering Morton a cup of tea but the hearing was due to start in ten minutes. He would take it as an invitation to reminisce and she'd never get him into the hearing room on time. Morton was famous for his indifference to punctuality. A former Conservative Member of Parliament and perennial backbencher, Morton had passed the latter half of his career in endless, meaningless discussions with constituents and colleagues once he had been passed over too many times for a cabinet post. He had lost the habit of meaningful speech and often announced that he preferred wit to wisdom, although both had been in short supply in the halls of Parliament.

"Two minutes; shall we go?" She was already rising and gathering her documents. "We have inexperienced counsel, someone named Lawrence Curdley, so I expect the direct examination to take a little longer. I just hope he isn't going to repeat everything in the PIF."

Morton rose gracefully to follow. "Oh how I detest lengthy rep-
etitions of the PIF. Almost as much as I detest the use of the
acronym itself." He sailed through the door, obviously pleased with
his bon mot.

The normal practice was for all parties to be seated in the hearing room in order for them to rise in unison as the members entered
through a separate door, in the manner of judges. The Board administration believed that a formal entrance set a serious tone for the
hearing and established the authority of the members. Hester preferred to be seated before the claimants entered so that she could catch
that first unguarded glimpse of the claimant as they entered the
room. She believed she got a better look at exactly who the person
was. She used it as a kind of before-and-after photograph to compare to the face or mask that presented itself during the testimony.

The claimant was a surprisingly tall, shambling man with unruly
hair, a large nose, heavy eyebrows, and a face that was closed to the
world. Not at all what she had expected. After all, he'd been beat-
en up several times. This man had the size to be physically imposing, although he sat with hunched shoulders, drawn into himself.
That could be an act. She glanced over at Morton to assess his reaction but found him fiddling with a button on his vest. John Morton was far and away the best-dressed member on the Board, man
or woman. It was rumoured that all of his suits were custom made
by a loyal Conservative tailor from his former riding.

Mischievously she passed her first note of the day. She was renowned for bombarding her second member with little yellow Post-
it notes during the hearing. She believed that whispering into the
ear of a colleague intimidated and distracted the witness. This one
read: *What do you think so far?* Morton scribbled back: *Which one
is the claimant?*

It was true that the lawyer's shirt and suit looked as though it
had been purchased from the same second-hand store as the
claimant's. He was unpacking his files from a frayed briefcase at
the interpreter's seat next to his client. Hester gently indicated
that the claimant's counsel should sit at the table to her left,
kitty-corner to his client, who sat facing the panel members. The
lawyer sat opposite the Refugee Claim Officer, who was there to
assist the members.

"Mr Curdly, is this your first case before the Board?"

"Yes, yes it is." He was placing papers in disorganized piles that suggested he was either ill prepared or nervous, and possibly both.

"By way of advice, may I suggest that you stick to the issues indicated in the disclosure letter. We do not need to hear a repetition of information in the claimant's narrative. We would like to complete the testimony well before the noon hour. Also make sure you allow the interpreter sufficient time to interpret your questions and comments. Some counsel tend to run on. Please do not do that."

Curdley nodded vigorously. "Of course. I will limit my questions to the relevant issues, Madam Presiding Member."

She detested that appellation. Madam Chairperson wasn't much better. She wasn't a lawyer herself and had never adjusted to the lawyer's penchant for bowing and scraping, which was unnecessarily sycophantic. She supposed they got it from court, this excessive deference, "Yes your Honour, If it please your Lordship." She saw it all as a kind of courtly priestcraft that did nothing but lengthen the proceedings and possibly impress a gullible claimant, although in her view, it was more likely to scare the pants off the poor fellow. She was interested in facts, not fancy posturing. She also wondered how "Madame Chairperson" would sound in Russian. A Somali interpreter had confessed to her once that he had interpreted her title as Big Lady.

Hester briskly went about the business of opening the hearing, introducing the parties, entering the written documents as exhibits, defining the issues. The claimant sat silently, disclosing nothing other than incomprehension. She completed the formalities as succinctly as possible. Many members would dally over the procedural niceties as would the lawyers, which caused her no end of irritation. More priestcraft. The formalities were mainly for the record, to satisfy the procedural requirements of the Federal Court. Claimants rarely understood the legal folderol and in her view it simply confused and alienated them, a poor way to begin a process where the claimant, not the members, was truly the star performer, the primary, and usually the only, witness.

Finally she asked the claimant to take an oath to tell the truth, the whole truth, and nothing but the truth. At one time she had closely watched the eyes and body language of claimants during the recitation of the oath but had finally given up, finding no correlation between a claimant's manner and the subsequent credibility of his or her story. Some of the most shifty-eyed oath takers had the most compelling stories and vice versa. Some showed their pain, at times openly displaying it like a beggar showing his stump in the street. Others hid everything and there was no way of knowing whether it was from a fear of authority, particularly her, or fear of being exposed as a fraud. She believed most claimants were frightened, although in appearance they ranged from manifest anxiety to a frozen rigidity. She did her best to help them relax, to reassure them that she was there to listen to their story, to communicate. Possibly a few even believed her.

"Mr Petrovich, please listen carefully to the questions and try to give a precise answer. If you do not understand a question, please say so." She paused between each short sentence to allow the Russian interpreter time to interpret, establishing a rhythm for the others to follow. "If you don't know the answer to a question, please say so. Please do not guess. You have just taken an oath to tell the truth. It is important that you tell the truth as you understand it."

The claimant nodded slowly after each instruction. Hester knew that many claimants were so desperate to give an answer to please the "judge" that any answer was better than no answer. It was particularly a problem for anyone coming from a harsh totalitarian regime, anyone who had been raised to please authority. The right answer was the one the interrogator thought was correct. Truth had nothing to do with it. It wasn't a question of lying, it was an overwhelming need to tell the questioner what he or she wanted to hear.

"And finally, please try to relax. Have some water whenever you need it." She indicated the water jug and glasses near the claimant. Invariably they poured and took a sip. Water had a certain universality and offering it suggested a small measure of hospitality. Some members disliked making any humane gesture, as though it exposed a weakness to be somehow abused by the false claimant, the dissembler. In Hester's view, kindness did not subvert her neutrality.

"We understand that this hearing is very important for you and that you are feeling anxious. Just try to listen carefully to the questions and answer as best you can."

Other than a slight nod and a glint of understanding in his eyes, there was no acknowledgment from the claimant. His eyes were deep-set, lost in the shadow of the overhanging brow. There were days when Hester wondered if she was wasting her breath and should just get on with it. Except with obviously frightened women. For them she would always take her time, softening her voice, and perhaps that was a form of sexism. Oh well.

"Counsel, it's your witness. We have the passport and identity documents so you need not take too much time on identity. Let's get to the incident at the school as soon as possible."

"Thank you, Madam Chairperson." The lawyer appeared nervous. He was still shuffling papers when he turned to his client. "Mr Petrovich, did you leave Russia because you are gay?"

Morton made a rumbling sound beside her. Reluctantly, Hester stepped in before the claimant could answer. She hated being intrusive so early in the testimony.

"Mr Curdly, this examination will go much more smoothly if you listen to my instructions and if you do not lead the witness. At this point you have not established that your client, sorry, Mr Petrovich, is gay. If I may offer as an example, 'Mr Petrovich, do you have a preference in the gender of your sexual partners, and if so, what is it?'" She silently cursed herself for being unnecessarily didactic even as the words came out of her mouth.

After the interpretation of her question, the claimant responded with a lengthy utterance in Russian. The interpreter, a brittle well-dressed woman, said, "He says that he is gay."

Hester sighed. It was going to be a long day. "Ms Alexandrova, it's important that you interpret literally everything the claimant says. Also, in the first person, in his exact words. Please refrain from editing. If the claimant's utterances are confusing, we will ask for clarification."

The interpreter nodded. "I understand, Madam President. He said, 'I don't know what she wants, my lawyer already asked me, tell her that I am gay."

Hester sighed inwardly. "Thank you, Ms Alexandrova. Mr Petrovich, please try to speak directly to me although you are speaking through the interpreter. It is Mr Morton and myself who must decide whether or not you are a refugee."

With the slightest of nods, the claimant mumbled something in Russian that the interpreter did not bother to interpret. Hester sighed again. It was definitely going to be a long day. The story was complicated enough without the impediments of a balky interpreter and an inexperienced lawyer. This large man in front of her claimed to be a mechanic and a homosexual. If true, his life had been a miserable one, hiding his sexuality from family, friends, and classmates as a youth, believing it to be an illness that he could not overcome, and finally surrendering to a seduction during a drunken student party at college, a polytechnical institute. He had been studying to be an engineer until caught in the dormitory with his seducer, who had become his lover. Both boys, young men really, had been discovered and beaten by their fellow students, both had been hospitalized. The claimant, his first name was Vasily, had pissed blood for a week; his partner had a broken nose and smashed eye socket. In one sense, it was a pity for the claimant that only his partner's body would bear any evidence of the beating. Hester always appreciated the objective certainty of a doctor's report; an x-ray of the smashed nose and socket would have been a refreshing certainty.

The partner had disappeared after his release from hospital. Both had been expelled from the institute for immoral conduct. Vasily had been called to the director's office to receive his documents and had been told he was lucky to escape with a beating. Sodomy was a crime as well as a sickness. If he hadn't been such a good student, the director would have reported the incident to the police. The director said he had a sickness but did not deserve the hell he would experience as a homosexual in prison. He had been a good student, he should mend his ways, although the director could never recommend him to another school.

Vasily returned to his home where his father beat him again, and he remained in his room for half a year. Former friends and strangers taunted him in the street, his family were ashamed, he was taken to doctors who understood nothing. Finally he left home for Leningrad, to lose himself in the city and find work as an industrial mechanic. He was fortunate, the director had made no entry in his student book, which had to be shown to the employer along with the internal passport. For a year he was safe, except that he was haunted by his feelings for other men.

Eventually he met a man and another and slipped into a downward spiral of covert meetings in alleyways, private rooms, once the apartment of a wealthy man where the other tenants did not seem to care. There were rumours, accusations by fellow workers and landlords, beatings, new jobs, new towns, entries in his work book, and more serious beatings, until he feared imprisonment and bribed the administrator of a fishing company to put him on a boat as a diesel mechanic, a boat travelling to international waters. Gay friends had said that the West accepted homosexuals. He hoped to go to England or to America, but his boat had gone north and he had jumped ship in St John's, Newfoundland, when they had come in for repairs.

On the surface the story made sense but there were gaps and nagging inconsistencies. He and a friend had twice complained to the police about beatings at a time when sodomy was illegal and the police had no respect for the civil rights of citizens. Suspicion was sufficient cause for detention and abuse. Gays, Jews, blacks, political dissidents, the deviant underbelly of Soviet society did not seek protection from the state. As well, it was not easy to find work with the international fleet. Everyone wanted the opportunity to return home with Western loot: blue jeans, boom boxes, Calvin Klein. How did a transient disaffected worker obtain such a privileged position? The fishing boat had stopped twice at Iceland: why hadn't the claimant left the boat at that time?

And then there was his size, Hester was still having trouble fitting the picture of this large man into the image of someone who was afraid of his fellow workers and skulked about the halls of his building fearing physical confrontation. Also he didn't look gay, not in any of the ways she understood, although the literature of the weekend had educated her on that point. Gays came in all shapes and sizes, eluding the stereotypes as often as matching them. It was territory as foreign as village culture in the Congo.

On the other hand, Hester wondered, who could dream up such a story if it were not true? He certainly didn't appear to have the demeanour or quickness of intelligence to create and carry off such an outrageous story. Did he buy it in some black market? Had someone written it and coached him in what to say? There were organizations in Moscow and Montreal that sold that kind of thing, all the elements of a false claim, phoney travel documents, a customized story with falsified evidence to prove it, instructions on what to say at the border, what to expect at the hearing. The rumours constantly floated through the Board about the invidious efficiency of Russian and Iranian passeurs. Smugglers. For some reason everyone used the French word. The passeurs knew everything: Board regulations, Board decisions, acceptance rates in the different regional offices. They got it off the Internet, they collected successful PIFs, they talked to the interpreters. Apocryphal stories circulated: a planeload of Iranians was intercepted with prepared PIFs in their luggage, a bound book of PIF narratives in Russian could be purchased in Montreal, a Refugee Claim Officer had been compromised in Toronto. Rarely were the stories confirmed in any concrete way.

Hester wasn't persuaded. Sure, documents were falsified and there was a brisk market in PIFs from previously successful claims, but there was little attempt to tailor the fabricated stories to particular claimants or to prepare them for the hearing room. So many were caught out because of outlandish stories that did not fit the claimant. Hester believed she could use reason, knowledge, and intuition to drill through the claimant's story. With patience and the right questions, you could discover the truth. Most often truth was discovered in the details, the small facts surrounding the large event. Small facts spontaneously rendered, that could not be prepared in advance. You had to look for the little things. She had to believe that, otherwise she would be the fraud, supplanting her reality for theirs. With effort, it was possible to separate fact from fiction. That was her job and it was worth the fight for the sake of the genuine claimants, who, in her opinion, were still in the majority.

"It was bad, very bad. I did not think they would do this thing to me. It was a big surprise." The words were uttered in the high, slightly nasal voice of the interpreter, Ms Alexandrova. Moments before Vasily had been shaking his large head while speaking in Russian but now he sat still as a stone during the interpretation. Hester had long ago accustomed herself to the out-of-synch quality of interpreted testimony. She had learned to carefully observe the body language of the claimant, knowing she would have to link it to the words that would only become meaningful several seconds later. It was a trick, a knack. Occasionally, with excellent interpreters and demonstrative witnesses, the unconscious splicing of sight and sound would create the illusion of simultaneous testimony, a synchronicity of word and gesture, the illusion of moving pictures.

That would not occur today. The dissonance between the mumble of soft-spoken Russian offered by the taciturn claimant and the brittle inflected English of Ms Alexandrova was jarring. Hester shook her head inwardly, thinking of the recent pronouncement by a prominent Federal Court judge on the importance of demeanour in assessing the credibility of witnesses. How could she assess demeanour with a thirty-second sound delay? What the hell did the judge know anyway? He only spoke with lawyers. He'd probably never met a real live claimant.

"I have these feelings about men that I cannot hide." It was almost funny watching the words come out of the mouth of Ms Alexandrova, like hearing the testimony of a ventriloquist's dummy. Vasily was describing his first encounter with his lover at the technical school. The description was sparse, a lean recounting that closely followed the written narrative in the PIF, offering none of the small enriching details that might suggest the story was true.

The lawyer, Curdley, was of little assistance. His primary means of questioning appeared to involve asking, "and then what happened?" giving no shape or direction to his client's testimony. Hester decided to shake the tree a bit to see if there really were apples up there.

"Mr Petrovich, I believe you said that some students came into the dormitory when you were with your lover, is that correct?"

The big head swung around towards her from the point on the lawyer's desk where his gaze had been fixed. Swinging as smoothly as an artillery gun, she thought, coming to bear on its target. It was difficult to see the eyes under the shaggy overhanging brow. Not his fault, she thought, overhead lighting.

"Yes."

"How many were there? How many students in the group?"

"Five."

"So tell me what happened. These five students enter the dormitory, you are with your lover. Tell me what happened. Tell me the details and take your time."

"We were surprised. We were not expecting that people would be coming. They spoke to us in a very harsh manner. I tried to respond but they did not want to listen. Then they beat us."

Hester was careful not to disclose any twinges of impatience. "Yes, I understand. That information is already in your PIF, your personal information form, but now I would like to hear more details. For example, what were your emotional reactions?" Perhaps she could nudge him along here without telling him what to say.

"My emotions were very strong. At first I was surprised and then I was afraid after they began to strike us."

Hester waited. Vasily looked straight ahead at the space between Hester and Morton. "Mr Petrovich, I don't want to put words in your mouth but it would be most helpful if you could provide us with more details about the beating." Even as the words came out of her own mouth she was wondering how the interpreter would handle that expression. A literal translation could be disastrous. Putting words in your mouth. How would that sound in Russian? What would it suggest?

A strained look passed over the claimant's face. He stared down at his lap, his hair falling further over his face. Finally he looked up, pushing the hair away from his eyes, and murmured a brief response. The interpreter had to lean forward to catch all of the words. Had she seen a flash of pain in those dark eyes? There was something, the merest glimpse before his hair fell back over his brow. She had seen something, pain, possibly fear, but real, the briefest opening of a curtain.

"I do not know what else to say. There were some students who shouted at us. I was very afraid and then they beat on us. What else do you wish me to tell you?"

Hester could think of a dozen things to say, if she had been there, if the experience had happened. The names of the assailants, who did the talking, who led the attack, who hung back, who was a friend or acquaintance, details of the beating, did they have any clothes on, how did they get to the hospital? So much could be said. She already knew that the experience of living an event was the richest source of detail, the little things you wouldn't think of unless you had lived them, the little things that were the wellsprings of life and memory, the little things you could not make up, not unless you were a brilliant method actor with a great imagination. Most liars had to work within a plot line, they couldn't relive the experience during the telling of it, they could only remember concocted facts.

She also knew that some witnesses could not tell their story, even if it were true. Their memories survived in a barren landscape, either because of trauma or because of an unconsciously cultivated ignorance, the sensory receptors long ago turned off from years of suffering, both physical and psychological. Others were simply inarticulate, either because they were frozen with fear at the prospect of being sent back to their country or because they were simply overwhelmed by the gap between the question and the answer, the dark chasm that lay between themselves and the white English judges who wanted so much information on the paper about things that were not important and then asked the same questions as though they had not read the paper; judges who knew nothing of their country except what was written in thick documents that did not truly tell about the country either. Hester knew the gap was sometimes too wide and so the claimant would not even attempt to leap it, balking with the animal certainty of a horse confronted with a jump he knows to be too far.

The good lawyers and good Board members understood these things and knew ways to build bridges or to find departure points from which frightened or paralysed claimants could leap the gap. Hester prided herself on her ability to find departure points that worked, images and metaphors that made sense to the claimant. She also knew she could not make it too easy for the dissembler to trip lightly across a bridge of her making. In this case, the claimant had failed to jump, quite possibly because the story was false. For the moment she would leave a huge question mark beside the incident and look for other opportunities later in the testimony. But she wondered about that flash of pain. What was he hiding?

"Counsel, let's move along."

The lawyer looked up abruptly from shuffling papers. Had he even been following the testimony? It was bad enough that he was inexperienced, he also seemed ill prepared, as though he had not clearly thought through the issues in the claim, had not clearly considered what evidence was critical to proving the claim. Bad lawyering. Hester detested it. How could they take the money and not even try to do the job? These were people's lives, for God's sake.

"Thank you, Madam Chairperson. Where would you like me to resume?"

Hester made a noise in the back of her throat. Even Morton stirred uneasily, shifting his weight from one haunch to the other.

"The hospital, it would be helpful to hear about the events at the hospital, Mr Curdley, the extent of his injuries and what efforts he made to seek state protection, if any."

By mid-morning they had made little progress, having sat through sparse recountings of Vasily's treatment at the hospital, dismissal from the school, and six months of shame in the family home. The high points of the morning's testimony were "My father was unhappy" and "My mother would not look in my face." Even Morton made an effort to elicit spontaneous information about the school director. Hester's only note read *Slim pickings*. Morton's scrawled response was *A country and western singer who knew more about homosexuality than this fellow*. Hester crumpled up the note and called a mid-morning break. Maybe the Earl would have some ideas.

The weather had progressed as little as she had. The hot tea was a comfort as she watched the gusts of wind-rain pummel the floor-length window of her office. The neighbouring office towers were blurred and distorted by the rain that smeared her window. Was that how it was with the claimant? Was it her window that caused the distortion? An exaggerated metaphor that didn't work. She had no gusty interior emotions at the moment. This fellow wasn't giving them anything. Nothing. He was shut down and she couldn't find a way to pry him open. She also couldn't pick up any hint of homosexuality, not a whiff. Not that she would know. She had to be honest. Apart from the weekend's reading, her only knowledge of gay culture came from books, movies, magazines. Stereotypes, media stereotypes. She knew less than zilch, as her daughter would put it. She could think of three former colleagues who were gay, all from the university. Two were women, both married, who had both cut their hair and discovered each other after lengthy divorces. Hester had always suspected that feminist politics drove the attraction more than sexuality, but the perception was unkind, she thought, and probably an indication of her own insensitivity. How about denial? Forget it. That was predictable and excessively self-indulgent. This wasn't about her. She had a comfortable if unspectacular marriage. Her husband was as comfortable as this reading chair.

Her third colleague, a close friend, had been gay for years. She almost spilled her tea barking out the laugh that followed the thought. It was such thinking that caused her to be sceptical about her own perceptions. If she still saw homosexuality as some kind of overlay, some kind of add-on to one's essential personality, she still didn't get it. Not as bad as the school director seeing it as a mental disease but also not taking it seriously as someone's innate and innocent sexuality, hardwired for a different form of human bonding. She had come of age in the age of permissiveness, different strokes for different folks, but she still didn't get it. Not really. She would have to watch herself very carefully.

She would also have to watch John Morton, who had dropped two mildly gay jokes on the doorstep of her office before wandering off for coffee. They lingered in the office like two slightly malodorous farts. The metaphor made her feel a bit better. She had always thought John Morton was full of hot air but not of that variety. Certainly neither of them were bringing to this claim the kind of instant empathy they both felt for the elderly Jewish cases from the former Soviet Union. They would both have to be watched.

"Mr Curdley, how do you intend to prove your client's sexual orientation? You are aware that it is an essential element in establishing your client's claim?"

They were off the record in a mid-hearing conference, the claimant and interpreter outside the hearing room. Since the break they had proceeded through two job losses for immoral conduct and one beating at the hands of fellow tenants. The testimony rarely strayed from the written narrative in the PIF. Hester had attempted two more interventions with little success. The claimant had not complained to the police. He had simply accompanied his partner who had made the complaint. Allegedly they had filled out a written complaint without incident. There had been no follow-up investigation and no problems with the police. Yes, the police were a problem for gays and he had no explanation for why his partner had made the complaint. He also had no explanation for not seeking asylum in Iceland. He did not think about leaving the ship in Iceland because he "did not know about that place." He had been told about Canada.

Hester had decided to switch tacks and come at the problem from another direction. If they could establish that the claimant was homosexual, they need not focus quite so much on the separate incidents of alleged persecution. She already believed that if the claimant were gay and working class in Russia, his life would be a misery. The documents were fairly clear on that point. She wasn't sure if Morton would be prepared to go that far but it would be ir-relevant if they weren't persuaded of the claimant's sexual orien-tation. She knew it was a slightly desperate tactic. If the fellow couldn't describe the acts of persecution, how would he be able to talk about his own sexual propensities, particularly if overburdened by a history of profound social stigma? Well, maybe she would look for that, shame or some sign that he had struggled with social and emotional barriers. Whatever. It would certainly have to be better than "My father was angry and I was unhappy."

The lawyer, Curdley, suddenly looked smug. "I have a witness, Madam Chairperson. He is a Canadian citizen and can attest to the claimant's homosexuality."

Again Hester made a low growl as though clearing her throat. "Mr Curdley, I don't like surprises. You should have informed us of any witnesses well before the hearing and should also have pro-vided an affidavit summarizing the content of his testimony." She paused to glance at Morton, who nodded in agreement

"Well, the witness is here, Madam Chair, and his testimony is es-sential to proving the claim. What else can I say?"

"An apology would be a good start, Mr Curdley."

She hadn't intended to be so curt but this lawyer appeared im-mune to her reprimand. She had expected some hint of chagrin or apology. He didn't seem to understand that members prepared for hearings by framing out the available evidence and narrowing the issues. It was difficult enough to compress all the testimony into three hours without last-minute witnesses. Or perhaps he just did-n't care. Perhaps she had underestimated him. He already knew they would have to hear the witness. The claimant's sexual orien-tation was critical. Morally, they could not refuse to hear essential

evidence because a lawyer did not comply with the rules of procedure. This wasn't a property tax issue over a few dollars. She might
have to adjourn the case and wait for the affidavit. She sent a quick
note to Morton. *Do you have an afternoon case?*

Morton took some time drafting his reply, using an expensive-
looking pen that he touched frequently to his lips. Hester ignored
the lawyer. Let him fidget. He had no right to be so cocky. She was
certain that the witness would be a gay Canadian, probably here to
say that he and the claimant were lovers, and Curdley assumed that
such testimony would make his case. That would explain the lack
of preparation. Well, the little twerp had a few things to learn. She
could feel her irritation rising like a flush along the side of her neck.

Morton's note read: *This is most inconvenient. I do not have a
hearing but do have a private appointment at 3:00 P.M. What are
the alternatives?*

He knew damn well what the "alternatives" were: an adjournment. Which would not faze John Morton in the least. He was renowned for leaving a trail of adjourned cases throughout the hearing
schedule. Often the continuation did not occur for two or three
months, at which point all the freshness of the testimony was lost.
It was like starting the claim over again. A private appointment
indeed. Probably his barber or accountant. Adjournments. Unfin-
ished business. Hester hated them. She was not going to let Morton
off so easily. There had to be a way at least to hear the corroboration witness. If his testimony was convincing it might not be necessary to hear anything else.

*Can we compromise? A short and early lunch then hear the
claimant and witness on his sexual activity in Canada? We should
be able to get it all in before 3:00.*

*Not an appetizing thought either before or after lunch but I sup-
pose your suggestion is the least offensive.*

"Mr Curdley your lack of disclosure has certainly inconve-
nienced the panel's schedule. However, we also acknowledge that
the testimony will be essential to the claim. I trust you are aware
that corroborating testimony must be heard immediately following
the claimant's testimony to prevent any possibility of collusion.
Without that assurance, the panel could accord far less weight to
the corroborating testimony. Do you understand that?"

She was going to make him squirm a little in front of his client. It was one of her few weapons against indifferent counsel. Essentially, the lawyer held the claimant hostage. She could not refuse a claim without making a full effort to hear the available evidence no matter how dilatory or indifferent the performance of the lawyer. But she could certainly make him squirm.

"Yes, Madam Chair."

"So we will take the lunchbreak now and return here at twelve fifteen, at which time we will ask the claimant about his relationship with the witness and immediately follow that with the testimony of the witness, who will of course remain outside the hearing room until he testifies. I assume the witness has an intimate relationship with the claimant?" Her abruptness was deliberate, to shake Curdley up a bit.

"Well, I don't want to serve as a witness, Madam Chair, but I believe that my client will be giving testimony to that effect."

The smug little upstart was not giving any ground. "Testimony to that effect." The pretentious twit. Curdley reminded Hester of Uriah Heep, in her view one of the most detestable characters in English literature. She would really have to watch herself for bias, not only against the claimant but also his legal counsel, and even, to some degree, her colleague. Come to think of it, she wasn't exactly inspired by the interpreter. That left the Refugee Claim Officer, who had been silent thus far and remained in Hester's good graces. Leaving the room, she thought, bias is a terrible thing in a judge.

Morton announced that he had eaten well despite the prospect of the afternoon's testimony. "I stayed away from the liver and onions, but a light spanakopita went down quite well, thank you. I actually managed to think of things other than the forthcoming testimony, pleasant things such as retirement in Portugal, the perfect combination of a cloudy economy in a sunny climate where the dollar is still worth more than a peso."

Hester wasn't biting. She had heard the Portugal spiel before. She had spent her own lunch hour poring over documents on the current security crisis in Russia. The post-perestroika world of 1993 was truly frightening – unchecked mafia spreading like a virus, middle-level KGB nasties re-emerging as the new security service, and, worst of all, corrupt regional warlords scooping up the military debris, including local nuclear arsenals, from the fractured Soviet state, with Yeltsin willing to give away the candy store for nominal gestures of loyalty. What was there to prevent a Saddam Hussein or Mu'ammer Gaddafi or any one of a dozen demagogues from getting their hands on second-hand nuclear weapons? Abruptly she shifted gears, none of this having any direct relevance to the persecution of homosexuals in the new Russia.

"Well, fearless leader, what is the strategy for the afternoon's drama? How are we to determine whether our laconic claimant is a fancy boy or a sly Slav? And may I suggest that frontal assault and rearguard action are both inappropriate expressions?"

Hester ignored the ribald humour, knowing that any objection, no matter how restrained, would only be taken as encouragement to further offend her perceived sensibilities.

"The issues are straightforward. This witness will be claiming to be his lover and our young lawyer friend assumes that makes his case, but it seems to me that he has to establish at least two facts: one, that the claimant has been his lover, hopefully on more than one occasion, and two, that if there has been sexual congress, it has not been done solely to provide evidence for a fraudulent claim. So we should be looking not only for evidence of a sexual relationship but whether he has shown other forms of involvement with local gay culture to suggest that he has a legitimate interest. In short, let's not focus solely on the sex."

Morton seemed bemused. He was like an intelligent dog who was constantly fretting at the leash but who always responded to a timely and gentle tug. "Well, that all makes sense. I suppose we could get on with it. Let's ask our RCO to do the legwork rather than Mr Curds and Whey."

"Good idea. And why don't you be the first to help out if Ms Goyer strays off track?"

"Sounds fine. Lead on, Macduff."

Walking out the door she vaguely wondered whether there was some veiled reference that she was missing, something in Macbeth. With Morton you never knew. Well, he was welcome to his clandestine humour, she had more than enough confusion and miscommunication in the hearing room without having to navigate the double entendres of her colleague. She already knew that the forth-coming testimony was a rich ground for duplicity. A few years be-fore she had done a series of claims by Russian and Ukrainian fishermen who had jumped ship in St John's. They had all claimed to be either Jewish or homosexual; some had claimed to be both. Morton called it separating the gays from the goys.

The false Jewish claims had ceased to work when Board members began sending the claimants' birth certificates to the RCMP forensic laboratory in Ottawa. Many were returned with evidence of tampering – the nationality of the parents had been altered to read Jewish. After that wave of unsuccessful claims, more and more Russian sailors were discovering their homosexuality. It was a nasty game, since any sailor who was legitimately gay would be treated with great brutality by the other sailors. All of the claimants would be able to describe in detail the brutality since they would all have seen it as victim, observer, or assailant.

Her personal favourites included the sailor who said that he had been caught in bed with another man but he truly wasn't gay. Personally, he disliked homosexuals. He had made a minor mistake out of loneliness for his wife. However, he would be perceived as gay by the other sailors and therefore feared persecution. Morton called it the case of the homosexual homophobe. Other claimants had paid Canadian homosexuals to give false testimony; the more desperate had entered into brief relationships. And some, of course, were gay and had plunged into the thriving gay culture on Water Street near the St John's harbour, amazed to go to clubs where men openly danced, necked, and even walked hand in hand down the street. A few felt they had come to a cold and wintry paradise.

Hester and the other members visiting Newfoundland had become reluctant experts in the arcane art of covert homosexual culture in the former Soviet Union: the clandetine meeting places in which parks, which theatres; the code words and signals such as the swinging of a watch fob in a park beside the statue of Catherine the Great. Hester had studiously avoided testimony on the more salacious aspects of sexual practice, although some of her colleagues revelled in it, musing over the details of penis rings and group couplings. The story of grafted mouse ears still popped up during after-hours discussions between members. Hester once said they were all missing the point, which only prompted more hoots of laughter.

Sometimes it was easy. She thought of the young Russian claimant, a ship's navigator, whose downy cheeks had turned a deep crimson on seeing his Cuban lover enter the hearing room to testify on his behalf. The first blush of true love. The intensity of emotion between the two young men was palpable to all and pleasurable to observe. Not even Morton's smutty innuendo about Hester giving an oral positive could diminish the moment. True love had invaded her hearing room and she was pleased to assure the lovers of Canada's protection.

She did not expect today's evidence to be so straightforward, and she was unfortunately correct. The claimant's demeanour had not changed noticeably from the morning, nor had his communication skills. It was like pulling teeth to get the simplest information, although the RCO, Francine Goyer, was doing her best, keeping the questions clear and simple.

"Where did you first meet Robert?" It had already been established that Robert was a Canadian citizen, unemployed, and a part-time university student."

"In a bar."

"Can you tell me the name of the bar and where it is located?"

"It is just a bar. I do not know the name. It is in a street. I do not know the street."

"Could you please describe the bar? Either the interior or exterior."

"I do not remember. It was just a bar. There are many bars. They are all the same."

"Mr Petrovich, could you please then tell us how many people were in the bar or some other aspect of your first meeting that you remember."

"I think there were some people, not too many. It was dark."

Eliciting meaningful testimony for corroboration required great skill. Hester knew this. The objective was to obtain clear statements of fact on material points from the claimant to be then confirmed by the witness. It seemed simple but facts were slippery. It was a subtle art. There were so many possibilities for confusion: language, perception, memory. If two witnesses saw, remembered, or described the same event differently, it did not necessarily mean they were lying. So there was a science to establishing clear facts that would be reasonably perceived and remembered in the same way by both witnesses. So far Francine Goyer had gleaned few hard facts despite her best efforts.

"Mr Petrovich." Hester could not help herself. "You have brought a witness who is sitting outside. I assume that person is going to tell us that he has had a relationship with you. It is our job to decide whether or not that is true." She waited for the interpretation.

"We need to hear the story from you first, then confirm it with your witness, Mr ..." her eyes searched for the name, "Danson, Robert Danson. We will ask him the same questions. But so far, your answers are too vague. Can you not be more precise? I assume that your first meeting was memorable to you in some way. Can you tell us something special or unique about your first meeting? Something that was important to you, that Robert might remember as well?"

She had broken her own rule, saying more than the interpreter could comfortably digest. Oh well. The interpreter seemed to be making her way through, stumbling only once. The claimant again shifted uncomfortably in his seat. Gloomy. He looked so damned gloomy.

"There was nothing special. He had a nice smile and a pleasant manner."

"What was he wearing?" Hester was aware that she had just taken over from Francine who may either be silently cursing or thanking her. A quick glance over to the RCO told her nothing. She was conscious of the three o'clock deadline and was determined to get something concrete out of this frozen stone.

"A shirt. I do not remember the colour. It was dark."

"No jacket or tie?"

"I do not think so."

"What were you drinking?"

"Beer."

"Mr Petrovich. What kind of beer?"

"I do not remember."

"You do not always drink the same kind of beer?

"No. I ask and the waiter brings. I do not know Canadian beer."
He added, after a pause, "Sometimes Molson."

It was so easy to find yourself on fruitless excursions to nowhere
wasting time on tiny irrelevant details, but she was not prepared to
give up.

"What does Robert like to drink?"

"He drinks whisky." Ah. A fact. Clear, simple, promptly rendered.
At last, a fact.

"What kind of whisky?"

"I do not know. It is just whiskey."

"That first time, you talked in the bar?"

"Yes."

"Did you dance?"

"No. It was not a dancing bar." Ah. Another fact. Progress.

"Did you leave together?"

"Yes. We leave together."

"You went home together?"

"No. We say goodbye, see you sometime."

"When did you first go home together?"

Vasily looked confused. Suddenly, in English, he blurted out,
"Home together? What is home together"?

Now Hester was leading the witness. In her impatience, she had
tried to take a shortcut, cut to the chase. But why was he suddenly
speaking English?

"Mr Petrovich, excuse me, I made an assumption that is perhaps
not correct. I assumed you and the witness, Robert Danson, were
lovers. Is that not correct?"

Again in English. "No. No lovers. Robert is a friend. But he knows
about me. He knows about my ..."

The claimant turned to the interpreter, saying something rapidly
in Russian. The interpreter replied, also in Russian except for one gar-
bled English word that sounded like tendency, or possibly, ecstasy.

"Tendencies! Yes, he can tell you about my tendencies."

Hester uttered a deep, heartfelt sigh. Morton groaned. She was
losing control of the hearing. Somehow the claimant was now testifying in English with untranslated asides to the interpreter in
Russian. His English was much better than she had been led to believe. And now it appeared that the lover-witness was not a lover.

This was not going to get out of hand. She paused a half beat to calm her voice. "Mr Curdley, a mid-hearing conference if you please. Mr Petrovich, you may leave the room for ten minutes while I speak with your lawyer. Do not speak to Mr Danson while you are outside of the room. Ms Alexandrova, please interpret that to the claimant."

The ensuing conference was brief. Hester chose her words carefully to avoid allegations of bias. For the same reason, she left the tape running. Everything on the record. She informed Curdley that his lack of preparation and disclosure had misled the panel and impeded the hearing to the detriment of his client. The detriment of the client bit was important. Sneaky lawyers would later claim that any criticism of them suggested a lack of impartiality on the Board member's part. The issue was not her convenience but giving the claimant a full and fair hearing and she was careful to say so.

Curdley offered a half-hearted defence, saying that an "intimate" relationship wasn't necessarily a "sexual" one. He admitted that he had not "fully explored" the details with his client. Hester reminded him that prior disclosure of the witness with an affidavit would have solved the problem. In addition, his client's English was far better than he had implied. Did he wish to continue the hearing solely in English? If not, then the claimant would testify consistently in Russian, without the English interjections.

For some obscure reason, Hester felt suddenly tired and dejected. She scribbled Morton a quick note. *This is going nowhere. Unless the witness surprises, I will do a written negative.*

Morton nodded, scrawling a brief addendum. *Fine with me as long as I can be out of here by three.*

Robert Danson's testimony was brief and disappointing. Manifestly gay, a chance acquaintance of Vasily's, he testified to seeing him regularly at Samosa's, a local gay bar. He did not recall the first time they had met. No, he had not slept with Vasily but his friend, Anthony, had been Vasily's lover for a period of time. Anthony was now somewhere in Vancouver. He thought Vasily had slept with other men but he could not give specific names. But there was no doubt that Vasily was gay. Anyone could tell that, at a glance.

Glancing at her watch, Hester saw that it was almost a quarter to three. She had only a few follow-up questions for Vasily.

Why was Anthony not available to testify, either in person or by video-conference from Vancouver? Apparently, Vasily no longer "had a relationship" with Anthony. And yes, Vasily had "passed time" with two other men but he only knew their first names and did not want to see them again. No, he did not wish to call other witnesses.

Exasperated, Hester glanced at Morton. It was five to three. She took one last shot. Something was wrong here, something didn't fit, but the claimant was impenetrable. His demeanour had not changed throughout the hearing. Every response was slow, implacable, untrusting. Where was the weak point? Where was the humanity that he wasn't disclosing?

"Mr Petrovich. You were an outstanding engineering student. You lost everything when you were discovered by your fellow students. Your parents have rejected you. You have been condemned to a life of miserable, physically difficult labour for which you are overqualified. You have been beaten by fellow workers. Is there anything else you want to tell us about your life? Tell us how it felt to live such a secretive, fearful life?"

"It was a difficult life. I did not like it. That is why I came to Canada."

Hester sighed. "Mr Morton, any further questions?" Morton simply shook his head.

"Ms Goyer?"

"No further questions, thank you, Madam Chairperson." Francine was experienced enough to know Hester's question was code for let's wrap it up. She would only raise an issue if she thought the panel had missed an important element of evidence that was needed to reject the claim.

"Mr Curdley?"

Curdley was still shuffling papers, probably stalling for time.

"No? Then we will adjourn. That completes the testimony. It's 3:00 P.M., Mr Curdley. The panel will require written submissions. Please deliver them to the registrar within seven days, that is, by November 29. Ms Goyer, it will be unnecessary to hear observations."

Again, this was code for the RCO. The panel had already decided negatively. They would not put her to extra work.

"Ms Alexandrova, Ms Goyer. Thank you both for your most helpful work." For Hester, this was a perfunctory but courteous closing of the hearing even though the interpreter's work had been sketchy at best. She deliberately omitted reference to the lawyer.

"Mr Petrovich, your lawyer will deliver written arguments to this office within one week to assist us in making our decision. After we receive that document and consider all of the written evidence and your testimony, we will make our decision. You will be informed in writing."

His demeanour did not change. Dark eyes hidden under heavy brows, heavy frozen face, communicating nothing. Fearful? Cunning? Hester had no way of knowing. He probably didn't understand a thing she had just said. It didn't matter. It was all administrative hocus-pocus now, inevitable, leading to only one result. Morton had already stood up. She quickly gathered all her documents, nodded to the claimant, and followed Morton's broad back out the door.

Morton was generous in his praise. "Well done, Hester. Right on the dot. And very tidily cleaned up, I must say. The reasons should be fairly straightforward, don't you think? Simply credibility. Insufficient evidence that he's gay or that he suffered the alleged acts of persecution."

Hester nodded wearily, thinking, you old hypocrite. Reasons were always easy for Morton as long as he wasn't writing them. He was already edging out the door to get to his precious appointment with his barber-tailor-lover. She wondered whether Morton did have a lover. A surreptitious glass of wine at the back of one of the local restaurants, an afternoon assignation on the clean sheets of one of the city's identical hotel rooms? He was sneaky enough, although probably too lazy. Also too cheap. Not even he would try to make some infatuated secretary pay for the room. No, probably his financial advisor, or maybe just home early because he had expected an open afternoon and had counted on it. Of course, why be so naive to think there even was an appointment? Hester shook her head. It didn't matter and Morton had already left.

It was after five before she left the office. The rain had stopped, the November light was fading. Standing at the curb, she looked along the sidewalk then across the street, hoping to see a tall shaggy-haired figure arm in arm with a lover. Male or female. It didn't matter. One small real observation, a certainty to clear her doubts, either way. Or maybe if he were cynically shaking hands with his questionable witness, Robert Danson, paying him off. That was funny, a questionable witness.

The claimant had not proved his case but she was still pierced by that one glimpse of pain that had transfigured Vasily's mask for just an instant. That was real pain, no doubt, and it had come in response to the question about the first incident at the school. But so what? What did it relate to? It was a crack in the story, nothing more. Where did it lead to? Maybe to the truth of his entire story. Maybe nothing. God. She wanted anything that would give her certainty. For one mad instant she thought of slipping into Samosa's in disguise, sitting in a back corner, watching for Vasily. Anything to help her with the true or false of the claim. But she couldn't and wouldn't.

The traffic light changed and Hester stepped onto the dark pavement, avoiding the puddle, thinking she would write the reasons on the weekend. Tonight she would review the evidence for the family of Hungarian Roma, tomorrow's case, a heart-rending story with some dubious facts.

AFTERWORD

Convention Refugees and the Canadian Asylum System

The central theme of these stories is the great difficulty and sometimes impossibility of deciding refugee claims accurately. It is a difficulty shared by the refugee and the decisionmaker as well as the
other participants within the refugee hearing: legal counsel, the
Refugee Claim Officer, the interpreter, although the burdens are not
shared equally. The refugee is the central figure, with the most to lose
or gain and with the primary obligation to prove his or her claim.
The IRB member, far less fearful than the claimant, still has the immense moral and legal responsibility of making the correct decision.

The hearing itself is a crucible in which fact and fiction, communication and miscommunication, fear and courage, passion and indifference, logic and bias, insight and ignorance, intermingle and
combine to form a story that may or may not capture the truth of
the refugee's experience. Every hearing is a human drama with its
players and its outcome, sometimes predictable, often surprising,
and occasionally shocking. There is great emotional intensity due
to the importance and uncertainty of the decision for the refugee
and the subject matter of the testimony, much of it concerning persecution and its myriad forms of suffering and humiliation. There
may also be a lingering sense of farce when the witness does not appear believable, words and gestures lose their power to persuade,
testimony becomes performance, and the hearing a hollow drama
with an unavoidable conclusion.

By way of confession, this book has both a didactic and advoca-
tory purpose. The stories seek to convey the realities of the hearing
room and implicitly describe the challenges confronting refugees and

any institution that must judge them. If Canadians, whether citizens or parliamentarians, wish to criticize or change their asylum system, they must first understand it. In contrast to the stories, this afterword provides a more explicit description of Canada's refugee system, including its strengths and weaknesses. It also argues that there is an urgent need for improvement and proposes some changes that will strengthen the integrity and viability of the system.

THE UN CONVENTION RELATING TO THE STATUS OF REFUGEES

The UN Convention Relating to the Status of Refugees was adopted by the United Nations in 1951.[4] The core of the convention, Article 33, is a promise that the signatory nations will not send any refugee back home if he or she could be persecuted there. In the refugee business, this is known as *non-refoulement*. There is a second series of promises, that the signatory nations will provide refugees with care and protection by extending to them basic civil rights that are available to legal residents such as the right to employment, education, justice, and religious freedom. The third promise is implied: that the signatory countries will not expel a refugee claimant until they can fairly decide whether or not he or she is a convention refugee in need of protection. Not all countries fully comply with this final provision. With a few exceptions, Canada does.

Canada did not ratify the convention until 1969, with good reason. Upon ratification, Canada surrendered its sovereign authority to turn certain foreigners away from its shores whenever it chose to do so. Nations do not like to give up power unless they are getting something tangible in return – a trade agreement for example. You accept my goods, I will accept yours. You recognize my passport, I will recognize yours. Amongst sovereign nations, it's a tit-for-tat world. The convention is different. It is a promise not to turn away strangers from our door if they need protection, not because other

---

4 *1951 Convention Relating to the Status of Refugees*, United Nations *Treaties Series*, vol. 189, p. 137.

nations will accept our refugees in exchange but because it's the right thing to do.

In that sense, the convention is a high-minded document. It was drafted in the aftermath of World War II by nations still bruised by post-Holocaust guilt, conscious of having denied entry to pre-Holocaust Jews. It was also a companion document to the Universal Declaration of Human Rights, which celebrated the rights and inherent dignity of the individual in relation to the state. The Universal Declaration also stated that everyone had the right to seek asylum from persecution.[5]

In 1951 Western democracies were ideologically opposed to the Communist states and were eager to grant asylum to those few freedom-loving souls who managed to escape from harsh totalitarian regimes. That's not the high-minded part. Others will tell you that none of it is particularly high-minded, at least from the view of the European nations. They would say that the convention was devised as a burden-sharing agreement, the burden being the human detritus of the Holocaust and massive displacements related to the Second World War, the thousands of stateless and homeless who at the time were still bound in camps or wandering aimlessly over shattered Europe. For most of the original signatory nations, their promise of protection was limited to victims of "events occurring in Europe before 1 January, 1951." Only in 1967 did the signatory nations expand the application of the convention to anyone fearing persecution anywhere at any time.[6]

Although the grounds for protection and the duties of the host state in caring for asylum seekers were closely negotiated during the drafting of the convention, scant attention was given to the evidentiary problems of deciding who was a refugee. Wouldn't it be obvious? The repressive nature of a state and the cruelty of its security apparatus would surely be well known. The claimant, an activist opponent of the state, would have the torture marks or the political reputation to easily explain his or her flight to freedom. Consequently, the convention says nothing about the *process* of deciding who is a refugee. That was left up to the individual nations.

5 Universal Declaration of Human Rights, Article 14, adopted by the General Assembly of the United Nations, 10 December 1948.
6 *1967 Protocol Relating to the Status of Refugees*, United Nations *Treaty Series*, vol. 606, p. 267.

Currently there are 141 signatory nations to the UN convention. Some have no formal system for deciding refugee status, some have rudimentary systems dispensing extremely rough justice based as much on government policy as on the merits of the refugee claim, some, in particular some of the African nations, have rudimentary systems that are extremely practical and effective in dealing with immense volumes of refugees, and some, including all of the Western industrialized nations of the world, have highly developed refugee systems based on complex administrative structures and quite legalistic interpretations of the convention refugee definition. Unfortunately legal sophistication does not ensure a just result and is sometimes the means by which nations engineer unjust results.

THE DEFINITION OF A CONVENTION REFUGEE

Most people understand the common definition of a refugee: someone who has fled harm in search of refuge. The literal meaning contains two separate notions: running away from harm and seeking protection. Some people think of legally recognized refugees as those fleeing political persecution. That assumption is much too narrow. There are many kinds of refugees fleeing many different forms of harm. On the other hand, the legal grounds for granting protection are not limitless. Not all who legitimately fear harm and seek protection are given it. For the purposes of granting asylum, countries define refugees in various ways but the primary ground for granting protection is based on the definition contained in the UN convention.[7] The convention definition forms the primary basis for granting refugee protection under Canadian law.[8]

The convention contains a legal definition of a refugee that includes some asylum seekers and excludes others. Essentially, the

---

7 Two other international accords are also used to grant asylum in specific regions. The Organization of African Unity's Convention Governing the Specific Aspects of Refugee Problems in Africa expanded protection to include all persons who have fled across borders from man-made disasters. The Organization of American States approved a similar definition in the Cartagena Declaration in 1984.

8 In June 2001 the Immigration and Refugee Protection Act expanded the refugee definition to include "persons in need of protection."

definition states that a refugee is someone outside her home country who fears persecution because of her race, nationality, religion, political opinion, or membership in a particular social group (for example, a labour union). The definition contains several limits on who merits protection. Four are particularly important.

1) The nature of the harm. The concept of "persecution" requires that the harm be serious and persistent. It does not necessarily have to be death or torture but it cannot be minor.

2) The reason for the persecution. It is not only necessary for claimants to prove that they would be persecuted but it must be for one of the five reasons contained in the definition. I fear being arrested or shot *because* I am a member of a particular tribe, religion, political party, etc. Those fleeing natural disasters such as flood, famine, drought, or personal disputes would not qualify. In some countries, those fleeing civil war and culturally accepted forms of violence would not be accepted.

3) Future harm. Claimants must prove that there is a reasonable possibility they *could be* persecuted if they returned to their country. Protection is only offered to prevent future harm, not to compensate for past harm. It is not even necessary for the refugee to have suffered persecution in the past. A threat of persecution is sufficient if it is reasonably possible that the threat would be carried out.

4) State protection. Even if refugees fear persecution, they must always show that their home country is unable or unwilling to protect them. This is a particularly important element when the persecutor is a non-state agent.

Here is the full definition. It may strike you as legalistic, complex and even incomprehensible. If it is difficult for you, think of refugees without education or any knowledge of English or French who try to understand whether or not their fear of persecution fits within the acceptable legal categories.

A convention refugee is any person who:

a) by reason of a well-founded fear of persecution for reasons of race, religion, nationality, membership in a particular social group or political opinion,

(i) is outside the country of the person's nationality and is unable or, by reason of that fear, is unwilling to avail himself of the protection of that country, or

(ii) not having a country of nationality, is outside the country of the person's former habitual residence and is unable or, by reason of that fear, is unwilling to return to that country, and

b) has not ceased to be a Convention refugee by virtue of subsection (2)

Subsection (2)
A person ceases to be a Convention refugee when
(A) the person voluntarily re-avails himself of the protection of the country of his nationality;
(B) the person voluntarily reacquires his nationality:
(C) the person acquires a new nationality and enjoys the protection of the country of that new nationality;
(D) the person voluntarily re-establishes himself in the country that the person left, or outside of which the person remained, by reason of fear of persecution; or
(E) the reasons for the person's fear of persecution in the country that the person left, or outside of which the person remained, cease to exist.

Subsection (3)
A person does not cease to be a Convention refugee by virtue of paragraph (2)(E) if the person establishes that there are compelling reasons arising out of any previous persecution for refusing to avail himself of the protection of the country that the person left, or outside of which the person remained, by reason of fear of persecution.[9]

To add to the complexity, not all refugee-receiving countries interpret the definition in the same way. The differences are profound, affecting large volumes of claimants. Both the Canadian courts and the IRB have developed liberal interpretations of the definition that should be a source of pride, not because they are liberal but because

9 Immigration and Refugee Protection Act, Sections 94 (2) and 95.

they strike closer to the truth of identifying those who genuinely need protection. Other countries have relied on technicalities within the definition to refuse refugees with a legitimate fear of serious harm. For example, some countries have denied protection to those fleeing civil war, no matter how high the likelihood of death or injury. Some countries have required that the persecutor be a state agent even though many refugees flee countries where there is no longer a viable government to protect them and their persecutors are uncontrolled militias or dominant ethnic or religious groups.

Many of the Canadian interpretations that were seen as groundbreaking in the early 1990s have become the standard for most of the industrialized countries. Recognition of persecution based on gender or sexual orientation, persecution by non-state agents and the persecution of particular groups of refugees caught in civil wars have all been more broadly recognized by most countries, often citing Canadian decisions. The few exceptions, such as Germany and France on some issues, are broadly seen as recalcitrant holdouts who are reluctantly moving towards more reasonable and compassionate interpretations of the definition.

In 2001 Canada expanded its refugee definition to include "persons in need of protection." This second ground for protection was intended to fill in some perceived gaps in the convention definition. Few claims have been granted solely under the secondary definition although it has significantly added to the legal work of lawyers and IRB members. Again, from the view of refugees, consider the following definition:

A person in need of protection is a person in Canada whose removal to their country or country of nationality or, if they do not have a country of nationality, their country of former habitual residence, would subject them personally

(a) to a danger, believed on substantial grounds to exist, of torture within the meaning of Article 1 of the Convention Against Torture; or

(b) to a risk to their life or to a risk of cruel and unusual treatment or punishment if

(i) the person is unable or, because of that risk, unwilling to avail themself of the protection of that country,

(ii) the risk would be faced by the person in every part of the country and is not faced generally by other individuals in or from that country,

(iii) the risk is not inherent or incidental to lawful sanctions, unless imposed in disregard of accepted international standards, and

(iv) the risk is not caused by the inability of that country to provide adequate health or medical care.[10]

There are sound legal and policy reasons for carefully defining various categories of protection but the final result, dressed up in the current vogues in legislative drafting, is a tortured prose that is virtually impenetrable to lawyers, lay persons, and certainly, refugees.

MAKING A REFUGEE CLAIM IN CANADA

Canada accepts approximately twenty-five thousand refugees per year through two separate refugee streams, an Overseas Program and an Inland Program. In the Overseas Program, refugees are selected by visa officers in Canadian missions abroad after an interview. Those decisions are rarely controversial since there is no public scrutiny. Refugee applicants are not represented by legal counsel and visa officer decisions are not ordinarily subjected to judicial review in Canada. In addition to the claimant's fear of persecution, the visa officer will also consider the claimant's ability to "successfully establish in Canada." A negative decision, whether just or not, will quietly send the claimant back to a refugee camp or into those vast itinerant populations of displaced persons floating in impoverished quasi-legal status throughout the Third World.

This book concerns Canada's second and more controversial Inland Program for those who claim refugee status in Canada. Canada's refugee status determination system has been frequently praised by the United Nations High Commission for Refugees (UNHCR) and other international bodies as a model for other countries to follow. It has often been referred to as the "Cadillac" of refugee systems. Other critics have called it the most expensive and most porous of

10 Immigration and Refugee Protection Act, Section 97.

systems. As usual, the truth lies somewhere in the middle. The Canadian system has merited neither all of the praise nor all of the criticism.

Here is a summary view of the refugee claim process. Upon arrival in Canada, whether by air, water, or land, people can make a refugee claim at the border. If they are already in Canada, they can make a claim at any immigration office. Claimants are photographed, finger-printed, and interviewed by an immigration officer. The interview focuses on security information and personal identity: who you are, your citizenship, where you have been, essentially information to assess security and criminality risks. Claimants are also asked why they fear persecution. At this stage, claimants do not normally have a lawyer. If required, an interpreter assists, whether by phone or in person. Sometimes the interpreter is a relative or friend. Sometimes the interviewer gets by on the claimant's passable English or French. Interpreters are expensive and difficult to schedule.

After the interview, the immigration officer decides whether the claimant is eligible to make a refugee claim. Ninety-nine percent of claimants are eligible and their claims are referred to the IRB for a refugee hearing. The few ineligibles are serious criminals, suspected security risks, or the odd person who has already been accepted as a refugee in another country.[11] The immigration officers do not assess the merits of the refugee claim itself. They have not heard enough information to do that fairly or accurately.

Once determined to be eligible, claimants are required to fill out a lengthy personal information form (PIF) containing detailed information about their life, names and dates of schools, residences, relatives, jobs, convictions, military service, and finally, an explanation of why they fear persecution. If the claimants are fortunate, they will have the assistance of a decent lawyer. Most claimants cannot af-

11 The Immigration and Refugee Protection Act expanded the categories of ineligibility to include repeat claimants who had made previous refugee claims in Canada or claimants who were entering Canada from the United States of America, pursuant to the Safe Third Country Agreement with the United States of America, which was not implemented until December 2004.

ford a lawyer. Legal aid is provided in four Canadian provinces.[12] However, by the time of the hearing several months later, most claimants will have some form of legal representation.[13] If claimants delay in sending the PIF, the IRB may declare their claim abandoned.

Once it receives the PIF, the IRB attempts to decide the claim as efficiently and as fairly as possible. If it is a very strong claim, it may be referred to the Expedited Process where it can be decided in a matter of weeks after an interview rather than a full hearing. In cases where claimants may themselves have been involved in the commission of human rights abuses or serious criminal acts, Citizenship and Immigration Canada (CIC) may choose to participate in the hearing to oppose a claim. In certain situations, CIC may suspend the claim process and seek an order declaring the claimant ineligible for a refugee hearing.

If there is a need for specific evidence, such as a forensic examination of identity documents or research into specific events in the claimant's home country, the Board will seek the appropriate information. The Board will also seek to narrow the issues and exchange all of the documentary information with the claimant's legal counsel prior to the hearing so that the testimony can be focused on the key issues. Hearing-room time is precious and the IRB expects members to complete most hearings within a half day. Exceptional cases may, however, require several days of testimony and argument. Very complicated cases may be adjourned and resumed several times. The half-day rule for hearings is only an administrative guideline. Members have an ethical obligation to ensure that all of the relevant evidence is heard before making a decision.

From the date of the initial claim, it will be a matter of months and possibly more than a year before the claim is heard. The IRB is a busy place, receiving more than thirty thousand refugee claims per

---

12 Ontario, Quebec, Manitoba, and Alberta legal aid plans fund some refugee claims. Generally, the legal tariffs for refugee lawyers are extremely low.
13 Section 177 (1) of the Immigration and Refugee Protection Act grants claimants a right to counsel but does not require that counsel be a lawyer.

year.[14] Unavoidably, it is to some degree a justice factory. Delays and line-ups are inevitable. At their hearings, claimants answer questions about their claim posed by their lawyer, the RCO, and the Board member(s). Most cases are decided on the credibility of the claimants along with the documentary evidence about the claimants' country. There are rarely supporting witnesses. After the testimony, the legal representative will make submissions stating why they think a claimant is, or is not, a refugee. Often the RCO will also comment on the evidence, usually in a more neutral manner.

The Board member will then render a decision with reasons, either orally from the bench or later in writing. The member is fully independent and has the power to decide the claim based solely on the law and the evidence presented. There is no authority for IRB management or the government to interfere or overrule the decision.[15] The reasons for most negative decisions are written after the hearing since the decision may be reviewed by the court. In theory, CIC may challenge a positive decision but rarely does.

If claimants are accepted as refugees, they may apply for permanent residence for themselves and their immediate family, including family members who are still abroad. A more thorough security review is completed prior to granting permanent residence. A few refugees are refused permanent residence, usually for minor criminality, but are permitted to remain in Canada since they are not returnable to their country of nationality due to Canada's obligations

14 Over the past 15 years, Canada has received approximately 28,000 inland claims per year. In 2001 the IRB received 45,000 claims; in 2002, 39,000; in 2003, 29,000; in 2004, 26,000. (numbers rounded to nearest thousand). With the tightening of US security provisions since September 11 2001, and the Safe Third Country Agreement, signed in Canada in December 2004, the number of refugee claims has fallen steadily. It is expected that fewer than 20,000 claims will be made during 2005.

15 Every rule has its exception. Where there has been an obvious breach of natural justice in a particular claim, the IRB may appoint a different member to rehear the claim. With a few notorious exceptions, the IRB and the government have been very respectful of the members' judicial independence. In this regard, the government's conduct has been admirable given that the outcome of some refugee claims, of both individuals and particular nationalities, have had potentially serious negative effects on Canada's economic and political interests.

under Section 33 of the UN convention. As noted earlier, approximately twenty-five thousand refugees from both the Inland and Overseas Programs are granted permanent residence annually, representing approximately twelve percent of the annual immigration flow to Canada.

If the claim is rejected, there are still several steps before a claimant is deported from Canada. Refused claimants have fifteen days to apply to the Federal Court for leave for judicial review. If leave is granted (about ten percent of applicants are successful), then the court will review the IRB decision. If claimants do not apply to the court, or if leave is denied, they become removable from Canada. However, they may still apply to remain in Canada on humanitarian and compassionate grounds. They may also apply for a preremoval risk assessment (PRRA) to decide whether they would be subjected to any serious harm if they were involuntarily removed to their country. They may also decide to leave Canada voluntarily, although claimants without valid travel documents do not have any means of legally leaving Canada.

The business of claimant removal is a difficult one. Refugee advocates say that the humanitarian and preremoval risk assessments are perfunctory administrative reviews with minuscule acceptance rates. They allege that claimants with genuine fears do not receive a fair hearing. Delays in processing impose years of uncertainty and painful separation from families abroad. From a different perspective, other critics of the system complain that these additional steps simply cause more delay, that the process can be strung out for years, and that the majority of refused claimants, most of them fraudulent, manage to remain in Canada because the process is too cumbersome and CIC is too inefficient. They allege that the low removal rate of failed claimants makes a mockery of the entire refugee system. From a third perspective, CIC officials say that they have lacked sufficient resources in the past to remove refused claimants, that the removal rate has improved in recent years, and finally, that removal is very difficult because of international law and the lack of cooperation from some Third World countries.

There is truth and exaggeration in all of these statements. It is very difficult to obtain accurate and meaningful refugee removal statistics for Canada or any of the developed countries.[16] Certainly CIC removal programs were at one time very inefficient and there has been significant improvement in the past several years. More could certainly be done including effective time management of the entire claim process, promoting voluntary removal programs, and expediting removals to high-volume refugee flow countries such as Costa Rica where state protection is available and almost all of the claims are without merit.

CANADA'S ASYLUM SYSTEM: CRITICISMS AND KUDOS

Canada's refugee system has been misunderstood and misrepresented by the media, the government, and the public for many years. Whether you measure on a per capita or total volume standard, Canada's received refugee flows are neither the highest nor lowest amongst the developed nations. We usually place in the middle of the scale.[17] Compared to nations of the developing world, in particular some African and Middle Eastern countries, our refugee numbers are disproportionately small.[18] Over the past decade, the number of refugees, persons outside of their country seeking protection, has normally ranged from 12 to 14 million people and most of them, more than ninety-five percent, have been located in the world's developing countries.

16 Few governments are straightforward about their removal data. In addition, it is extremely difficult to track refugees who are at various stages in the claim process over a period of two or three years. As a generality, it can be said that Canada has traditionally removed fewer than half of its refused claimants.

17 Over a ten-year year period, 1992–2001, Canada averaged 29,000 claims per year. The annual flows in Germany (160,000), the US (126,000), and the United Kingdom (57,000) were far higher. The Netherlands (36,000), France (28,000), Belgium (22,000), Sweden (23,000), and Switzerland (23,000) were in the same range. All statistics, rounded to the nearest thousand, are based on UNHCR data.

18 In 2002 Canada's total refugee population was 78,000 (claimants and accepted refugees). Iran had more than two million, Pakistan more than one and a half million. China, India, Tanzania, Zambia, Sudan, Lebanon, Kenya, and Thailand all exceeded a quarter of a million.

Canadians have good reason to be proud of their refugee system. In many ways, it works well. They also have cause for discomfort and even embarrassment. There are obvious and correctable flaws in the system that result in too many bad decisions. The consequences of refugee decisions, both negative and positive, are too important not to seek obvious improvements.

Genuine refugees confront many inherent impediments to proving their claim: lack of identity documents, lack of documentary evidence, lack of witnesses, and most seriously, an inability to testify effectively due to language, culture, past traumas, and current fears. By granting claimants a quasi-judicial hearing before an independent decisionmaker, refugees normally have a full opportunity to tell their story. It is a system that makes allowances for a refugee's inability to articulate fear of persecution and recognizes the importance of establishing a solid evidentiary base for the decision.

The Canadian refugee claim process is unique among nations. We are the only country that seeks to make the initial decision the best and definitive one. In most countries, a government official, normally an immigration or border official, will initially decide the claim after a brief interview. Often claimants do not have the time, opportunity, or understanding to present their cases fully. Decisions are relatively quick, based on meagre evidence and a sketchy legal and factual analysis. The decisionmaker is often poorly trained, ill informed, and not fully independent, meaning that the claim may be decided according to government policy rather than the facts and the law. Most of the European nations follow that initial decision with appeals to administrative tribunals and courts, resulting in high overturn rates, inefficiency, and delays in removal of refused claimants.

All of these countries have very low acceptance rates under the UN convention but subsequently grant alternative forms of temporary protection under other refugee legislation. The refugees' status is periodically renewed until circumstances change in their country, and then they are sent home. At first glance, such systems appear to make fast decisions with high rejection rates. A closer look discloses lengthy, complex asylum systems that yield ambiguous, unfair, and inefficient results.

One of the most unjust criticisms of the Canadian system has been the repeated comparison of the IRB's high acceptance rates under the UN convention to the far lower European rates, with the unstated presumption that the Europeans got it right. Such comparisons do not include the secondary grounds for protection in Europe. They also do not account for the European determination to prevent excessive immigration levels through restrictive interpretations of the convention.[19]

In Canada, claimants receive a thorough hearing during which they are usually represented by legal counsel, an interpreter is available, and they have the opportunity to testify, call witnesses, and submit documentary evidence to support their claims. In addition, the IRB submits documentary evidence about the claimant's country, recognizing that claimants often do not have the skills and means to obtain all of the relevant evidence. The IRB's country research centre is world renowned for the quality of its reports. The system is intended to give claimants a fair and efficient hearing and a full opportunity to explain why they fear persecution.

Unfortunately our national pride must be tempered with some honest humility. We excel partially by comparison to the other developed countries who have been deceitfully stingy in granting refugees a legitimately fair opportunity to tell their stories. Moreover, there are darker sides to the Canadian system, most notably our method of selecting our refugee decisionmakers, our failure to effectively review negative decisions for error, and our failure to provide consistently effective legal counsel for a process that is legally intricate. In the most problematic cases, these three flaws reinforce

19 To provide a more realistic comparison, the IRB did attempt to compare "protection rates" of various countries taking account of protection decisions at all levels of each asylum system to produce a blended rate. Such comparisons are fraught with technical difficulties given the variables in refugee flows, time periods for measurement, and different methods of data collection. Despite these variances, the results still provide a more accurate picture than the simplistic comparisons of acceptances under the refugee convention. Here are some sample comparisons of overall protection rates for 2001, drawn from *Comparative Rates of Industrialized Countries* (Ottawa: Immigration and Refugee Board 2001). The percentage indicates number of claimants accepted out of a total annual claimant population: Denmark and Canada, 58 percent; Great Britain, 51 percent; United States of America, 56 percent; Australia, 37 percent; Germany, 32 percent. (additionally, it is estimated that 50 percent of failed claimants remain in Germany on other residency grounds).

one another; incompetent or mediocre IRB members, hindered by inadequate counsel, can produce incorrect decisions that are not caught by the limited form of judicial review available in the Federal Court.

The federal cabinet holds the sole authority to appoint members to the Board. Unfortunately, not all members have been as competent as they could and should be. From the beginning of its history in 1989, the Board has been burdened by patronage appointments. I define patronage narrowly as the appointment or reappointment of politically connected members who are not able to do the job. Obviously, the finest judicial process in the world is neither fair nor effective if the decisionmaker is incompetent. Over the years the Board's morale and reputation have suffered because of a minority of weak members making bad decisions.

Poorly decided cases, both positive and negative, rarely reach the public eye. For the protection of refugees, hearings are confidential. Until 1999,[20] members were not required to provide reasons for their positive decisions unless requested to do so by the Minister or the claimant. Badly decided positive decisions rarely attracted the attention of the Minister and were seldom challenged. Due to the high volume of claims and the limited judicial review process, many incorrect negative decisions also escaped public and judicial scrutiny. Sloppy reasoning and shoddy hearing practices were not always identified and corrected by the courts or by the IRB. With relative impunity, the federal cabinet was able to reappoint notoriously weak or biased members. Covert political influence trumped member evaluation. Excellence was not necessarily rewarded, political connection was. The cumulative effect, particularly in the early history of the Board, led to a culture of cynicism for both members and the public service staff within the Board.

Patronage is principally driven by the regional caucuses of the governing party. Appointments are normally made on a regional

20 Under the Immigration Act, 1989, members were not required to give reasons for positive decisions unless reasons were requested by successful claimants or the Minister. In 1999 the IRB implemented a policy requiring that reasons be given for all decisions. That policy became law under the Immigration and Refugee Protection Act in 2001. Throughout its history, many of the Board's better members routinely gave reasons for all of their decisions.

basis to the regional offices of the Board, the two largest being Toronto and Montreal. IRB appointments are eagerly sought and the power to make them jealously guarded. Intense horse trading occurs between regional ministers who have no subsequent accountability for the performance of their nominees or apparently little interest in the Board's effectiveness. They do not see or wish to see the institutional and individual damage caused by bad appointments. Their interests are political and remote, not operational and immediate.

Incrementally, the government has improved the appointment process, placing more emphasis on the merit of applicants and granting the Board a greater role in the process. But the shadow of patronage still hovers over the IRB as the federal cabinet continues to delay or deny the reappointment of superior members while reappointing manifestly mediocre ones. Similarly, strong candidates without political credentials are repeatedly passed over and many potential candidates do not bother to apply. Such a practice continues to undermine the morale of the entire IRB and the effective authority of Board management. Given its early history, it is difficult to restore the full integrity of the Board with such reluctant half measures.

However, the patronage issue should not be overstated. Over the past several years, the majority of IRB members have done a very difficult job well, hearing thousands of cases each year with an admirable record of consistency. Despite the cynicism and indifference of political overseers, a remarkable number of Board members and staff have served with great dedication. Their loyalty and commitment have been founded on the importance and nature of the work itself, the work of deciding who needs protection and who does not. There is great power in the stories of genuine refugees, not only in the horror and pathos of their suffering but in the courage and fortitude that so many display. Despite the unctuous pieties of the politicians and Public Service mandarins, many IRB members and staff have continued to believe in the humanitarian values underlying the Board's work.

The second weakness in the Canadian refugee system is the lack of a meaningful appeal for refused claimants. An effective appeal is necessary. Even good members make mistakes and poor members make many more, some of them quite egregious. This weakness was exacerbated by the new Immigration and Refugee Protection Act, which mandated that refugee claims be decided by a single member instead of two-member panels where a split decision would be decided in favour of the claimant. Unexpectedly, the government failed to implement the new appeal process in the act, which was intended to provide a safety net for single-member decisions. After four years of unfulfilled promises, the government announced in November 2005 that it would not implement the Refugee Appeal Division. That decision merits the harshest criticism. The Board's least competent members, now alone in the hearing room, undoubtedly commit more errors that remain undetected with the present system of judicial review.

Refused claimants are limited to the old system of asking the Federal Court for permission to apply for a judicial review of the Board's decision. Approximately ninety percent of applicants are denied permission, after an unavoidably cursory review of the application by the court, which does not give reasons for its refusals.[21]

Judicial review in itself is not a full appeal. The court has a limited authority to quash the IRB decision if it is incorrect in law or "patently unreasonable" in its findings of fact. Even if the court does quash the decision, it may only return it to the IRB to be heard by a different decision maker. The court cannot substitute its own decision. Most international agencies, including the UNHCR, criticize Canada for not providing an effective appeal for refused claimants.

A third weakness in the Canadian system is the inconsistency of legal counsel. It is ironic that many of the procedural protections of the quasi-judicial process, due to their complexity, make the process less accessible to refugees who lack the assistance of skilled counsel. Claimants have a right to counsel at the hearing but only at their own expense. Most refugees cannot afford a lawyer. Only four provincial legal aid programs currently pay for legal counsel. At the hearing, the great majority of claimants have some form of representative, most often a lawyer but sometimes a consultant, a support agency worker, or a relative. Many representatives lack the training

21 Approximately twenty-five percent of refused claimants do not seek judicial review. Their reasons for not doing so are unknown. Speculative suggestions from lawyers and community workers include false claims, discouragement after lengthy delays, and the inability to retain a lawyer for the court proceeding.

and skill required to represent the claimant effectively.[22] Too many claimants proceed with badly prepared cases where important documentary evidence has not been obtained, where mistakes and omissions in the PIF have not been addressed before the hearing, where potential witnesses have been ignored, and where claimants have not been adequately prepared to testify at the hearing.

There are some excellent refugee lawyers providing impeccable legal service for very modest wages and many less-diligent ones who continue shoddy legal practices with near impunity. Provincial law societies have shown little interest or effectiveness in regulating the problem. Their disciplinary proceedings are complaint driven. Refused refugee claimants facing deportation lack the capacity to pursue a complaint. With a few notable exceptions, refugee consultants lack adequate legal training and advocacy skills. Many of them prey on claimants of their own ethnicity or language group who are unable to assess their competence and naively believe them to be more sympathetic to their case.

It is extremely difficult to identify and root out the causes of counsel incompetence since counsel are also protected by the confidentiality of the hearing process. The IRB's efforts to institute a code of conduct for counsel to place more accountability on legal representatives was not supported by the Minister of Citizenship and Immigration.[23]

In modest ways, the presiding Board member's inquisitorial role can offset the failures of counsel. In legal terms, a refugee hearing is an *inquiry,* at which the decisionmaker can directly engage in the gathering of evidence in a manner not available to a judge in an adversarial proceeding. With the assistance of RCOS and Board researchers, members can request additional evidence that is essential for their decision or take a more direct role in the questioning of the claimant. On the other hand, the role of legal counsel can be critical. They have far earlier and more intimate access to the

22 Approximately fifteen percent of claimants are unrepresented at hearings. It is generally thought that the majority of claimants are represented by lawyers but the IRB does not statistically track different types of legal counsel.
23 Along with new Rules of Practice following passage of the Immigration and Refugee Protection Act in 2001, the IRB presented a Code of Conduct to the Minister of Citizenship and Immigration, Denis Coderre, who declined to sign it.

claimant to understand the true nature of the claim and to gather critical evidence to prove it. Their advocacy role is essential when the member does not clearly understand the evidence or the law. Board members have a far easier decision when a claim is well prepared and well presented, and undoubtedly many claims have been incorrectly rejected because of inadequate legal representation.

ASYLUM REFORM

Along with virtually all of the developed countries, Canada has consistently sought the same goal, "a fast and fair refugee system." To date, that goal has not been achieved by Canada or any of the developed countries. To Canada's credit, the greater emphasis has been on the fairness of its process while many of its fellow countries have emphasized speed at the cost of fairness. The practical measure of "fast" is the time required for the entire asylum process, from date of claim to the date of either granting protection or removal of a refused claimant. In that sense, none of the developed countries are fast and few, if any, can provide accurate data about their entire asylum process. A comparable definition of "fair" would be a process that allows claimants a legitimate and reasonable opportunity to tell their story to an independent decisionmaker.

A discussion about asylum policy in the developed countries would be incomplete without acknowledging government preoccupation with the sheer volume of refugee claims. Unexpectedly high flows can overwhelm asylum systems, imposing delays that are unacceptable from the point of view of genuine refugees, the public, and the government. Excessive delay itself can attract false claimants who hope that a two- or three-year claim process will allow them either to remain permanently in Canada or at least to earn sufficient money to justify their venture.

Within Canada, any proposal for refugee claim reform inevitably invites a question about its "draw factor." Government officials will always consider whether a proposal will make Canada comparatively more attractive to both genuine and false refugee claimants.

Undeniably, volume can affect the quality of decisionmaking. High refugee flows can overextend judicial resources causing delays, time pressures, and a greater emphasis on administrative rather than judicial priorities. Within the IRB, there has frequently been a tension between increased efficiency and maintaining reasonable standards of fairness. At the same time, distinctions between fast and fair can also create a false dichotomy. Many of the IRB's best initiatives have improved both the quality and speed of decisionmaking.

Unfortunately, most asylum reforms in Europe, North America, and Australia have focused on denying access to asylum proceedings rather than reforming the systems themselves. Various methods have been employed to deter refugees from coming to a particular country, to intercept refugees before they arrive at borders, or to deny them access beyond the border. In Canada's case, those strategies have included increased visa requirements from particular countries, the assignment of Canadian immigration officers to international airports to detect false documents, carrier sanctions on airlines carrying falsely documented passengers, and the Safe Third Country agreement with the United States. Under the agreement, refugees coming from the United States are not permitted to make a claim at a Canadian port of entry.[24]

Canada has not engaged in some of the unsuccessful deterrence strategies of some countries such as the universal detention of refugee claimants or the denial or reduction of social assistance benefits.[25]

The essential criticism of such interdiction policies is that they do not distinguish between the genuine and false claimant. Canada has imposed new visa restrictions on countries such as Zimbabwe when many citizens were fleeing the country with a genuine fear of per-

24 The Safe Third Country Agreement was implemented on 29 December 2004. Refugee advocates have criticized the agreement since the US interpretation of the convention is narrower than Canada's and the US detains far more refugee claimants. Refugee claims coming from the US have declined significantly since implementation. Some claimants are exempt from the agreement; these include claimants with relatives already legally resident in Canada, claimants from "moratorium countries," which Canada views as particularly dangerous countries, and refugees claiming from inside of Canada.

25 The most extreme detention policies were instituted by the United States, Australia, and New Zealand. Great Britain increased detention and sought to reduce welfare benefits. The United States does not provide claimants with welfare or employment authorizations. There is no evidence that any of these strategies have reduced refugee flows.

secution. Similarly, a person intercepted in Singapore or Kuala Lumpoor airport with a false document may well be a genuine refugee who is being turned away in a country that does not grant refugee protection.

Many governments have been attracted by the success of the Australian interdiction program, the so-called "Pacific solution." In 2001 Australia imposed extremely tight visa controls on all air travel to the country and diverted waterborne refugees to the tiny island of Nauru, a separate country, to have their claims determined there or in Papua-New Guinea. The strategy has been successful in the sense that the refugee flows out of Southeast Asia have been choked off. Desperate refugees will risk their lives to reach genuine protection or will even endure years of prison as they did in Western Australia, but they will not risk themselves and their families to go nowhere.

The "Pacific solution" also highlights the essential problem. Most of the people on the diverted boats were genuine refugees from Iran, Iraq, and Afghanistan who were trapped in Indonesia and Malaysia, countries that are not signatories to the UN Convention Relating to the Status of Refugees. They must now remain in those countries with no legal status, vulnerable to criminal and government abuses until they find the means to escape to some other country, if they can afford to do so.[26] Having first fled persecution and then the destitution and hopelessness of the refugee camps parked on the edges of civil war, they become part of the human flotsam and jetsam, drifting throughout the world with no country or organization willing or able to provide them with genuine protection.

The interdiction and diversion of refugees to other jurisdictions is a short-term and cynical strategy that undermines the strength of the convention and its underlying committment by the signatory nations to share the burden of refugee protection cooperatively.[27] Canada is capable of producing an asylum system that is able to decide claims fairly and efficiently, a system that is capable of deterring

26 The United States has also intercepted refugees at sea, particularly Haitians, and forced them to return to Haiti in direct violation of their convention obligations.
27 Ironically at a ceremony in Geneva marking the fiftieth anniversary of the UN Convention in December 2001, the signatory nations unanimously re-affirmed the Convention to be the cornerstone of international refugee protection.

excessive flows of manifestly unfounded claims without resorting to extreme interdiction strategies. Here are four obvious reforms that would contribute to that result.

1 *Selection of decisionmakers.* The government, specifically cabinet, must completely remove itself from the selection process. Their interests are essentially political, not operational. An efficient system cannot afford that indulgence. The IRB's best decisionmakers have been excellent. They have been capable of producing far more and better-reasoned decisions in less time. The decisionmaker, although part of a much larger support team, is the lynchpin participant in the process. A well-designed racing car with a poor driver wastes everyone's effort. Member mediocrity and incompetence have imposed a large and hidden cost in wasted hearing-room time, wasted support services, excessive training, excessive management, inconsistent decisions and, worse, bad decisions. There is a pool of potential candidates within Canada with no political connection that could spectacularly improve IRB performance. Refugee decisionmaking is too difficult and too important not to use the best available resources.

2 *Effective legal counsel.* Some Board members and most government officials see lawyers as obstructions to the refugee claim process. Bad lawyers are, good lawyers aren't. Given the complexities of the definition of a refugee and the inherent incapacities of most refugees to gather the relevant evidence or speak for themselves, legal counsel are essential. They are in the best position to frame the essential elements of the claim early in the process and to gather the relevant evidence as quickly as possible. The current system of providing indirect and partial funding for legal aid service through provincial governments that in turn pay for some or none of the necessary legal service has not worked well. Efficient and reliable refugee decisions require skilled, consistent, and accountable legal counsel. There are judicare models that can provide it. The federal government must acknowledge its responsibility for refugee determination and directly fund the appropriate model on a national basis.

3 *Appeal process*. It is apparent from the stories, I hope, that refugee decisions can be complex, subtle, and confusing. No one gets it right all of the time. Yet the outcomes, particularly the negative ones, can potentially threaten a claimant's life, liberty, and security of the person. If Canada is going to return refused claimants firmly and promptly to their countries, we must do so with the confidence that they do not have a well-founded fear of persecution. That confidence requires a meaningful review of the original refugee decision. Just to be sure. As any good carpenter would say, measure twice, cut once.

There is no perfect appeal model. Courts tend to be more authorative but slower, more cumbersome, and more expensive. A tribunal model can be faster, procedurally more agile, with a more specialized expertise in refugee decisions. However, its decisions would be ineffective if the courts insisted on a third level of review. The great majority of refused claimants must be removable after a single appeal decision.[28]

4 *Prompt removal*. After decisions by the IRB and the Federal Court, refused claimants have additional means of remaining in Canada, notably an application to remain for humanitarian and compassionate reasons and an application for a preremoval risk assessment as well as applications to the Federal Court to review those decisions. The current process is vague and seemingly interminable. Moreover, it is not viewed administratively as a single process but rather as a series of different administrative stages with little accountability or communication between them.

The asylum process requires integrity and finality. Interminable postappeal proceedings are unnecessary and render the asylum

---

28 There are tremendous hidden costs to delays and errors in refugee determination; many of them, such as social assistance, education, and social services, are borne by the provinces. A faster, more efficient system could pay for itself, although funding would have to be reallocated from other envelopes. It is a question of enlightened self-interest.

system vulnerable to abuse.[29] Some claimants have genuine humanitarian reasons for leaving their country that do not come within
the refugee definition. Such issues must be identified early in the
claim process (again with the assistance of legal counsel) and resolved prior to the appeal decision. Once their claim has been denied at the appeal level, claimants must be promptly removed to
their country of origin. The removals program would benefit from
more positive and proactive approaches, including assisting voluntary returns and even instituting aid programs to assist meritorious
returnees.[30] Not all refused claimants have intentionally abused the
asylum system. For those who have, prompt return to their own
country is the most effective deterrent for them and others who
would follow.

CONCLUSION

One of the most gratifying moments for Board members at the conclusion of refugee claim hearings, having understood and accepted
the truth of the claimants' fear and suffering, is to be able to tell
them they have been accepted as refugees, that they are safe and will
not be sent back to the persecutions of their previous life. It is a
powerful moment, often accompanied by tears from any one of several participants as comprehension slowly or suddenly dawns on
claimants that beyond all of the legal gibberish, they are indeed
safe, that ancient fears will no longer rule their lives.

At such moments, members understand that they are the
spokesperson for their country and that the grant of protection belongs to the Canadian people, not themselves. Such an experience

29 While experts may agree on the issues, they do not agree on the solutions. For
    those with a strong interest in potential solutions, a *Summary Report of the
    Roundtable on Canada's Refugee System*, March 2004, may be obtained at the
    website of the Human Rights Research and Education Centre at the University
    of Ottawa Law School, www.cdp-hrc.uottawa.ca.

30 The Swiss government in particular has undertaken some innovative programs
    to substantially assist individual refugees and build community infrastructures
    in regions such as Kosovo.

can inspire members to have great pride in a country that has the capacity and willingness to protect the fearful and dispossessed of the world and the foresight to listen well before deciding. These are not casual emotions. There is a sense of being the point of the pencil for Canada's collective generosity. The liberalism of Canada's refugee law and asylum process is a construction shared by all of its builders: Parliament, the courts, the IRB, government, legal counsel, and ultimately, the Canadian people.

Canada's asylum system is worth appreciating and saving. It contains intelligence, integrity, and compassion that is embedded in Canada's refugee law and finds expression in the hearing rooms of the IRB every day. Undoubtedly there are increasing migration and security pressures that will test the efficiency of any asylum system, but the solutions do not lie in wholesale offshore exclusions of refugees. With sensible reforms, the system can be so much better. The traditions and rudiments are there, the capacity is there, and it is again an opportunity for Canada to lead the world in kinder and saner directions.